Joshua

TEACH THE TEXT COMMENTARY SERIES

John H. Walton
Old Testament General Editor

Mark L. Strauss
New Testament General Editor

Volumes now available:

Old Testament Volumes

New Testament Volumes

Visit the series website at www.teachthetextseries.com.

TEACH the TEXT
COMMENTARY SERIES

Joshua

Kenneth A. Mathews

Mark L. Strauss and John H. Walton
GENERAL EDITORS

ILLUSTRATING THE TEXT

Kevin and Sherry Harney
ASSOCIATE EDITORS

Donald C. Porter
CONTRIBUTING AUTHOR

BakerBooks

a division of Baker Publishing Group
Grand Rapids, Michigan

Published by Baker Books
a division of Baker Publishing Group
P.O. Box 6287, Grand Rapids, MI 49516–6287
www.bakerbooks.com

Printed in the United States of America

Library of Congress Cataloging-in-Publication Data
Mathews, K. A.
      Joshua / Kenneth A. Mathews ; Mark L. Strauss and John H. Walton, general editors ; Kevin and Sherry Harney, associate editors ; Donald C. Porter, contributing author.
          pages cm. — (Teach the text commentary)
      Includes bibliographical references and index.
      ISBN 978-0-8010-9217-6 (cloth)
      1. Bible. Joshua—Commentaries. I. Title.
   BS1295.53.M38 2015
   222′.207—dc23   2015022803

To My Dad
Charlie M. Mathews
December 22, 1915–December 14, 2003

Contents

Welcome to the Teach the Text Commentary Series

Why another commentary series? That was the question the general editors posed when Baker Books asked us to produce this series. Is there something that we can offer to pastors and teachers that is not currently being offered by other commentary series, or that can be offered in a more helpful way? After carefully researching the needs of pastors who teach the text on a weekly basis, we concluded that yes, more can be done; the Teach the Text Commentary Series (TTCS) is carefully designed to fill an important gap.

The technicality of modern commentaries often overwhelms readers with details that are tangential to the main purpose of the text. Discussions of source and redaction criticism, as well as detailed surveys of secondary literature, seem far removed from preaching and teaching the Word. Rather than wade through technical discussions, pastors often turn to devotional commentaries, which may contain exegetical weaknesses, misuse the Greek and Hebrew languages, and lack hermeneutical sophistication. There is a need for a commentary that utilizes the best of biblical scholarship but also presents the material in a clear, concise, attractive, and user-friendly format.

This commentary is designed for that purpose—to provide a ready reference for the exposition of the biblical text, giving easy access to information that a pastor needs to communicate the text effectively. To that end, the commentary is divided into carefully selected preaching units, each covered in six pages (with carefully regulated word counts both in the passage as a whole and in each subsection). Pastors and teachers engaged in weekly preparation thus know that they will be reading approximately the same amount of material on a week-by-week basis.

Each passage begins with a concise summary of the central message, or "Big Idea," of the passage and a list of its main themes. This is followed by a more detailed interpretation of the text, including the literary context of the passage, historical background material, and interpretive insights. While drawing on the best of biblical scholarship, this material is clear, concise, and to the point. Technical material is kept to a minimum, with endnotes pointing the reader to more detailed discussion and additional resources.

A second major focus of this commentary is on the preaching and teaching process itself. Few commentaries today help the pastor/teacher move from the meaning of the text to its effective communication. Our goal is to bridge this gap. In addition to interpreting the text in the "Understanding the Text" section, each six-page unit contains a "Teaching the Text" section and an "Illustrating the Text" section. The teaching section points to the key theological themes of the passage and ways to communicate these themes to today's audiences. The illustration section provides ideas and examples for retaining the interest of hearers and connecting the message to daily life.

The creative format of this commentary arises from our belief that the Bible is not just a record of God's dealings in the past but is the living Word of God, "alive and active" and "sharper than any double-edged sword" (Heb. 4:12). Our prayer is that this commentary will help to unleash that transforming power for the glory of God.

The General Editors

Introduction to the Teach the Text Commentary Series

This series is designed to provide a ready reference for teaching the biblical text, giving easy access to information that is needed to communicate a passage effectively. To that end, the commentary is carefully divided into units that are faithful to the biblical authors' ideas and of an appropriate length for teaching or preaching.

The following standard sections are offered in each unit.

1. *Big Idea*. For each unit the commentary identifies the primary theme, or "Big Idea," that drives both the passage and the commentary.
2. *Key Themes*. Together with the Big Idea, the commentary addresses in bullet-point fashion the key ideas presented in the passage.
3. *Understanding the Text*. This section focuses on the exegesis of the text and includes several sections.
   a. The Text in Context. Here the author gives a brief explanation of how the unit fits into the flow of the text around it, including reference to the rhetorical strategy of the book and the unit's contribution to the purpose of the book.
   b. Outline/Structure. For some literary genres (e.g., epistles), a brief exegetical outline may be provided to guide the reader through the structure and flow of the passage.
   c. Historical and Cultural Background. This section addresses historical and cultural background information that may illuminate a verse or passage.
   d. Interpretive Insights. This section provides information needed for a clear understanding of the passage. The intention of the author is to be highly selective and concise rather than exhaustive and expansive.
   e. Theological Insights. In this very brief section the commentary identifies a few carefully selected theological insights about the passage.

4. *Teaching the Text*. Under this second main heading the commentary offers guidance for teaching the text. In this section the author lays out the main themes and applications of the passage. These are linked carefully to the Big Idea and are represented in the Key Themes.
5. *Illustrating the Text*. At this point in the commentary the writers partner with a team of pastor/teachers to provide suggestions for relevant and contemporary illustrations from current culture, entertainment, history, the Bible, news, literature, ethics, biography, daily life, medicine, and over forty other categories. They are designed to spark creative thinking for preachers and teachers and to help them design illustrations that bring alive the passage's key themes and message.

Acknowledgments

I am indebted to many who encouraged and assisted me in various ways during the research and writing of this volume.

I am grateful to Dean Timothy George, Beeson Divinity School, and Samford University President Andrew Westmoreland and Provost J. Bradley Creed for providing the opportunity and resources to write the book.

Students who helped by reading the manuscript at its different stages and making suggestions for illustrative helps were Lauren Doss, Matt Harber, Ben Smith, and Daniel Williams.

I also express a special thank you to general editor John H. Walton, for his kind invitation to participate in the series, and to the editorial staff at Baker Publishing Group, especially James Korsmo, who supervised the editorial production.

Most important, Dea Mathews, my wife and chief encourager, was instrumental in boosting my efforts to complete the manuscript during many health crises in our family.

Abbreviations

Old Testament

Gen.	Genesis	2 Chron.	2 Chronicles	Dan.	Daniel
Exod.	Exodus	Ezra	Ezra	Hosea	Hosea
Lev.	Leviticus	Neh.	Nehemiah	Joel	Joel
Num.	Numbers	Esther	Esther	Amos	Amos
Deut.	Deuteronomy	Job	Job	Obad.	Obadiah
Josh.	Joshua	Ps(s).	Psalm(s)	Jon.	Jonah
Judg.	Judges	Prov.	Proverbs	Mic.	Micah
Ruth	Ruth	Eccles.	Ecclesiastes	Nah.	Nahum
1 Sam.	1 Samuel	Song	Song of Songs	Hab.	Habakkuk
2 Sam.	2 Samuel	Isa.	Isaiah	Zeph.	Zephaniah
1 Kings	1 Kings	Jer.	Jeremiah	Hag.	Haggai
2 Kings	2 Kings	Lam.	Lamentations	Zech.	Zechariah
1 Chron.	1 Chronicles	Ezek.	Ezekiel	Mal.	Malachi

New Testament

Matt.	Matthew	Eph.	Ephesians	Heb.	Hebrews
Mark	Mark	Phil.	Philippians	James	James
Luke	Luke	Col.	Colossians	1 Pet.	1 Peter
John	John	1 Thess.	1 Thessalonians	2 Pet.	2 Peter
Acts	Acts	2 Thess.	2 Thessalonians	1 John	1 John
Rom.	Romans	1 Tim.	1 Timothy	2 John	2 John
1 Cor.	1 Corinthians	2 Tim.	2 Timothy	3 John	3 John
2 Cor.	2 Corinthians	Titus	Titus	Jude	Jude
Gal.	Galatians	Philem.	Philemon	Rev.	Revelation

General

AT	author's translation	i.e.	*id est* ("that is," "in other words")
ca.	circa ("around," "about")	lit.	literally
cf.	confer, compare	NT	New Testament
chap./chaps.	chapter/chapters	OT	Old Testament
e.g.	*exempli gratia* ("for example")	pl.	plural
ibid.	*ibidem* ("in the same place")	v./vv.	verse/verses

Ancient Versions

| LXX | Septuagint |
| MT | Masoretic Text |

Modern Versions

ASV	American Standard Version
ESV	English Standard Version
HCSB	Holman Christian Standard Bible
KJV	King James Version
NAB	New American Bible
NASB	New American Standard Bible
NET	The NET Bible (New English Translation)
NJPS	*The Tanakh: The Holy Scriptures: The New JPS Translation according to the Traditional Hebrew Text* (1985)
NKJV	New King James Version

| NLT | New Living Translation |
| NRSV | New Revised Standard Version |

Secondary Sources

| *ANET* | James B. Pritchard, ed. *Ancient Near Eastern Texts Relating to the Old Testament*. 3rd ed. Princeton, NJ: Princeton University Press, 1969 |
| *HALOT* | L. Koehler, W. Baumgartner, and J. J. Stamm. *The Hebrew and Aramaic Lexicon of the Old Testament*. Translated and edited under the supervision of M. E. J. Richardson. 5 vols. Leiden: Brill, 1994 |

Introduction to Joshua

Joshua and the "Great Story"

Usually readers think of the book of Joshua as the story of Israel's conquest of Canaan, and indeed that is the *narrative* plot. Yet, the message is not primarily historical, although the book's message is inseparably bonded with real historical events. Its message is the story's two theological affirmations: (1) God's word is truthful and authoritative; and (2) the fulfillment of his promise of land is coming to pass. For the Israelites this means they settle in the land of Canaan, as the Lord first promised Abraham, and they prosper as a nation free from the hostilities of their enemies. For Christian readers Joshua shows that the revealed word and its promises in Christ and in the Scriptures are true, reliable, and authoritative in the Christian life (Acts 2:42; 1 Tim. 4:6, 13). Joshua is

The fulfillment of God's promise to Abraham to give him the land of Canaan, which began with the rescue of the Israelites from Egyptian slavery, continues in the book of Joshua as the Israelites actually move into the land. This sarcophagus relief from the fourth century AD depicts God's deliverance of his people at the Red Sea. God miraculously parts the waters so that the Israelites cross on dry ground and then defeats Pharaoh's army as the waters return and engulf them.

Theology of Deuteronomy

1. The people enter into covenant with the Lord, the God of their fathers, at Mount Horeb (= Sinai). Whereas most references in the Old Testament show preference for the word "Sinai," Deuteronomy uses the place name "Horeb" (except Deut. 33:2). Despite their departure from Mount Horeb, God's presence with his people will continue in the land through their obedience to *torah* (= "teachings").
2. The presence of God is realized in the land through the people's faithful worship of the Lord alone.
3. The people recognize the lordship of God over every facet of their lives in the land by obedience to torah's commandments.
4. Living under torah means adapting and applying the (timeless) teachings of torah to the new circumstances of the land. By means of torah the words of the Lord go with them.
5. The Lord authorizes prophets to interpret torah for the people, despite the absence of Moses. Torah is the successor to Moses, not any person (Joshua and the elders).[a]

[a] These points are derived from Vogt, *Deuteronomic Theology*; see especially pp. 227–31.

a reminder that Christians also receive an inheritance (Eph. 1:11–14, 18; 1 Pet. 1:3–5).

The book of Joshua is critical to the unfolding revelation of God found in the "Great Story"—that is, Genesis through 2 Kings (excepting Ruth) in the Hebrew arrangement. Joshua provides the transition from Israel's life *outside* the land of Canaan to life *inside* the land. The book advances the story of Israel's deliverance from Egypt and their journey to the land of their fathers (Genesis–Deuteronomy) by reporting the (partial) fulfillment of the land promise made to Abraham (Gen. 12:1–3; 15:18–21). The books of Joshua through 2 Kings tell what happens to God's people in the land and explain why they eventually go into exile. Since Joshua through 2 Kings is composed primarily as history in genre

and content, these books appear in the Septuagint (LXX, the Greek OT) and in the Protestant Old Testament canon under the rubric "Historical Books." In the Hebrew Bible's arrangement, however, they are part of the collection "Prophets."[1] Why? As with the Pentateuch (Torah) and the Writings sections, the rabbis considered them the same voice of God as delivered by the classic prophets, such as Isaiah. These books are "thus saith the LORD" too, giving the Lord's interpretation of Israel's story to the ancient Israelites and to Christian readers today.

That Joshua through 2 Kings fits together is shown by the continuum in plot, use of similar language, and the same theological viewpoint on history. Some scholars even theorize that the books constitute a single composition, the "Deuteronomistic History," which underwent a number of literary embellishments (redactions) from different time periods in Israel's history (eighth to sixth centuries BC). Although I do not find this reconstruction compelling, it points up the scholarly consensus that Deuteronomistic theology (see sidebar) influenced the theology of Joshua and the subsequent books in the "Great Story."

The ministry of Joshua and his generation relies on the presence of God and the revelation given to Moses. The presence of God is symbolized by the ark of the covenant located in the portable tent of meeting (tabernacle). The revelation given to Moses at Mount Sinai is provided through the "written" torah of Moses, which is what continues to live as the standard for measuring Israel's fidelity to its covenant with God—inside or outside its land. In particular Deuteronomy's legislation collection is the orthodox expression of traditional Yahwism to be practiced in the land. Moses is dead and buried, and Sinai must remain behind. The tent of meeting functions *as* Sinai, and indicates the revelation and presence of God in the land (Exod. 40:34–38; Lev. 1:1). Although Joshua and the people do not any longer have Moses as leader and mediator or reside at Sinai, they receive "rest" from their enemies and prosperity in the land because of God's fulfilling of the promise and Israel's obedience to torah as the community of God.

Outline

1. Claiming the land (chaps. 1–5)
2. Conquering the land (chaps. 6–12)
3. Distributing the land (chaps. 13–21)
4. Living in the land (22:1–24:28)
5. Resting in the land (24:29–33)

The covenant relationship formed between God and Israel at Sinai is one of the key theological themes in the book of Joshua. Jebel Musa, shown here, is the traditional location of Mount Sinai.

Chief Theological Themes

The following six theological themes are prominent in the book and need to be kept in mind when the book of Joshua is read. Although they are listed here separately, they must be read as interdependent themes, not isolated from one another, lest the themes lose their full expression and meaning.

God's Word

For Israel the writing of history (historiography) included the accounts of the events but also the interpretation of the events by the revelatory word. The covenant revelation at Sinai provides the focal theme and unity of the revelation in Old Testament Scripture. Therefore, the book of Joshua gives special attention to the instructions of Moses and presents the idea of *torah* ("teaching") in diverse manners: "Book of the Law [of Moses] . . . written" (1:8; 8:31, [32], 34; 23:6); "the law" (1:7; 8:34; 22:5); "Book of the Law of God" (24:26); "as I [the LORD]

promised Moses" and its variant expressions (e.g., 1:3, 5, 17; 3:7; 4:12, 14; 8:31, 33; 11:12, 20; 13:14, 33; 14:2; 21:8); and "You have done all that Moses . . . commanded you" (22:2). The book of Joshua shows that God's promise of inheritance is unfailing and that he is able and willing to achieve it (e.g., 21:43–45). Success is dependent on the people's observance of the law of Moses, not by their military competence. Continued possession of the land means observing the requirements of the commandments of the law of Moses that regulate the life of Israel (24:25; cf. Deut. 4:4–5). The land is sacred because it is the Lord's and he requires a consecrated people (see below, "Holiness"). It is, however, important to state clearly that the commandments do not redeem the people of God, for that is typically considered to have occurred at the exodus-Passover. The "Book of the Covenant" (Exod. 24:7; cf. Deut. 31:24), with its ordinances, is given *after* the liberation of Israel from Egypt. Nonetheless, settlement and continued life in the land require obedience to the covenant's obligations.

The dynamic of divine promise and human obedience produces a narrative and theological tension. The literary genre of narrative explains in part the apparent juxtaposition of elective love and human obedience in the book of Joshua. Narrative gives a real-world viewpoint, not a systematic presentation of an abstract set of biblical doctrines. The nature of history telling (historiography) inherently involves human actors in concrete historical circumstances. Joshua's narrative, like those of the rest of the Great Story, shows that human decisions are causal for the outcomes of blessing and curse. These decisions are real,

not phantoms. Readers identify with the narrative because they too make decisions that are causal, producing certain effects.

Covenant

The prominence of the "covenant" relationship God formed with Israel at Sinai is evident in every part of the book of Joshua—either explicitly or indirectly. Joshua 8:30–35 and 24:25–27 are renewals of God's covenant with Israel, which requires obedience to the "Book of the Law" (1:7–8; 8:31, 34; 23:6; 24:26; cf. 7:11, 15; 23:16). The "covenant" under which Israel lives is the "covenant of the LORD" (7:15; 8:33; cf. 24:16) and is expressed personally by God as "my covenant" (7:11). The "ark of the covenant," or "ark of the LORD," symbolizes God's presence among his people, and it visually dominates the narration in the crossing of the Jordan and the defeat of Jericho (e.g., chaps. 3–4; 6; cf. 7:6, 23; 8:33; 18:1). Failure to keep covenant loyalty leads to death for the culprit, war, or expulsion from the land (e.g., 7:24–26; 22:12; 23:15–16; 24:20). Also, any covenant treaty between Israel and an individual (e.g., Rahab, 2:12–14; 6:22–23) or a nation requires loyalty to the agreement, for it is entered into by Israel under oath to God (e.g., Gibeon, 9:6, 15–21).

Holiness

Essential to appreciating the message of Joshua is grasping the idea of holiness in relation to the land and the people of Israel. The word group "holy/sanctified/consecrated" (*qdsh*) appears many times in the book of Joshua (e.g., 3:5; 5:15; 6:19; 7:13 [2x]; 24:19, 26; not counting the place name "Kedesh/Keshion"). But the concept of what is "sacred" is fundamental to understanding the book as a whole, both in its message and in the narrative actions described in the book. God alone is inherently holy (24:19). People, land, and things are counted as "holy" only because they are in a contingent relationship to the All-Holy One. The "holy" is whatever is moved from the ordinary realm to the sphere of the holy (Lev. 10:10). The people are distinguished as holy because of their covenant connection to God (Lev. 11:45; 20:22–24). Among the people is another grade of holiness—the Levitical priests, as well as the sanctuary (Exod. 30:30; 40:9). The land is sacred space, since it is God's land and he dwells in it (Lev. 25:23; Deut. 23:14). Therefore, the people must be holy if they are to continue in the land; this is possible through obedience to God's commandments so that they might remain holy (Lev. 20:7–8).

The book of Joshua assumes that the audience/reader understands the concept of holiness that is expressed concretely in specific actions at key moments. The people "consecrate" themselves through ritual ceremony in preparation for carrying out the actions of God (3:5; 7:13). The appearance of God in their midst involves holy space (5:15), and those things devoted to God cannot be profaned by Israel taking them for their own use (e.g., Achan, 6:18–19; 7:1, 10–15). The "setting apart" of the six cities of refuge from among the cities of Israel indicates a special grade of sacred space, since they in a unique way serve God's purposes (20:7). The practice of *haram/herem* ("put to destruction" / "devoted things") reflects God's judgment on the wicked and his demands for a consecrated people (e.g., 6:17, 21; 8:26; 10:28; 11:11–12; cf. Deut.

The territory allotted to each tribe is shown on this map of the promised land.

7:2; 20:13–18). For the significance of this practice for Christian readers, see below, "Christian Interpretation."

Inheritance of the Land

The first principle regarding the land (*'erets*) and its possession by Israel is recognition that the land belongs to God. This fundamental teaching has its anchor in the creation itself, for the Lord makes the "earth" (*'erets*), and he differentiates the "land" (*'erets*)—in which he plants a garden, wherein God and humanity live together—from the waters and sky. Eden

Introduction to Joshua

is the theological prototype for interpreting the gift of the land to Israel. The tent of meeting in the land indicates the presence of God. The presence of Israel and the bounty of Eden have their counterpart in Canaan, "a land flowing with milk and honey" (5:6; cf. Deut. 6:3). Since the Lord owns the land, he may bestow it or withhold it as he chooses, making Israel its tenant only (Lev. 25:23). He promises it to the fathers of Israel and their descendants on the basis of his elective love (Gen. 12:1; Deut. 1:8–9; 4:36–38). Possession of the land signals that God is faithful to his promises (e.g., 1:6; 21:43). The land represents "rest"—meaning security and prosperity in the land, not inactivity (e.g., 1:13; 5:14; 10:14; 11:20, 23; 21:44; 23:4). However, for Israel to acquire the land they must obey the Lord's commands, the chief of which is sole worship of the Lord God (e.g., 1:7–8; 7:1; 22:5; 23:6–8; cf. Deut. 11:22–23). Failure results in expulsion in accord with the Lord's moral requirements, not on the basis of ethnicity, for the Israelites too face expulsion should they adopt the evil practices of the land's former inhabitants (see above, "Holiness"). It is this reason that the former nations experience ruin at the hands of the Israelites (Lev. 18:24–26).

The land, therefore, is indicative of the covenant relationship between God and the people. Possession of the land has stamped the psyche of the Israelites and their identity. Since the land is distributed down to the level of families, it is the practical means by which the individual in Israel claims the covenant. Moreover, each family is responsible for recognizing that continuing possession and familial inheritance are dependent on fidelity to the divine Owner. This is best

illustrated in the detailed boundary descriptions in Joshua 13–19, which divide up the land by tribe and ultimately down to family farms (cf. Zelophehad's daughters, 17:3–4). This feature of familial ownership is important for future redemption of lost properties (Lev. 25:23–24) and the unity of the villages diversified by geographical locations, showing that they all have a common stake in the covenant blessings (cf. the tribal tension created by a second altar, Josh. 22).

The land motif also entails a tension that corresponds to the earlier discussion of divine promise and human obligation. Israel only partially possesses the land, despite the Lord's promise that all will be theirs (e.g., 1:3). The book shows this apparent inconsistency in three ways. First, explicitly the text says that the whole land falls into the hands of the Israelites (e.g., 10:40; 11:23). At places it is "Joshua" who wins the land (e.g., 10:40; 11:16, 23), but more often it is the "LORD" who is credited. He is the Divine Warrior who fights for Israel (e.g., 10:42; 23:3, 9–10). In other texts the book admits that there are inhabitants yet to be dispossessed (e.g., 13:1–7, 13; 15:63; 16:10). This apparent contradiction, however, is not a true contradiction created by opposing viewpoints of the conquest. Younger has shown that in conquest accounts in the ancient Near East, hyperbole is a typical rhetorical device when describing a king's victory.[2] That the book describes the complete settlement of the land and defeat of all of Israel's enemies is a consistent feature of this literary genre (see "Historical and Cultural Background" in the unit on 11:16–12:24). Second, the contingency of obedience is tied to the perpetuity of occupying the land. Williams points to 14:9, the request of Caleb for his inheritance, as a clear example of the two factors in conjunction.[3] Whereas the Genesis promises are expressed as eternal gifts (e.g., Gen. 13:15), the subsequent history of Israel shows that continued occupation is qualified by obedience. Third, Hawk shows that the geographical descriptions of the land promised to the fathers and the actual possession of the land in the book of Joshua do not correspond. The land progressively "shrinks" from the vistas of patriarchal promise to the actual occupation under Joshua, indicating

Joshua is chosen by God to succeed Moses as leader of the Israelites, and he is "filled with the spirit of wisdom because Moses had laid his hands on him" (Deut. 34:9). This watercolor design drawing for a stained-glass piece depicts the scene.

that Joshua's generation does not meet the ideal, due to the failure of the people to follow through.[4] As was the case with Moses and Israel, which Joshua personally witnessed (Deut. 31:14–21), Joshua predicts that the people will soon commit apostasy (24:19), and the narration implies this was the case (24:31; cf. Judg. 2:7). But not all is lost, for the Lord will use the remaining Canaanites for his purposes by testing the loyalty of the people and teaching them warfare (Judg. 2:20–3:2).

Unity

Maintaining unity so that "all Israel" might enter into the promises is important to the success of the conquest. Unity is dependent on the people's allegiance to the same covenant Lord. Submission to the covenant is the ideological glue that transcends tribal differences. "All Israel" (or "all the Israelites") commonly occurs in the book of Joshua, expressing the solidarity of the community as a holistic entity (e.g., 3:1, 7; 4:14; 7:23, 25; 8:24), but the idea is also expressed by the actions taken by the community. "All Israel" participates in crossing the Jordan (3:1–7) and receives the call to covenant renewal (24:1). Inheritance is for all (e.g., the lax seven tribes, chaps. 18–19), and there is unity within a tribe (e.g., the voice of Joseph's sons, chaps. 16–17). Israel's identity as covenant people transcends geography (e.g., the Transjordan tribes are "fellow Israelites," 22:8; cf. chap. 13), crosses generations (e.g., the ancestors and future descendants, 24:6, 19, 31), and includes ethnic groups (e.g., aliens/foreigners, 8:33, 35; 20:9). Even towns of refuge are provided for manslayers so that they might remain in the community in safety

Introduction to Joshua

rather than fleeing to a foreign land (chap. 20). And there is community accountability and appropriate sanctions levied against mutiny and breaking covenant (e.g., 1:18; 7:16–24; chap. 22).

Leadership

The book describes the transition in leadership to Joshua, the new Moses, who is the next "servant of the LORD" (compare 1:1 and 24:29). God, however, is the nation's ultimate leader, whose appointed representatives only carry out his commands. Joshua's appointment is acknowledged by the people (e.g., 1:16–18) and repeatedly confirmed by the narration (e.g., 4:14; 6:27; 10:40; 24:31). The Pentateuch remembers Joshua was with Moses on Sinai (Exod. 24:13; 32:15–18), assisted him at the tent of meeting (Exod. 33:11; cf. Acts 7:44–45), and received the "spirit of wisdom" when Moses laid hands on him (Deut. 34:9). As the second Moses, Joshua sends out spies (chap. 2), leads Israel across dry land at the Jordan (chaps. 3–4), distributes land (e.g., 13:7–8; 14:1–21:45; 22:7), and gives Israel a covenant (chap. 24). Although Joshua is plainly depicted as Moses's successor, there is no obvious successor to Joshua's leadership. In the priesthood, however, Phinehas is the clear successor to Eleazar (22:13). The settlement period relies on the leadership of the Levitical priests, but as the books of Judges and Samuel show, the leadership fails, and the Lord turns to selected civil leaders ("judges," Judg. 2:10–23) and the monarchy (1 Sam. 16:1, 13).

Historical Background

For those who accept the book of Joshua as historically reliable, the setting of the conquest is generally accepted to be in the second half of the second millennium BC, but the specific dating is disputed by scholars. Traditionally, it is dated at the end of the fifteenth century (ca. 1400 BC), according to the biblical chronology of 1 Kings 6:1's 480 years. Others attribute it to the thirteenth century primarily on the basis of Egyptian and Palestinian evidence, understanding 1 Kings 6:1 as a symbolic timetable (ca. 1290/1270 BC). The 480 years refer to twelve generations of an ideal forty years each. What the two views hold in common is establishing the historical setting in the Late Bronze Age (1550–1200). In this period Canaan was carved up among independent kinglets who established walled cities and standing armies. The major political powers—the Hittites, Egyptians, and Assyrians—were at a standoff, freeing Canaan from outside interference. The Amarna Letters from Egypt (ca. 1350) describe the power struggles within Canaan. Kings of Canaanite city-states wrote letters to Egypt's pharaohs, seeking help in dealing with raiding bands of outlaws, known as the Habiru/'Apiru. The term "Habiru/'Apiru" should not be equated with the word "Hebrew" ('ibri) as an ethnic designation, referring exclusively to the Israelites. Rather, the word designates a member of a social group, "outlaw/mercenary," that existed on the margins of settled society. As a consequence of this instability in Canaan, Israel did not face a unified power, such as the Egyptians, when settling the land.

Composition

The authorship of the book is uncertain since Joshua is anonymous. Critical scholars reconstruct the composition's history in terms of early and late sources, tying it to the proposed dates of the books of Deuteronomy and Judges (seventh–sixth centuries). According to this interpretation, a series of indicators in the book shows different perspectives on the events, reflecting a long process of supplements by different editors.[5] Others, however, show that the book does not reflect the late date that tradition-history scholars propose, providing historical and rhetorical grounds for dating the book earlier in the monarchy.[6] The book itself sets the events sometime after the exodus and before the monarchy. The geographical and historical descriptions, settlement patterns, names, and cultural characteristics reflected in the book fit its chronology of the second half of the second millennium BC. Jewish tradition, taken up by Christian tradition, ascribes the book to Joshua, written soon after the events, but there is evidence of later contributions. The book involves both eyewitness testimony (e.g., 5:1, 6; 6:25; 8:32; 18:9; 24:26) and later sources (e.g., "to this day," 4:9; 5:9; 7:26; 10:27; 13:13). The book was probably based on early testimony, both oral and written sources, and was supplemented by an author no later than the early monarchy. The presence of the "Jebusites" (cf. 15:63 with 2 Sam. 5:6–9) and the Canaanite possession of "Gezer"

Israel is conquering Canaan at a time of instability in the region. The Amarna letters, several shown here, reveal that there was no unified power, just small Canaanite city-states that were writing Egypt for help against invading outlaws and mercenaries.

reflect a time before the monarchy (cf. 16:10 with 1 Kings 9:16).

Joshua the Man

Joshua, who is renamed (originally Hoshea, "Salvation") by Moses (Num. 13:16; Deut. 32:44), is an Ephraimite. The name "Joshua" (*Yᵉhoshuaʻ*) means "the LORD is salvation." The short form of "Joshua" (*Yeshuaʻ*) is *Iēsous* ("Jesus") in Greek. Joshua is best remembered as Moses's servant and successor (1:1–9; cf. Exod. 24:13; Num. 27:18–23; Deut. 31:7–8, 14, 23; 34:9), who leads the armies of Israel (Exod. 17:10–13), conquering and distributing the land (cf. Num. 34:17; Deut. 31:3, 7). Only Joshua and Caleb from their generation are permitted to enter Canaan, because of their faith in God's promise (Num. 14:6, 30, 38). Joshua dies at 110 years old and is buried in his allotted land in Canaan (24:29–30; Judg. 2:8–9). He serves as an example of courage and faith (24:14; Acts 7:45; Heb. 11:39).

Christian Interpretation

Christian readers face two especially important interpretive challenges in the book of Joshua. The first concerns the morality of the actions depicted in the book. Second, what is the significance of the land promise made to ancient Israel for Christ and the church?

First, the moral tension faced by Christian readers is the apparent contradiction

Introduction to Joshua

between the command to eradicate certain Canaanite cities (Deut. 7:2; Josh. 6:17–21) and Jesus's teaching to love our enemies (Matt. 5:44). It is a mistaken idea that the Israelites eliminated all the Canaanites in a bloodthirsty, wanton onslaught. Although this ethical dilemma cannot be fully resolved, understanding the special situation helps explain Israel's actions.[7] (1) The practice of *herem*/*haram*—meaning "devoted thing" (*herem*, noun) and "put to destruction" (*haram*, verb)—in which captives and property are devoted to the gods is known in the ancient Near East (2 Kings 19:11; 2 Chron. 20:23). (2) Israel's practice, however, is limited to certain cities, under specific conditions and for one generation (Deut. 20:10–15; cf. an exception in 1 Sam. 15 with Num. 21:1–3). (3) The Canaanites initiate the wars and plan to eradicate the Israelites (9:1–2; 10:1–5; 11:1–5). (4) Israel's policy is only at a divine command based on a moral principle. The practice is often expressed in terms of maintaining holiness.

God uses Israel to destroy the Canaanites because of their idolatry and most-evil conduct (Gen. 15:16; Lev. 18:24–30), which in turn has the effect of weakening their influence on Israel (Deut. 20:17–18). If captives and property are devoted to the service of the Lord, there is no economic incentive for waging war. Moreover, the motivation is not racial superiority or nationalism (Deut. 9:4–5), for the Hebrews are also subject to annihilation if they are equally wicked (Deut. 13:11–16; Josh. 6:18; 7:15).

Second, Christians must answer the question of whether the land promise to the fathers is a promise that is fulfilled in Israel's history, under Joshua's conquest or King David's monarchy, or is a promise yet to be fulfilled. Further, if yet to be fulfilled, is the land promise intended for a future redeemed Israel, or is it fulfilled in

The book of Joshua serves as a bridge between the accounts of Israel's life outside the land of Canaan and those of its life inside the land. This view taken from Mount Nebo looks west across the Jordan Valley, into the land God promised to Abraham and his descendants.

the Christian church? Or, for that matter, in some sense is it fulfilled in both? Is the land promise realized in an actual geopolitical Israel/Palestine, or is it a type of the spiritual realities of Jesus Christ and his church (antitypes)?[8] We cannot answer the questions in a satisfying discussion, since they deserve a thorough hearing, but we can indicate the position of this commentary and explain why. This commentary takes a mediating position by positing that the land promise finds its fulfillment in the life of Jesus and the church. Yet we recognize that the land promise has importance for a future reign of Christ on earth, showing that he is Lord of heaven and "earth" (Phil. 2:10). (1) The conquest of the land is only provisionally fulfilled, not fully and not forever. The conquest is progressive over many years and not complete (e.g., Exod. 23:29–30; Josh. 13:1–7; 15:45–47), which comports with Hebrews 4:8–9. The theme of "land" is used metaphorically for the Christian life, from its inception to the eternal rest (Heb. 4:1–15). The associative idea of the "temple" in the geopolitical center of the land (holy space; cf. Num. 35:34) has its presence in the person of Jesus Christ and the church (John 2:21; 1 Cor. 6:19). (2) The New Testament downplays the importance of the land promise (Rom. 9:4), although other features of the Old Testament promises are given their due, such as "seed" and "blessing" (Gal. 3; Rom. 4). There are explicit references to a metaphorical fulfillment, stating that the land is not the ultimate goal of the promises (Heb. 4:9; 11:10; 13:14). (3) The Old Testament itself suggests that the land promise is not a territorial gift that is historically bound but a gift reaching beyond space and time. This is well illustrated in the inheritance of the Levites, who possess no land tract comparable to the other tribes. Their inheritance is God himself (Josh. 13:33; cf. Deut. 18:1–2). Similarly, those in Christ receive as their inheritance the Lord and his eternal blessings, not a land grant reminiscent of the former era of Israel. (4) The possibility of a land possessed by the saints on earth exists and will not be exclusively Jewish (Rom 11:26; Rev. 20:1–6).

Preparing to Possess the Land

Big Idea *The word of God reveals God's will for his people, and his presence enables them to achieve his purposes.*

Understanding the Text

The Text in Context

Chapters 1–5 describe the preparations made by Israel to confront their enemies (chaps. 6–12). In concert with Joshua 2, chapter 1 introduces themes that will dominate the subsequent stories of Israel's battles. Chapters 1 and 2 establish that it is the Lord, not the people, who brings them victory as their Commander in Chief. He orders Joshua and the people, directing strategy and execution. The effectiveness of the directives, some of which are quite odd, transforms the people's initial apprehension into courageous confidence. To instill confidence in Joshua and the people, the Lord himself formally inaugurates the leadership of Joshua. The Lord speaks to Joshua directly, as he has done with Moses, who held the esteemed position of "the servant of the LORD." Joshua is his successor, "the servant of Moses," but he is yet to prove his valor in the eyes of the people. By leading the people across the Jordan on dry ground, the Lord shows Israel that he is leading Joshua as he has led Moses (3:7). By the end of the book, readers are pointedly informed that Joshua too has become "the

servant of the LORD" (24:29). Joshua's response to the commands of the Lord demonstrates that the success of Israel rests on the promises of God, not on a particular man, whether it is Moses or another.

Chapter 1 describes the inauguration of the divine purpose for Israel by the call and succession of Joshua to Moses. "After the death of Moses" is a hinge that connects the book of Joshua with the preceding account of Moses's message and recorded death in Deuteronomy. The phrase swings back by bringing to mind all that the reader knows from Israel's prior history and swings forward by anticipating the post-Moses life of the people. The wilderness generation reaches the plains of Moab, where they encamp east of the Jordan River.

The structure of chapter 1 reinforces the idea of Joshua's and the people's united compliance. The flow of the narrative moves in parallel lines, with (1) God preparing Joshua for the task of entering the land (1:1–9) and (2) Joshua preparing the people to obey (1:10–18). The Lord's exhortations to "be strong and [very] courageous" (1:6, 7, 9) are echoed by the people in their loyalty oath to Joshua (1:18). Joshua and the people begin in sync in following the Lord's commands. These are the same words he has received from his mentor, Moses, and from God at his commissioning service (Deut. 31:6, 7, 23). Joshua's ordination was a public event, made in view of the people; now, by echoing the divine charge to Joshua to "be strong and courageous," the people acknowledge his calling and urge him to fulfill it.

Another structural feature is the correspondence in content between the opening paragraph (1:2–5) and the arrangement of the whole book's outline. The paragraph serves as a précis. "Cross the Jordan River" (1:2) anticipates the preparations for crossing the Jordan narrated in chapters 1–5. "[The land] I will give you" (1:3) corresponds to the conquest of the land found in chapters 6–12. Chapters 13–21 report the land tracts distributed to the tribes, which correspond to the description of Israel's "territory" in 1:4. For the final section of the book, chapters 22–24, the expression "all the days of your life" (1:5) anticipates the closing exhortations to be faithful to the covenant's stipulations so that they might remain in the land all their days.

Historical and Cultural Background

The primary message of Joshua is God's gift of the land to his people. The

Key Themes of Joshua 1:1–18

- God promises to lead his people through his revealed word and his appointed leader Joshua.
- God calls for Joshua and his people to be obedient and to persevere with courage, despite opposition.
- The people pledge to obey Joshua's instructions, calling on Joshua to be faithful to the revelation given him by God.

format of the book corresponds generally to a royal land grant from the early second millennium.[1] Abbael, king of Aleppo in northwest Syria, grants the city Alalakah to his loyal vassal King Yarimlim. The land grant and the structure of Joshua share in these major features: (1) a narrative explanation for the land grant (chaps. 1–12); (2) description of the allotment (chaps. 13–21); (3) an oath of loyalty by the vassal (chaps. 22–23); and (4) witnesses to the completion of the transaction (chap. 24). The correlation in Joshua shows that the Lord is the great King who bestows Canaan on his vassals, the Israelites, conditioned on their exclusive and continued loyalty to God.

The arrangement of the book of Joshua is similar to royal land grants found in the ancient Near East. Like the book of Joshua, the land grant shown here contains an explanation for the gift of land, a description of the land boundaries, and witnesses to the transaction (Babylon, eleventh century BC).

Interpretive Insights

1:1 *the servant of the LORD.* "Servant" (*'ebed*) is a different word from "servant [*mᵉsharet*] of Moses," which describes Joshua's subordination to Moses (but cf. 4:14; 24:29). Moses retains pride of place as the unique vessel of revelation (cf. Num. 12:7–8). Moses's instruction equates to God's word, which is to be observed by succeeding generations (1:7–8).

1:4 *from the desert to Lebanon.* The parameters are generally stated and described from the perspective of central Canaan: south (desert) to north (Lebanon), east (Euphrates River) to west (Great Sea = Mediterranean). The promise resembles Deuteronomy 11:24–25, showing that God is about to make good on his pledge (Gen. 15:18–21). The boundaries are given in principle since the people do not reach them in the limited wars of Canaan. The regime of David/Solomon comes closer to the ideal (1 Kings 4:21; cf. Ps. 72:8).

1:5 *As I was with Moses.* Although the expression may refer generally to God's superintendence, it probably refers to Moses's victory over the Transjordan kings Sihon and Og (Deut. 31:3–8). God now grants Joshua victory over the Cisjordan nations.

1:6 *Be strong and courageous.* When these words occur in tandem, they often describe military resolve (e.g., 2 Sam. 10:12). The Canaanites are described as determined "enemies" of Israel (21:44).

1:7 *Be careful to obey.* The same expression occurs in Moses's exhortations to Israel (Deut. 28:1, 15; 32:46).

to the right or to the left. This merism (contrasting parts that express totality) indicates complete obedience (Deut. 26:14).

successful wherever you go. This is not a comprehensive promise of success at everything the Israelites attempt. "Wherever you go" is a figure of speech indicating "wherever you go in conformity to God's instructions."

1:8 *Book of the Law.* "Law" (*torah*) occurs nine times in the book (1:7, 8; 8:31, 32, 34 [2x]; 22:5; 23:6; 24:26) and means "instruction," often given in law collections (8:31; 23:6; 24:26). This probably refers to the written laws derived from Deuteronomy (30:10; 31:24–26), although Moses recorded other laws and events (e.g., Exod. 17:14; 24:4; 34:27; Num. 33:2).

meditate on it day and night. "Meditate" (*hagah*) does not refer to a repetition of mystic words (mantra) or to reaching a heightened level of spiritual awareness. It describes contemplation for the purpose of understanding and obedience. The merism "day and night" means "continually" (cf. 2 Tim. 1:3). Vigilant study of God's instructions must characterize the king (Deut. 17:19) and the wise person (Ps. 1:2).

1:9 *Do not be afraid . . . discouraged.* This expression anticipates military conflict (8:1; 10:8, 25; 11:6) but assures Joshua that Israel will prevail.

1:10 *officers.* As one of three groups, including elders and judges, that exercise civil authority (3:2; 8:33; 23:2; 24:1), the officers assist the leading elders (Deut. 1:15). A line of authority reaches from Joshua to the officers to the people, but all are under the rule of God, which is mediated through the Book of the Law (including future kings, Deut. 17:18–20; 1 Kings 2:3).

1:11 *Three days.* If not a full three days, the reference is to parts of three days or is simply the idiom for a short period of time (e.g., "yesterday, three days ago" is the idiom for "aforethought, beforehand" [20:5]). The precise chronology of "three days" mentioned in 2:16, 22 and 3:2 is uncertain.[2] That the narrative gives such details suggests an eyewitness to the events.

take possession of the land. This states the purpose of crossing the Jordan—to dispossess Canaan's inhabitants (Deut. 1:8).

1:12 *the Reubenites, the Gadites and the half-tribe of Manasseh.* These three receive their inheritance from Moses at Israel's victory over the Amorite kings in Transjordan. They must, however, join their brother tribes in conquering the land across the Jordan (Num. 32; Deut. 3:18–20). That the Transjordan tribes already receive their inheritance is reassurance that *all* Israel will do the same.

1:15 *the LORD gives them rest.* "Rest" is prominent in the book, meaning peace and prosperity (Deut. 12:10). "Rest" does not mean a state of inactivity or an indisposition to activity. The Lord, who fights Israel's battles (21:44; 23:1), secures their "rest." The keynote of "rest" is figurative for spiritual salvation in Hebrews 4:1–13.

1:18 *Whoever rebels.* The people recognize that defiance by some would mean judgment for them as a whole (e.g., Achan's sin, 7:1). The ancient concept of community

solidarity meant that individual behavior impinged on the accountability of the collective community.

be put to death. This phrase often describes capital punishment carried out by the community against transgressors (e.g., murder, Exod. 21:12). Since Joshua's commands are tantamount to divine instructions, those who oppose Joshua's directives are punished as violators of God's law. Obedience is a matter of life and death.

Theological Insights

The authority of the word of God is the primary theological idea. Divine authority and human obedience are ideas repeatedly visited in this chapter. The authority of Moses and Joshua lies only in their

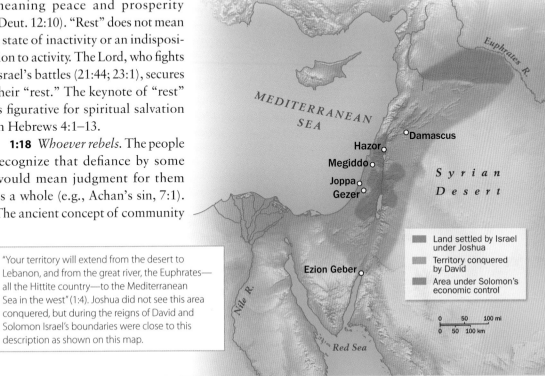

"Your territory will extend from the desert to Lebanon, and from the great river, the Euphrates—all the Hittite country—to the Mediterranean Sea in the west" (1:4). Joshua did not see this area conquered, but during the reigns of David and Solomon Israel's boundaries were close to this description as shown on this map.

Land settled by Israel under Joshua

Territory conquered by David

Area under Solomon's economic control

Joshua 1:1–18

conformity to God's instructions, not in the position of the men per se. Their authority is derived from their special appointment by God. When they faithfully speak the word of the Lord, the proper response of the people is to obey. In doing so they recognize that God has called Joshua to this assignment. From the outset and throughout the book there are repeated reminders that the conquest is in response to God's command to enter the land, not the action of a greedy land seizure. A contributing theological idea is the presence of God. As obedience is required for successful entrance into the land, the enabling presence of God is equally necessary. God is the Divine Warrior who fights Israel's battles (Exod. 15:3; Josh. 10:14, 42). The imperative of God's presence reflects the same sentiment as Moses, who has acknowledged that unless God goes with the people they should not attempt to enter the land (Exod. 33:14–15).

Teaching the Text

This passage shows that God's promised blessing will be realized when the people are faithful to God's revelation (1:7–9), in contrast to the former generation, whose disobedience resulted in failure to enjoy the blessings of the land (Num. 13–14; Heb. 3:7–4:13). The passage emphasizes obedience to the authority of God and the verbal nature of revelation. The passage calls for the Israelites to know and act ("careful to obey," 1:7; "careful to do," 1:8) on the Scriptures as the sure word of God. The lesson for Christians is that persevering faith means continuing in the blessings of Christ. It is Christ alone who has perfectly

obeyed God on behalf of the unrighteous, and because of him they receive the righteousness of Christ (2 Cor. 5:17–21).

The references to "this Book of the Law" and "written" (1:8) show that the revealed word is not for Joshua's audience alone but is written (inscripturated) for the instruction of future generations. That the Lord is present with Israel when they enter the land ("will be with you," 1:9) is what will assure their settlement. The combination of the themes of word and presence in the chapter communicates that God's personal integrity and presence stand behind his promises. For Christian readers, the New Testament teaches the centrality of the Scriptures for Christian faith and service (Rom. 10:17; Col. 3:16–17; 2 Tim. 3:15–16). Christ secures for believers the blessings of divine promise and presence (Eph. 1:3, 13–14).

Although the idea of leadership is present in the text, to teach principles of godly leadership is secondary to the purposes of the passage. The chapter may illustrate useful leadership lessons, but it does not give prescriptive directives as a model. The exhortation "be strong and [very] courageous" (1:6, 7, 9, 18) occurs in a context that shows God calls Joshua to a special task. The Lord strengthens Christians for *his* purposes (1 Cor. 16:13; Eph. 3:16), not for whatever goals they might want to achieve.

Illustrating the Text

Be committed to knowing God's Word.

Quote: *The God Delusion*, by Richard Dawkins. The atheist Dawkins makes an astonishing observation about the state of

Bible knowledge among Christians today: "I must admit that even I am a little taken aback at the biblical ignorance commonly displayed by people educated in more recent decades than I was."[3] Dawkins puts his finger on the reason why some Christians stumble theologically and morally. We cannot be obedient to what we do not know. Challenge your listeners to consider their commitment to know, understand, and apply the Word of God.

Honor the authority of God's Word.

Autobiography: *Just As I Am,* **by Billy Graham.** In his autobiography, evangelist Billy Graham describes his encounter with theological liberalism and his subsequent struggle with accepting the authority of the Bible as God's Word. He describes how he took an evening walk in the woods and prayed, "O God! There are many things in this book I do not understand." Then he surrendered his questions to God: "Father, I am going to accept this as Thy Word—by *faith*! I'm going to allow faith to go beyond my intellectual questions and doubts, and I will believe this to be Your inspired Word."[4] Not long after this evening, Graham preached in the Los Angeles campaign that began his lifelong work

as one of the twentieth century's greatest evangelists. Our finite minds are incapable of comprehending God and the universe, and ultimately there must be a decision of faith to accept God's Word and authority. As Billy Graham discovered, such a decision can change the world.

Be strong and very courageous.

News Story: In 2014, Meriam Yahya Ibrahim, a twenty-seven-year-old Sudanese woman, was sentenced to death for refusing to renounce her Christian faith. She was accused of converting from Islam to Christianity and then marrying a Christian man. She was also sentenced to one hundred lashes for having a child with her Christian husband. All of this could have been avoided if Meriam would have simply denied Jesus, as many before her had done in order to escape punishment and a death sentence. But Meriam refused to recant her faith, and, without ever compromising her commitment to Christ, she was later released.[5] Ask your listeners to consider what it means for them to "be strong and very courageous" as they live out their Christian faith in an increasingly hostile world.

Scouting the Land

Big Idea *God reassures his people that his promises will be fulfilled.*

Understanding the Text

The Text in Context

The spying of the land continues the steps of preparation given in chapters 1–5 for the people's entrance into the land. Chapter 1 describes God's instructions to Joshua to ready the people to enter, and chapter 2 demonstrates that God has prepared the way. As the first chapter is cast in the image of Moses and his exhortations in Deuteronomy, the spying of the land episode recalls the dispatch of the twelve spies sent by Moses in Numbers 13–14. Taken together chapters 1 and 2 set the present generation in a situation similar to that of their fathers. They must decide if they will go forward in faith or refuse to enter out of fear. We learn that fear rests with the Canaanites, not with the Israelites. Chapter 3 narrates the response of Joshua to the good report by the spies.

Chapter 2 is made up of four key parts. (1) The chapter is framed by Joshua's orders to the spies and by their report (2:1, 24). (2) The interaction between the king of Jericho and Rahab in verses 2–7 presents the cause for the oath between Rahab and the spies. (3) The oath is mutually agreed to in verses 8–21a. (4) Verses 21b–23 narrate the spies' escape and return to Joshua. The same term "sent" occurs for Joshua sending forth the spies to Jericho and for Rahab sending forth the spies for their return (2:1, 21b). The king of Jericho also has "sent" for Rahab (2:3).

Two dialogues direct the episode: (1) the king of Jericho and Rahab and (2) the spies and Rahab. Rahab dominates the two primary scenes. Her significance is twofold. First, she is responsible for protecting the spies, and second, she gives the perspective of the Canaanites toward the imminent invasion of the Israelites. The fear in Jericho that she reports to the spies is in turn reported to Joshua by the spies, affirming that God is with them (2:9, 14, 24; cf. Judg. 7:13–15). The spies realize that the Lord has instilled the terror that he has promised (Deut. 2:25; 11:25).

Historical and Cultural Background

The events of Joshua occurred in the latter half of the second millennium (Late Bronze Age, 1550–1200 BC). In addition to the Bible, our sources for understanding the cultural setting of Canaan are the contemporaneous texts from Amarna (Egypt) and Ugarit (northwest Syria). Ugarit's religion was a naturalistic polytheism. The gods and goddesses were inextricably tied to the phenomena of the heavens and the earth. For example, Baal was "the Lord of the Earth," who with Anath, the goddess of war and love, provided seasonal fertility. The confession of Rahab reflects a striking difference in worldview. Her admission that "the LORD [Yahweh] your God is God in heaven above and on the earth below" (2:11) shows that she has embraced Israel's God as Creator and acknowledged the history of Yahweh's victories over Israel's enemies. The focus on the city wall in chapters 2 and 6 reflects its importance as the major defense against hostile invasions. Rahab's house was built *in* the wall or was in some way connected to the wall, which explains the spies' undetected departure. Archaeological evidence from this period shows cities with a continuous band of connected houses forming the perimeter "wall." Ancient texts from the second millennium describe an association between prostitution and innkeepers. The Babylonian Law of Hammurapi (eighteenth

Key Themes of Joshua 2:1–24

- God protects his people and defeats the enemies of his purposes.
- The people of faith (Rahab and the spies) risk their lives and persevere with courage.
- God reassures Joshua that the promise of possession will be inevitably accomplished.
- As the Lord is certain to discharge his oath to Israel, the Israelites are expected to discharge faithfully their commitments.

century) requires prostitutes to hand over criminals who are in their house. Rahab risks her life by housing the Hebrew scouts.[1]

Interpretive Insights

2:1 *two spies from Shittim.* The location was probably in the hills of Moab opposite Jericho, east of the Jordan River (Num.

Rahab's house is described as "part of the city wall" (2:15), which made it easier for the Israelite spies to escape Jericho undetected, by rappelling from her window. City architecture from this period shows evidence of houses whose back walls were part of the city wall construction. The archaeological remains at Beersheba, shown here, reveal several pillared houses whose back walls are connected to the city perimeter wall.

An aerial view of Tell es-Sultan, the ancient city of Jericho.

33:49). Ironically, this site from which Israel initiates its victory is also remembered as the place where Israel worships Baal of Peor (Num. 25; Ps. 106:28–30). References to the "two" men (2:1, 4, 23) echo the "two" of the twelve spies in the first generation who give the good report (Joshua, Caleb) and who alone are permitted to enter the land (Num. 14:6–9, 30).

entered . . . prostitute named Rahab . . . stayed. That the men begin at the house of Rahab may be no more than a practical decision since the location of her house, built in (or atop) the wall of the city, would be easily accessible. It may be that travelers visiting a prostitute would not cause suspicion; even so, they are detected, including their identity and their mission (2:2). The nature of her prostitution is uncertain since in ancient cultures both street prostitution and temple prostitution were common. There is no evidence in the text that she is connected with the cult in Jericho, however. The terms "entered" (*bo'*) and "slept" (*shakab*, "to lie down"; NIV: "stayed") can describe sexual relations (e.g., Gen. 30:15–16). What is more, the sexually charged expression "the men

came to me" is spoken by Rahab (2:4), which can be an idiom for sexual relations (e.g., Gen. 6:4). However, when "stayed" means sexual contact, it includes the preposition "with" ("to lie down with"; e.g., Gen. 19:32, 33; NIV: "sleep with"), and the context is usually explicit. Since the text does not state sexual relations occur, it should not be assumed by the reader. The recurrences of *bo'* ("came," 2:4) and *shakab* ("lay down," 2:8) may nonetheless intensify the tension in the story by subtly reinforcing in the reader's mind the risk of temptation. Rahab's profession of loyalty to Israel and acknowledgment of the supremacy of the Lord are the first reported incident of new allegiance in the book.

2:9 *has given you.* This recurring expression "the Lord gives the land" (2:14, 24) also appears in the promise that God makes to Israel's ancestors regarding their descendants (Exod. 6:4, 8). The verb "has given" (*natan*) indicates that although the Israelites have not yet taken possession, the decree has been declared and the result is certain.

fear of you. The word "fear" (*'emah*), sometimes translated "dread" or "terror," also occurs in the Lord's promise to inspire fear in the nations (Exod. 15:16; 23:27). The Lord can terrify (Job 9:34; 13:21), and invading armies can stir alarm (Ezra 3:3). In this case what the Lord has done in Egypt and the defeat of the two Transjordan kings are what produce panic.

2:10 *completely destroyed*. "Put to destruction" (*haram*) means to devote a person/thing to God's exclusive service, "to ban from common use" (e.g., Lev. 27:21; NIV: "devoted"). In reference to warfare it means that the Israelites devote the cities and their populations to the Lord by utterly destroying them (Deut. 2:34). Achan breaks the ban by stealing "devoted things" (*herem*) from the captured spoils of Jericho (7:1). For the significance for Christian readers, see "Christian Interpretation" in the introduction.

2:11 LORD *your God is God*. Rahab's confession is remarkable in light of the nations' polytheism. Heaven and earth are the realms of pagan gods. The name "LORD" (*yhwh*, Yahweh) is the distinctive covenant name of God that specifies that the "God" she refers to is the God of the Hebrews, who has made covenant with Israel at Sinai (Exod. 3:18; 6:2–8). That Rahab acknowledges Yahweh as God shows that the Canaanites are culpable for their refusal to submit to the Israelites. See the sidebar "Abraham's Ancestral Gods" in the unit on 24:1–18.

2:12 *shown kindness*. "Kindness" (*hesed*) typically refers to acts of loyalty, such as faithfully carrying out the pledge of an agreement. Rahab's protection of the spies is an act of loyalty that deserves a reciprocal response. Operating on the principle of family solidarity, the spies extend her protection to family members.

2:14 *Our lives for your lives!* The spies' oath offers the guarantee that no harm comes to her family, or else the spies' own

Jericho

Jericho was one of the oldest cities in Palestine and was almost continuously occupied in antiquity. The modern site, Tell es-Sultan, is not large—approximately ten acres. That it was located at a natural spring and strategically guarded the passage from the Jordan River to the central highlands made it a prized site. It was an important transit point for travelers (cf. Luke 10:30–35). Jericho is an archaeologically complex site that has produced widely divergent views regarding its testimony to the biblical account. Moreover, scholars differ in dating the conquest, placing it either in the mid-fifteenth century or the mid-thirteenth century BC. The biblical account cannot be definitively confirmed or falsified by the archaeological record at Jericho.

lives are held accountable. The stipulation of the pledge is the continued loyalty of Rahab.

2:15 *house . . . city wall*. For the relationship between the house and the city wall, see "Historical and Cultural Background" above. Mention of the "wall" points ahead to the salvation that Rahab's household experiences, afforded not only by the spies but also by the superintendence of God. Although the city's walls will collapse at the sound of the trumpets, she and her family will survive (6:5). Since the gate to the city has been closed, the spies are in effect captured. Rahab's lowering of the spies by a rope provides the only escape route available. This aspect of the story underscores the vulnerability of the spies and their dependence on Rahab's favor and ingenuity.

2:19 *their blood will be on their own heads*. The idiom refers to the question of guilt for failure to keep the oath (Lev. 20:9; Ezek. 18:13; Acts 18:6).

2:22 *three days*. Rahab has ample opportunity to reverse her pledge while the men are hiding west of the Jordan, but their safe return shows the spies that Rahab has kept her oath.

Theological Insights

God's faithful confirmation of his promises is the chief theological contribution of this chapter. Not only does the Lord reveal his plans for his people, but he also reassures them of the fulfillment of his promises. Any opposition to the purposes of God is ultimately defeated. The Lord inspires courage and endurance in the life of a believer through his revelation and abiding presence. The proper response of his people is perseverance in faithful obedience, trusting God for the fulfilling of his promises.

Teaching the Text

Spying the land is *not* an episode that addresses moral issues, such as prostitution or lying. The primary message is God centered. The realization of the promises is dependent on the Lord, who has given them purely by his grace (Deut. 7:7–8). Although Rahab is a Canaanite and a prostitute, her deliverance shows that God's grace extends to any person who confesses him. Her neighbors also hear of the Lord (2:9–11), but only Rahab surrenders to his purposes. Also, the text does not *teach* that immorality as a means to an end is acceptable when the outcome is moral (6:25; cf. Exod. 20:16; Col. 3:9). The text only *describes* the events and does not render a judgment on Rahab's occupation or the lie that she tells the king. She is commended for her faith, and the Bible is silent about her deception (Matt. 1:5; Heb. 11:31; James 2:25). God works out his will in a sinful, fallen world, using less-than-ideal people and circumstances to advance his purposes (e.g., Isa. 10:5). For instance, the disagreement between Paul and Barnabas regarding Timothy leads to the spread of the gospel (Acts 15:37–40).

Another lesson is the assurance of Israel's victory over their enemies. The passage specifically states the enemies' impending demise but also shows this indirectly by depicting the king of Jericho in an unfavorable light. That the king is tricked by Rahab, a woman of low social order, lampoons the king, making him appear inept (cf. Jael and Sisera, Judg. 4). The purpose of exposing the king's weakness is to strengthen the people's resolve to move forward in faith. Christian readers have the assurance of the victory that the cross of Christ has secured (1 Cor. 15:54–58; Col. 2:13–15; 1 John 5:4). Christian living involves battling spiritual powers and suffering under oppressive authorities. What comforts, however, is the knowledge that the *ultimate* outcome has been won and secured by Christ.

A further insight is the relationship of God's mighty acts to human faith. Mighty acts convince Rahab that the Lord God is indeed the Lord of all creation and is alone worthy of her devotion. God performs his mighty deeds to demonstrate his power and his grace (24:17; Exod. 10:1–2). In the New Testament the miracles performed by Jesus and the apostles are "signs" that engender faith (John 3:2; Acts 14:3). God's saving works in the Western world today are not typically accompanied by miracles, but witnessing the power of the gospel to transform lives encourages faith in the life of believers.

Illustrating the Text

Amazing grace! God can use even you!

Hymn: "Amazing Grace," by John Newton. Newton drew the lyrics of this hymn from the experiences in his own life. Walking away from the faith of his Christian mother, Newton took to the seas and eventually joined a slave-trading ship. In his own words Newton lived a life of moral abandon: "I not only sinned with a high hand myself, but made it my study to tempt and seduce others upon every occasion."[2] But the Lord captured his attention on a journey in which his ship was struck by a life-threatening storm. After giving his life to Jesus during that storm, he later became a pastor and the author of numerous hymns.[3] As we see in the story of Rahab, God can use anyone, regardless of his or her past. Will you trust in his amazing grace and allow him to use you?

Trust God in the face of great odds.

Church Missions: Andrew van der Bijl ("Brother Andrew") is a Christian missionary who smuggled Bibles into communist countries during the height of the Cold War. In his autobiography, *God's Smuggler*, Brother Andrew tells the story of his first entry smuggling Bibles into communist Romania. The six cars in front of him had been inspected so thoroughly that one even had its engine taken apart. Watching these intense inspections, he prayed, "Lord . . . , I know that no amount of cleverness on my part can get through this border search. Dare I ask for a miracle? Let me take some of the Bibles out and leave them in the open where they will be seen. Then, Lord, I cannot possibly be depending on my own stratagems, can I? I will be depending utterly upon You."[4] When it was his turn at the crossing, he got over the border in less than thirty seconds; the guard only looked at his papers and waved him through. There are times when God calls us to take risks in order to accomplish his purposes. We obey knowing that we are not alone and that he is a God of miracles.

Develop courage and perseverance.

Literature: *A Wrinkle in Time*, by Madeleine L'Engle. In L'Engle's work, the main character, Meg, is on a mission with her brother and friend to rescue her father from an evil planet. In the early stages of their journey, she feels the need to hold their hands as a way to steady herself. However, once they arrive on the dark planet, she realizes that this mission is too serious for her to be afraid and completely dependent on her companions. Meg knows that she alone is close enough to her father to get through to him. She is scared but goes alone anyway. The Lord calls us to live a life of faith, which requires us, by the very definition of faith, to let God do through us what only he can do. Such a life requires courage, perseverance, and trust in God.

Crossing the Jordan

Big Idea *God demonstrates his power so that people might believe that he is the living and true Lord God.*

Understanding the Text

The Text in Context

Chapters 1 and 2 prepare for the crossing of the Jordan River in chapters 3–4, the central event of chapters 1–5. Chapter 3 continues the setting at Shittim and contains allusions to chapters 1 and 2 (e.g., comparison of Joshua to Moses). The ark of the covenant takes center stage in chapter 3. The word "ark" occurs ten times in the passage, and third-person references to the ark ("it") appear four more times. The title "ark of the covenant of the LORD" begins and ends the account (3:3, 17), and in between are variations on the name. The flow of the narrative reflects the movement of the ark. It is the heart of the chapter from both literary and visual perspectives, for the people are to keep their eyes on the ark, and the advancement of the ark dictates the movement of the assembly.

Chapters 3 and 4 are overlapping narratives, describing the same event (cf. 4:10).[1] Chapter 3 details the crossing itself, and chapter 4 details the two memorials to the event. These chapters share many particulars that create a literary cohesion. For example, "Today I [God] will begin to exalt you [Joshua]" (3:7) anticipates the fulfillment, "that day the LORD exalted Joshua" (4:14).

Chapter 3 recounts the journey in two steps: first, from the base of operations (Shittim) to the staging area at the river's banks (3:1–2), and second, the crossing (3:14–17). Sandwiched between are speeches that slow the action: (1) the officers, probably in accord with Joshua's directives (as in chap. 1), instruct the people how to proceed (3:3–4); (2) Joshua instructs the people to prepare spiritually (3:5); (3) he commands the priests who carry the ark to cross over (3:6); (4) the Lord encourages Joshua (3:7–8); and (5) Joshua addresses the people, exalting the Lord and forecasting what is about to take place (3:9–13).

Interpretive Insights

3:1 *Shittim . . . to the Jordan.* (See the comments on 2:1.) The Jordan River is the major physical feature that separates the tablelands of Transjordan to the east from the central highlands of Canaan to the west. The river valley is elongated in shape and is eleven miles at its widest point near Jericho. The length is about sixty miles (as the crow flies), but the river's winding course covers about two hundred miles.

3:3 *ark of the covenant.* The ark is the chief symbol of God's presence (Num. 10:33–36), and it is God's attendance that ensures the people's success (Josh. 3:11–12). The ark, however, is not an image of God, nor is God limited by the presence or absence of the ark (Num. 14:44; 1 Sam. 4:1–11; 1 Kings 8:27). (See also the comments on 4:16.)

3:5 *Consecrate yourselves.* The language "consecrate yourselves" (*qadash*) is related to the vocabulary of sanctuary worship. The crossing, therefore, is cast as a sacred act of worship. Their ritual activity probably entails ritual washings (Exod. 19:10–11). The measure of space between the people and the ark (about a half mile) has practical and theological aspects. Practically, it gives a better line of sight for the people, enabling them to follow its route. Theologically, it makes clear that it is God, not Joshua, who is in charge of the procession. It also reinforces the idea of God's holiness, serving as a protective barrier between the people and the danger of the holy ark (Exod. 19:12; 1 Sam. 6:19; 2 Sam. 6:6–7). To trivialize the ark by treating it as a magical amulet would result in their failure (1 Sam. 4:3).

3:10 *living God.* The passage tells the reader more about God than it does about the armies of Israel. Unlike the deities of the nations, the God of Israel is "living" and thus able to fulfill his promises to Israel. The name "God" (*'el*)

Key Themes of Joshua 3:1–17

- The Lord, represented by the ark of the covenant, leads his people into the land of inheritance.
- The people prepare themselves spiritually before taking action.
- The Lord assures Israel of ultimate victory over their enemies by demonstrating his power in drying up the river.
- "All Israel" acts in unity of purpose and with precision.

underscores the power of God, whose supremacy will vanquish the formidable walled cities of the nations.

Canaanites, Hittites, Hivites, Perizzites, Girgashites, Amorites and Jebusites. There are many diverse lists of the Canaanite nations, but these seven nations constitute an

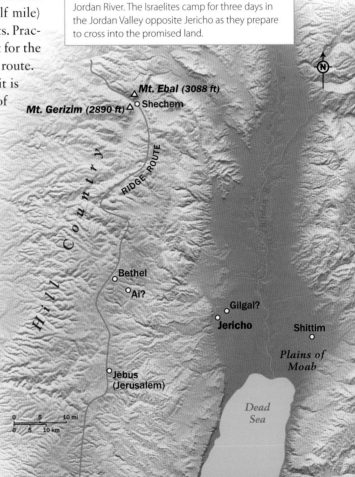

The eastern boundary of the promised land is the Jordan River. The Israelites camp for three days in the Jordan Valley opposite Jericho as they prepare to cross into the promised land.

ideal list and are described as stronger and more numerous than the Israelites (Deut. 7:1). This same list in 24:11 shows that the Lord, as the one and only "living God," has defeated the nations.

3:11 *Lord of all the earth.* Israel's God is Master of the earth. The Hebrew word "Lord" (*'adon*) differs from the covenant-specific name "LORD" (Yahweh). The emphasis of "all the earth" proclaims the limitless reign of God, whose majesty is evidenced by the breadth of his authority. The word translated "earth" (*'erets*) can be translated "land," which would refer to Canaan, not the whole earth. Since the same title occurs in contexts that refer to the whole world, it is better to render the word in that sense (Ps. 97:5; Zech. 6:5). The Lord's rule has no borders and no rivals.

3:13 *stand up in a heap.* The term "heap" describes the wall of water at the exodus crossing (Exod. 15:8; Pss. 33:7; 78:13; see ESV). The Jordan crossing is linked to the miracle of the exodus event. The Lord God is the almighty Creator who gathers the waters by his unmatched power.

3:15 *Now the Jordan is at flood stage.* This parenthetical aside highlights the marvel of the miracle since it shows that the drying of the riverbed is not by lucky coincidence or natural means. The river is at its highest point and at its most dangerous moment; during spring harvest the waters surge from above and empty into the Dead Sea.

3:16 *Adam . . . Zarethan . . . Dead Sea.* Adam is usually identified as Tell ed-Damiyeh, which sits eighteen miles north of Jericho on the east side of the Jordan, just south of the Jabbok River. Its location

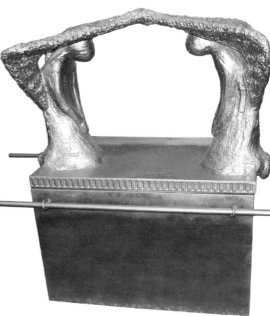

The priests carrying the ark of the covenant, the symbol of God's presence, are the first to enter the Jordan River to cross into the promised land. This replica of the ark of the covenant is part of the tabernacle model at Timna, Israel.

is a strategic place for crossing. Zarethan's location is uncertain; recommendations include sites east of the Jordan and north of Adam. That the water gathers above Jericho means that the river's flow from that point south to the Dead Sea completely dries up.

Theological Insights

God achieves "amazing things" (3:5; cf. Exod. 34:10) among his people to show that he alone is God and he alone is worthy of their utmost trust (e.g., 2:10–11; 9:9–10). The main objective of the miracles he achieves is to build the people's faith in the Lord. Also, the overall impression of the story is the orderly progress of the assembly, which is obedient to the instructions of its leaders, who in turn follow carefully the prior instructions of the Lord. There is a smooth coordination of actions that portrays the idea of command and obedience. The participants are the commander Joshua, the civil officers, the cultic priests, and the general population—all Israel. They each know their role and abide by it. At the head of the processional is the ark, which represents the presence of God. The Lord alone is the one who achieves this great wonder. It is not the process itself nor the ark functioning as a magical box that performs the deed (cf. 1 Sam. 4:3).

Teaching the Text

This miracle crossing should not be presented as one of many magic shows in a carnival. The passage profiles God, who is the magisterial, living God; his authoritative power transcends human comprehension or achievement. He is also the holy God who exhibits moral perfection in all his attributes and deeds. This is reflected in the admonition that the people are to consecrate themselves (3:5). The crossing is presented in the text as an act of reverential worship.

Some readers may explain away the "miracle" in terms of natural phenomena alone. For instance, rock slides in the Jordan River that stop the river's flow have been reported in the past. The dichotomy of "natural" and "supernatural," however, is a modern imposition on the text. Theologically, the Bible shows that all things are attributed to God's power and purpose. Whether the Lord uses "nature" or not, the biblical story points out two features of the crossing that indicate it is a mighty work of God. First, the river is at flood

Ark of the Covenant

The ark was a rectangular box, made of acacia wood, measuring forty-five inches long, twenty-seven inches wide, and twenty-seven inches high. It was overlaid with pure gold inside and out. The lid, called "the atonement place" (kapporet), traditionally known as the "mercy seat," also was pure gold. Two golden cherubim were at the two ends of the lid, facing each other and looking down at the cover, with their wings raised above (Exod. 25:10–22). The cherubim were guardians of the divine presence. The ark housed the tablets of the testimony revealed to Moses, and for this reason the ark was also identified as "the ark of the covenant law" (Josh. 4:16). The significance of the ark was shown by its place and function in the tent of meeting. It sat in the most sacred room of the sanctuary, "the Most Holy Place" (Exod. 26:34; Heb. 9:3). It is from above the ark that the Lord spoke to Moses (Exod. 25:22; Num. 7:89). The Lord was identified with the ark, though not coterminous with it, and it is referred to as the place above which God is enthroned (e.g., 1 Sam. 4:4) and is called his "footstool" (e.g., 1 Chron. 28:2). The high priest on the annual Day of Atonement entered the most holy place, presenting the blood of the slaughtered goat to make atonement on behalf of the nation (Lev. 16:15–16). The Greek Old Testament renders the lid hilastērion ("place of atonement"). In the New Testament, hilastērion is the place where Jesus's blood functions as a sacrifice for the forgiveness of sins (Rom. 3:25; cf. Heb. 9:5). The writer to the Hebrews in chapters 9 and 10 draws an analogy between the earthly and heavenly sanctuaries. The heavenly most holy place is entered by Jesus, who offers his blood on the ark (Heb. 9:12). "By the blood of Jesus," Christians may enter into the most holy place, confident in the perfect, permanent redemption achieved by Christ and where we by faith receive forgiveness and are sustained spiritually (Heb. 10:19).

stage, making the total cutting off of the waters remarkable ("dry ground," 3:17; 4:22). Second, the stoppage occurs on the third day, just in the timing and in the way the Lord has said it would. The crossing happens just at the moment the ark enters the river (3:15–17). It is better, therefore, to focus on the divine intention of the act than to explain the "how" of the drama. The miracle strengthens the relationship of God and Israel by promoting Israel's faith. The miracles that Jesus performs show his special relationship to the Father, bring people to faith, and reveal the Father's love and compassion (Matt. 14:14; John 7:31; 11:41–42).

As in previous chapters, the passage exhibits the significance of God's presence (3:10–11). God's presence leads Israel through the wilderness and against formidable enemies (Exod. 33:14–15; Deut. 4:37–38). The Lord promises to pave the way (1:5; Deut. 31:6, 8; Heb. 13:5). Now the people must move forward at the Lord's command, trusting him to prevail over the mighty Canaanites. This dramatic crossing reveals that they are not alone; they receive the favor and power of God in their midst. By the ark's lead, the people can see and know that the Lord is at the head of the processional, not Joshua or the tribal elders. The holy priests are living reminders of their awesome God, who demands their

loyalty and complete obedience. Their enemies have no reason to fear the vagabond Israelites but have every reason to fear the God of the Israelites. Christian readers take comfort from knowing that the work of Jesus is supreme and transformative (Phil. 1:6), overcoming any authority that opposes his salvation purposes (Rom. 8:38; Col. 2:13–15; 1 Pet. 3:22).

Illustrating the Text

You can't know that God is faithful until you take a step of faith.

Film: *Indiana Jones and the Last Crusade.* The ending of this movie provides a vivid illustration of the truth that the faithfulness of God is experienced once we are willing to take a step of faith. The father of Indiana Jones is mortally wounded, and the only way to save him is for Jones (played by Harrison Ford) to overcome a series of cryptic obstacles and find the Holy Grail. At one point Jones must step by faith off a

That the Israelites cross the Jordan River on dry ground when the river is in flood stage emphasizes God's miraculous power at work. This photo taken of the flooded Jordan in 1935 gives an idea of the width of the river at flood stage. The bridge seen midcenter would normally have spanned its banks.

cliff, believing that once he takes the step an actual step will appear and save him from a sure death. Jones moves forward off the cliff, and a bridge becomes visible and enables him to cross the chasm. Had he not taken the step, he would not have discovered the way forward. The only way we discover that God is faithful is by taking steps of faith based on his promises. Are you living by faith or by sight?

God has the power to transform your life.
News Story: Velma Margie Barfield was a fifty-two-year-old grandmother who was executed after being convicted as a serial killer. She was the first woman executed after the death penalty was reinstituted in 1976 in North Carolina, and the first woman to die by lethal injection. While on death row Barfield gave her life in faith to Jesus Christ, and she was transformed. She became a counselor and helped other inmates learn to cope with their life in prison.

She also cowrote a book titled *Woman on Death Row*, which was a collection of her memoirs.[2] After her execution, evangelist Billy Graham preached at the prison, using John 3:16 as well as Barfield's Christian witness, and two hundred people responded to the invitation to trust in Jesus for their salvation. God has the power to transform your life as well![3]

The marvels of God strengthen the faith of his people.
Testimony: After talking about how the miracle of the crossing of the Jordan River strengthened the faith of the Israelites, it would be helpful to present a contemporary example of this same principle. Ask a member of your congregation to share (through video or in person) an example of how God's intervention in that person's life strengthened his or her faith (expressed in terms of future trust and obedience).

Remembering God's Grace

Big Idea *Memorials to the Lord's glorious deeds are reminders to future generations of the Lord's faithfulness to his promises.*

Understanding the Text

The Text in Context

Chapters 1–5 recall the preparations that set the stage for Israel's advance against their enemies, which is narrated in chapters 6–12. Chapters 3 and 4 work in tandem, but with different emphases (see "The Text in Context" in the unit on 3:1–17). Chapter 4 continues the story of Israel's crossing of the Jordan (chap. 3) but focuses on the two memorials, celebrating the marvel of God's grace. The passage brings the past to the fore by referring to Moses (4:10, 12, 14). Chapter 1 calls for obedience to the directions of Moses, and chapter 4 shows the nation in full compliance.

Chapter 4 consists of three parts. (1) Verses 1–9 describe two memorials: twelve stones taken from the riverbed and placed at the camp, Gilgal (4:1–8, 20); and twelve stones set *in* the riverbed (4:9). Scholars differ on whether Joshua set up one or two memorials. The NIV's text reflects the view that there was one memorial by its translation, "set up the twelve stones that *had been* in the middle of the Jordan" (4:9; italics mine). The NIV's textual note offers the alternative translation, which indicates a different, second memorial, "Joshua *also* set up twelve stones" (italics mine; cf. NET, NLT, NJPS). (2) Verses 10–13 briefly repeat the actual crossing, already reported in chapter 3, with verses 12–13 providing parenthetical information about the army's warriors. (3) Verses 14–24 describe in detail the final stages of the crossing, highlighting the purposes of the memorials and the crossing.

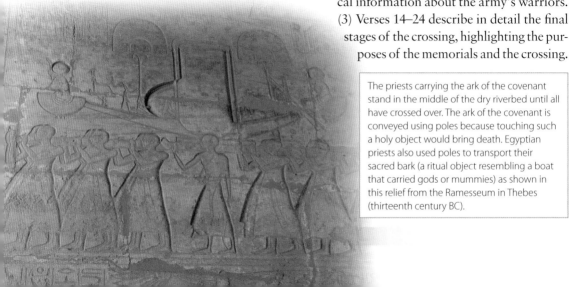

The priests carrying the ark of the covenant stand in the middle of the dry riverbed until all have crossed over. The ark of the covenant is conveyed using poles because touching such a holy object would bring death. Egyptian priests also used poles to transport their sacred bark (a ritual object resembling a boat that carried gods or mummies) as shown in this relief from the Ramesseum in Thebes (thirteenth century BC).

This part tells the different effects of the crossing on the nations and on the Israelites. A parenthetical statement precisely dates the event, venerating the crossing (4:19).

Interpretive Insights

4:3 *twelve stones.* The representative number "twelve" refers to the full assembly of twelve tribes (4:5; cf. 4:8, 9, 20). "All," when referring to Israel, repeatedly appears in chapters 3 and 4, showing that the promise to Israel is inclusive (3:1, 7, 17; 4:1, 11, 14). Although the altars of worship built for the Lord were made of uncut stones, the memorial stones were not for use in worship (cf. Exod. 20:25; 1 Kings 18:31–32). The text specifies the purpose of the gathered stones as a "sign" (4:6; cf. the replica altar incident, 22:25–29).

4:6 *What do these stones mean?* The question reappears in verse 21, eliciting the confession of Israel (4:22–23). The repetition underscores the catechistic purpose of the memorial.

4:7 *memorial . . . forever.* "Memorial" (*zikkaron*) is related to the terms "remind" (*zakar*) and "remembrance" (*zeker*; cf. Ps. 111:4). As a pedagogical device, future generations relive the crossing (4:21; cf. Deut. 6:4–9). Events and special days are memorials to God (e.g., Passover, Exod. 12:14).

4:9 *to this day.* This phrase is common in Joshua, indicating a historical perspective on the events the book narrates (e.g., 5:9; 6:25; 9:27; 15:63; 16:10). The eyewitness accounts in the book (e.g., 5:1) have been supplemented by contemporaneous or near contemporaneous sources.

4:10 *just as Moses had directed Joshua.* The chain of command is reiterated in this verse. God commanded Moses, and Moses

instructed Joshua (cf. 11:15, 23; Num. 32:20–33; Deut. 31:7).

The people hurried over. Since there was a clear line of authority and a consistent obedient response, the people passed across the river without delay or hesitation.

4:13 *About forty thousand armed for battle . . . war.* On the number, see "Historical and Cultural Background" in the unit on 8:1–29. The redundancy of "battle" and "war" reinforces the anticipation of warfare.

4:14 *exalted Joshua . . . just as . . . awe of Moses.* God's promise to exalt Joshua in 3:7 is fulfilled. "Awe" (*yare'*, "to fear, reverence") indicates respect for Joshua and the realization that he is the servant of God, as was Moses (Exod. 14:31). The same term describes submission to God (4:24; 24:14; NIV: "fear").

4:16 *ark of the covenant law.* "Covenant law" (*'edut*, "testimony") refers to the stone tablets of the Ten Commandments in the ark (Exod. 31:18; 40:20). (See the sidebar "Ark of the Covenant" in the unit on 3:1–17.)

4:18 *No sooner.* The detail of the timing adds to the reader's marvel at God's power.

4:19 *tenth day of the first month.* The specific date highlights the unique event in the community's memory. The first month,

Following the priests, soldiers from the tribes of Reuben, Gad, and Manasseh lead the Israelites across the Jordan. They do not need to swim like the soldiers in this Assyrian relief because God stops the waters of the Jordan, providing a dry path to walk on. Battle reliefs like the one shown here indicate that armies crossing a river too deep for fording would use small boats to transport equipment and inflated animal skins to support swimmers (Nimrud, 865–860 BC).

Aviv (Exod. 13:4; also known as Nisan), was in March–April, which correlates with the river's annual flooding. The "tenth day," when the Passover lamb is chosen (Exod. 12:3–6), anticipates its celebration (Josh. 5:10).

Gilgal. "Gilgal" (*gilgal*) sounds like "to roll away" (*galal*); the name commemorates the first circumcision by the new generation (5:9). Sadly, the place where the Israelites launch their possession of the land becomes a notorious site for false worship (Hosea 9:15; Amos 4:4). Amos 5:5 employs wordplay on the name "Gilgal" (*gilgal*) by predicting Israel's "exile" (*galah*). Gilgal is just east of Jericho (4:19; 5:10), although the specific location is unknown. It is the site for the first Passover in the land (5:10–12) and is the staging area for wars in central and southern Canaan (chaps. 6–10). It is probably the locale for the distribution of tribal allotments in chapters 15–17 (cf. 14:6).

4:22 *on dry ground.* Israel's confession (4:22–24) emphasizes the nature and purpose of the historic crossing. That the riverbed is "dry / dried up" is mentioned three times in two short verses.

4:23 *the* LORD *your God.* Four times in verses 23–24 God is identified by the covenant name "the LORD" (Yahweh) (cf. Exod. 3:13–15). Future generations learn their identity and unique heritage through the recitation of historical confessions (e.g., Exod. 12:26; 13:14).

until you had crossed over. The phrase "until you/we had crossed over" occurs twice in verses 23–24, repeating the marvel of God's grace that has secured the entrance of all Israel.

4:24 *so that . . . so that.* The two purposes for the extraordinary crossing center on the response to the majesty and power of God. (1) It is a witness to the pagan nations that the God of Israel accomplishes this wonder (5:1; see also 2:11; 9:24–25; Exod. 15:11; Isa. 61:9). (2) It motivates enduring faith among God's people.

Theological Insights

The Lord God alone is deserving of worship because by his mighty power and gracious love he delivers his people, as at the Red Sea and the Jordan River. Israel's memorials are tributes to God, not to human achievements. They reflect a living faith in the Lord that he receives with favor (Lev. 2:2; Matt. 26:13; Acts 10:4). Together, the stone memorials—one in the river and one at Gilgal—are constant reminders of what God has done for Israel. By reciting God's historic acts, Israel achieves a union of past and present and of individual and nation (cf. Deut. 26:3–11). Memorials are for the living, not the dead, to contemplate and reverence the Lord God. Although they are tributes to God's works in the past, they call for change in the present. The awesome power of God inspires fearful submission by the nations (Josh. 2:9–11; 9:24) and obedience by his people (Deut. 31:12–13). The passage also shows the necessity of the Lord's presence for victory (Exod. 33:14–16; Josh. 1:5; 3:7). Israel's defeat at Ai is directly attributable to the absence of God's favor (7:12).

Teaching the Text

The chief interest of the text is the exaltation of God. The remarkable events of the crossing and the memorials are not in themselves the object of the people's attention. Teaching the passage must focus on the power and grace of the Lord, not on the miracle of the crossing alone. The purpose of what transpires is to incite worship. The events of the story lead to a call for humility and devotion to the Lord. The memorials function as reminders of these great events.

Miracles

Joshua includes three astounding "miracles" that are topics of special discussion: the crossing of the Jordan, the collapse of Jericho's walls, and the sun standing still. Today, "miracle" means an extraordinary event that is inexplicable, usually attributed to divine intervention. The biblical terms "wonderful/marvelous" (*nipla'*, Exod. 34:10), "sign" (*'ot*, Deut. 26:8), and "fearful/awesome" (*nora'*, Deut. 10:21) describe miracles but focus on the cause (God) or effects (fear/awe) of the wonder more than on the event itself. The New Testament terminology speaks of "(miraculous) powers" (*dynameis*; NIV: "miracles"), "wonders" (*terata*), and "signs" (*sēmeia*) (Acts 2:22). The purpose of miracles is to show the power and glory of God (Josh. 4:24; John 11:4). In the scientific era, natural and supernatural events are standard conceptual categories. Natural law depends on the principle of repeatable phenomena, evidenced by experience and observation, in order to explain and define reality. Supernatural events are considered "unreal," not observable, so that they cannot be explained. Ancients did not think of reality in these terms, although they certainly knew the difference between the "normal" and the extraordinary. Both were explained by the power of the deity. The God of Israel, however, transcends nature and therefore is of a completely different order than pagan deities. There is a place to consider natural explanations for miracles, such as rock slides that dam up the Jordan, but this does not satisfy the biblical requirement of a miracle. Biblical understanding of miracles requires divine control of the so-called natural elements, especially since the timing of the event is not a mere "coincidence" but involves specifically divine causation.[a] Christians acknowledge *all* reality, including the existence and involvement of the transcendent God. Limiting reality to "natural law," as is the case with empericism, excludes the possibility of a personal Creator.

[a] Dubbed a "coincidence miracle"; see the discussion of Williams, "God of Miracle and Mystery," in McConville and Williams, *Joshua*, 154–70. The recent rise in interest in miracles testifies to the limitations and failures of modern empiricism to satisfy the human spirit. For example, see the extensive apologetic of Keener, *Miracles*; see also, Collins, *God of Miracles*; Geivett and Habermas, *In Defense of Miracles*; and C. S. Lewis's classic work *Miracles*.

They have the effect also of unifying the identity of the covenant people across generations as members of the called-out family of God. Christian readers are reminded that unity is in the Lord as his one body (Eph. 4:1–16). The body of believers is not yet full, since future generations will come into the faith (Heb. 11:39–40; Rev. 6:11). The Lord provides two memorials to recall the story of Jesus for Christians: baptism and the Lord's Supper. These two are gracious gifts designed to keep the church's focus on the death, burial, and resurrection of Jesus Christ (e.g., Matt. 26:26–30; Rom. 6:3–5; 1 Cor. 11:17–34; 1 Pet. 3:21).

Illustrating the Text

Symbols can be used to help us remember and to express emotion.

Popular Culture: Show pictures that have meaning and that create emotion for your particular culture. For example, you might want to show the symbol for the Red Cross, a swastika, a baby, and the cross (no matter what symbols you choose, finish with the cross). Project or hold each picture before the audience and ask them to respond (either verbally or silently) to these questions: What words or phrases come to mind as you consider this image? What emotions do you feel as you look at this image? Explain that images can be a meaningful way to stir our hearts and help us remember events that should never be forgotten (memorials, such as the Vietnam War Memorial, could help illustrate this point). These images can also stir emotions that remind us of the importance of these events. Throughout the Bible the Lord encourages his people to use images (for example, the bread and the cup for the Lord's Supper) to remember as well as to stir our hearts.

Use symbols to tell God's stories to future generations.

Props: Symbols have historically been used by Christians as a reminder of God's love, strength, and help. For example, in the early centuries of the church the anchor became an important symbol for Christians during Roman persecution. It reminded the people that Jesus is their anchor and that he can be trusted to fulfill his promises (Heb. 6:17–20).[1] Bring objects that remind you of the Lord's provision and power in your personal life. Hold each item separately and tell the story of how it represents an example of God's intervention in your life. Read Joshua 4:21–23a and challenge your listeners to consider gathering objects they can place in their homes and in their workplaces to represent the Lord's power, goodness, love, and faithfulness. These symbols become an opportunity to tell others about the Lord!

The memorial of twelve stones at Gilgal is to remind the Israelites of God's power. Symbols have always been used as reminders for God's people. At the time when the early church was suffering persecution from Rome, the anchor symbolized the trustworthiness of God. This funerary stele of Licinia Amias includes the anchor symbol (early third century AD, Rome).

Keep your focus on faith and not on fear.

Object Lesson: In an article from *Leadership Journal*, Jack R. Van Ens writes, "In the midst of controversy, one of the first casualties is perspective." Van Ens goes on to say that we lose perspective because we are often too focused on what he calls "the close-up" rather than on the wide-angle view. He provides the example of looking at a harmless spider under a microscope. From this "close-up" view the benign spider looks like "a hairy, horrible monster." With this view none of us would ever want to tangle with even a harmless spider. However, from the wide-angle view we realize that we are much larger than the spider and have nothing to fear.[2] When it comes to living the Christian life, many of us focus too closely on the challenges and the obstacles, forgetting to take the wide-angle view that the Lord is bigger and more powerful than any obstacle we will face. Why did the Israelites cross the Jordan River at the peak of its flow? Because the Israelites focused on the wide-angle view and remembered that the Lord was sovereign over the Jordan River. We would all do well to face life's challenges while remembering the wide-angle view of the greatness of our God!

New Life in Canaan

Big Idea *The Lord prepares his people spiritually so that they might enter into the life of his promises.*

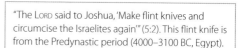

Understanding the Text

The Text in Context

After crossing the Jordan River (chaps. 3–4), the people begin a new life in Canaan. Chapter 5 completes the preparations for possessing the land (chaps. 1–5). Restoration of circumcision and Passover prepares them spiritually for victory (5:1–12) in the same way that consecration prepared them to cross the Jordan (3:5, 15). The fear of the nations and the location of Joshua at Jericho (5:13) anticipate the destruction of the city in chapter 6.

Chapter 5 begins and ends with two contrasting responses to the crossing of the Jordan. Verse 1 describes the paralyzing fear of the nations, which frees the Israelites to celebrate circumcision and Passover. Verses 13–15 describe the submissive response of Joshua to the "commander of the Lord's army," which prepares him for receiving marching orders (6:2–5). The introduction of a new character in 5:14, simply called the "commander," and his dialogue with Joshua in 5:13–15 signal a new division, so these verses are treated separately in the next commentary unit.

> "The Lord said to Joshua, 'Make flint knives and circumcise the Israelites again'" (5:2). This flint knife is from the Predynastic period (4000–3100 BC, Egypt).

Verses 1–12 consist of two parts: (1) the act of circumcision recalls the inheritance of the promises made to Israel's forefather, Abraham (5:1–9); and (2) the Passover celebration recalls the formation of the nation Israel at the exodus and Mount Sinai (5:10–12). Thus, the new act of circumcision and the new celebration of Passover prepare them for the new life in Canaan.

Historical and Cultural Background

The renewed practice of circumcision among the Israelites was a signal moment between the former Israelite community in the wilderness ("rolled away the reproach of Egypt," 5:9) and the new Israel about to enter the promised land. Circumcision is the removal of the loose foreskin of a male's penis, which is practiced in Israel on the eighth day after a boy's birth (Gen. 17:12; Lev. 12:3). It is a physical sign marking the household of Abraham as the recipients of the covenant. In a patriarchal clan society, the males made the decisions for the clan, and therefore their dedication was the determining factor. Since male members represented the whole household, male circumcision symbolized the whole household as coparticipants in the covenant. Circumcision is also a symbol for spiritual devotion to God (Deut. 10:16; Jer. 4:4; Rom. 4:11; Col. 2:11). Circumcision among the Egyptians and some West Semitic groups (Jer. 9:25–26) was a puberty or marriage rite. Hebrew circumcision differs by its unique religious significance. The technique in Egypt made dorsal incisions in the foreskin that partially exposed the penis. Some scholars speculate that the "reproach" (cf. 5:5) removed from the Israelites is this incomplete Egyptian form of circumcision.

Interpretive Insights

5:1 *Amorite kings west of the Jordan . . . Canaanite kings along the coast.* The verse emphasizes the widespread fear of the nations, echoing the alarm shown by Jericho (2:1, 9–11). The region encompasses the land from Jericho westward to the Mediterranean Sea. The inhabitants of Canaan present a complex ethnic and political picture. The Amorites and the Canaanites represent all the diverse people groups (24:15; Deut. 11:30; cf. "seven nations," Deut. 7:1; Acts 13:19).

their hearts melted. The figurative language indicates fear and loss of will to fight. The verb "to melt" (*masas*) describes the dissolving of wax (Ps. 68:2). "Melted" recalls the terror generated by the crossing

at the Red Sea (2:9, 24; Exod. 15:15). This parallel to the exodus shows God's favor and presence (Exod. 33:14–17).

5:2 *Make flint knives and circumcise.* The word for "flint" (*tsor*) occurs one other time in the Old Testament where Zipporah, due to Moses's delinquency, circumcises their son (Exod. 4:25). Although subtle, the allusion to Moses's failure may be a reminder of Israel's disobedience in the desert (Num. 13–14) and thus contrasts with the faithfulness of Joshua.

again. The word (lit., "a second time") assumes the first circumcision of the exodus generation. They suspended the practice during the desert wanderings (5:5). Renewal of circumcision is necessary because only circumcised men may eat the Passover (Exod. 12:48–49). Circumcision and Passover are two significant indicators that a Hebrew family belongs to the covenant community. Since the exodus generation was ethnically diverse (Exod. 12:38), circumcision as an outward sign of covenant membership has special importance.

5:3 *Gibeath Haaraloth.* The name, literally "the hill of the foreskins," memorializes the epic event; the place is located near Gilgal (5:9).

5:5 *that came out . . . born in the wilderness.* The contrast between the two generations involves not only their geographical origins but also their geographical destinies. God has sworn that those twenty years and older would die in the wilderness but their children would possess the land (Num. 14:28–33). What was promised to their parents is now theirs to enjoy.

5:6 *forty years.* The author contrasts the former and present generations by the rite of circumcision. Although "all" of the former generation were circumcised, their disobedience brought death (Num. 13–14; Ps. 95:10–11; Heb. 3:11–4:3). Physical circumcision does not assure God's favor. Circumcision of the "heart"—an internal spiritual commitment to covenant—is required (Deut. 10:16; 30:6).

the men who were of military age . . . had died. Literally, "men of war" (*'anshe hammilhamah*), this is a technical expression for armed soldiers (Num. 31:28; NIV: "soldiers"); men twenty years and older are registered for the army (Num. 1:45). Those of the former generation suffered God's wrath for Israel's disobedience (Num. 14:29; Deut. 2:14, 16), but the "men of war" of the new generation successfully possess Jericho (6:3; NIV: "armed men"). "Died off" or "perished" (*tamam*) creates a wordplay on "finishing" (*tamam*) the circumcision of the new generation (5:8; see ESV). The text heightens the contrast between the outcomes of the two armies.

sworn . . . solemnly promised . . . milk and honey. Twice the word "swear / solemnly promise" (*shaba'*) occurs, emphasizing that the promise is irrevocable. The implication is that the first generation failed, not God. "Milk" (*halab*) reflects the lush pastures that support large herds (Deut.

32:14), and "honey" (*debash*) indicates lavish agricultural products (2 Kings 18:32; 2 Chron. 31:5). This description recalls the promise made to Moses and his generation (Exod. 3:8).

5:8 *until they were healed.* Joshua shows his complete trust in the Lord. By circumcising his army at the Lord's command, Joshua disables his soldiers, leaving them vulnerable to attack (cf. Gen. 34).

5:9 *rolled away the reproach.* "Rolled away" (*galal*) is a play on the name "Gilgal" (see the comments on 4:19). "Reproach" (*herpah*) refers to the shame of slavery in Egypt or of having refused to enter the land (Num. 13–14).

5:10 *Passover.* At least on one occasion the desert Israelites celebrated the Passover (Num. 9). The Passover is on the fourteenth of the first month, followed immediately by the Feast of Unleavened Bread on the fifteenth to the twenty-first days of the month. The celebration in the land occurs four days after arrival at Gilgal. The passage focuses on the Feast of Unleavened Bread because upon entering Canaan the people celebrate God's provision (see 5:12).

5:11 *that very day.* The significance of this event is highlighted in the text by its chronological prominence (cf. 10:27). This same expression describes the original institution of the celebration (Exod. 12:17; NIV: "this very day"). The feast calls for the people to eat unleavened bread for seven days, a remembrance of the immediate departure from Egypt (Exod. 12:33–34). Roasted grain is offered as firstfruits following Passover and Unleavened Bread at the spring's harvest (Lev. 2:12, 14; cf. Exod. 23:16; Lev. 23:9–14). Offering the first outgrowth expresses thanksgiving and

The promised land is regularly described as a "land flowing with milk and honey" (for example, Exod. 3:8; Num. 13:27; Josh. 5:6). Honey most likely refers to date honey from the date palm, shown here.

recount the two historic benchmarks in Israel's relationship with God—the giving of the covenant and the exodus from Egypt. By reviving these two ceremonies the people acknowledge the Lord as their God and make their claim on the inheritance. It is a new day, and the people are full of hope. That they commemorate these two identifying rites in the land of promise shows that the Lord is fulfilling his oath. Once in the land they must appear before the Lord three times a year, including Passover / Feast of Unleavened Bread, to renew their oath of devotion (Deut. 16:16).

The people's consecration is necessary, for the land is holy—the place of God's dwelling—and they must not defile the land (Num. 35:34; Josh. 22:19). They consecrate themselves for crossing into the land (3:5). Moreover, they must be sanctified as warriors (7:13; 1 Sam. 5:21; Isa. 13:3) who carry out the task of facilitating God's wrath against the wicked inhabitants of Canaan.

recognition that God has delivered them and led them into the land (Deut. 26:1–11).

5:12 *manna stopped.* The diet of manna, the "bread from heaven" (Exod. 16:4; John 6:31–33, 41, 50), during the long wilderness sojourn is no longer necessary. Now they must trust God to provide a new way for their sustenance. They harvest what they do not plant by dispossessing the Canaanites (Deut. 6:10–12). The Lord fulfills this promise, and it is remembered in the covenant renewal ceremony (24:13).

Theological Insights

The primary theological significance is the spiritual preparation of the people who submit obediently to the Lord. He reinstitutes two historic rituals that recall the rule of God over his people. Circumcision points back to the promises to and protection of the patriarchs (Gen. 17:10–11). Passover remembers the salvation that he provided Israel, and it is to be practiced as a memorial in perpetuity in the land (Exod. 12:24–25). One might say that history is on Israel's side! Circumcision and Passover

Teaching the Text

This passage magnifies God's commitment to his promises and the people's response of obedience and confidence in the Lord. First, by reinstating circumcision and Passover, the Lord shows his continued commitment to the descendants of Israel (5:2). By eating from the fruit of the land, Israel experiences the fulfillment of the promise of blessing made to the patriarchs (5:12). Second, both circumcision and Passover remember the obedience of their ancestors: the fathers in

Joshua 5:1–12

the land and the Israelites in Egypt (Gen. 17:23, 26–27; 22; cf. James 2:21–24; Exod. 12:25–28, 50). Christians are called to devote themselves wholeheartedly to the Lord. The expressions of our faith, such as baptism and the Lord's Supper, differ from the ancient Israelites, but they are no less important to our Christian profession.

The text also indicates the importance of consecration by the Israelites as they undertake the Lord's commission to enter the land in faith. The people must exhibit as a nation rekindled devotion to the Lord as the unique covenant people of God. Ritual circumcision and Passover reinforce their national identity, for they must be a holy people who serve a holy God. Ritual observance of the law was intended to be a reflection of a person's spiritual (interior) reality (22:5). The people were to have circumcised hearts (Deut. 10:16; 30:6; cf. Ps. 40:6–8; Rom. 4:11). Similarly, for Christian identity the institutions of the Lord's Table and water baptism function as ritual witnesses to spiritual realities (Matt. 26:26–29; Rom. 2:25–29; 1 Cor. 5:7; Col. 2:11) and must be observed with the same solemnity that Israel experienced (1 Cor. 11:27–30). These outward signs of communion and baptism are significant for us only if they mirror our authentic "inner being" of devotion to God (Eph. 3:16–17; cf. 1 Pet. 3:21).

Another lesson derived from the text is the impact of former generations on their descendants (5:4–7). Although the new generation of Israel does not initially possess the sign of circumcision due to the failure of their parents, they do not suffer the guilt of their parents' disbelief. Succeeding generations typically imitate the character of their parents (Exod. 34:6–9), but each

generation is responsible for its own behavior (Deut. 24:16; Jer. 31:29–30; Ezek. 18:14–18). God has eliminated the blot of the past *and* its influence (5:9). The New Testament indicates the same perspective on personal responsibility (John 9:2–3, 41; 1 Cor. 3:8, 13; Rev. 2:23). Christians are responsible for their own actions but also for the influence they have on others. We are to exhibit positive influence as examples of God's grace and as witnesses to his salvation (Matt. 5:16; Phil. 2:15; 1 Pet. 2:12).

Illustrating the Text

Obedience to God is a supreme expression of our trust in him.

Sports: As amazing as it might sound, people who are visually impaired can be taught to downhill ski. In fact, there is a manual for teaching visually impaired skiers that includes these instructions for communication between the instructor and the visually impaired student:

> Before going onto the hill, determine emergency commands like "slow down," "sit down," and "stop." . . . Directional commands are as follows: "right turn, left turn," or "turn, turn, turn." "Hold, hold, hold" can indicate traverse. Keep them short and simple for on the slope. Tapping your ski poles can provide a constant connection for your student to cue in on. Remember to always maintain verbal contact with the student.[1]

In order for those who are visually impaired to ski down the mountain, they must be willing to place their trust in the instructor. Imagine skiing down the hill, unable to see trees, moguls, other skiers, and so on, but simply responding to the commands of the instructor. Trust is marked by obedience to the commands of the skiing companion. In the same way, trust in the Lord is expressed by obedience to his commands, even when we may not fully agree or understand. Like the visually impaired skier, we are not in a better position to contradict the Lord's commands.

Every promise of the Lord will be fulfilled.

Finance: A "promissory note" is defined as "a financial instrument that contains a written promise by one party to pay another party a definite sum of money either on demand or at a specified future date."[2] The willingness to loan money based on a promissory note would depend on the character of the one loaning the money as well as the character, collateral, and credit history of the person who is to pay the money back. In other words, the note is only as good as the one who is making the promise to pay. The promises of God are based on his character, his ability to fulfill the promise, and his faithfulness over generations. As we consider putting our faith and trust in the Lord's promises, we must always remember that he is and always has been faithful, and that he has the power to do whatever he has promised. When God makes a promise the future is certain. A wise person acts today with the assurance that the future promises of God will be fulfilled.

The Lord's forgiveness provides a clean slate.

Film: *Holes.* In 2003 Disney Studios released the movie *Holes*, which was based on the 1998 novel of the same title by Louis Sachar. The story involves a boy from a family that has a history of bad luck, all stemming from an ancient family curse. By the end of the movie the main character, Stanley Yelnats, is able to break the curse of the past, thereby freeing the family forever. Similarly, there are people who allow the sins of previous generations to influence their own lives as they choose to follow the bad example set for them. But the Lord has the power to set us free so that the sins of previous generations no longer have power over us. The forgiveness that comes through faith in Jesus Christ provides a clean slate.

The Commander of Israel's Armies

Big Idea *The Lord assures his people that he is present and will give them victory.*

Understanding the Text

The Text in Context

After the spiritual preparation of circumcision and Passover is completed (5:1–12), the people are ready to enter the land at the Lord's command. Yet there is one more necessary element—the presence of the Lord (5:13–15). The sudden and mysterious appearance of the "commander" recalls Moses's experience at the burning bush (Exod. 3). Scholars offer different explanations for the identity of this enigmatic person. This is especially the case since the commander does not answer Joshua's question, "Are you for us or for our enemies?" (5:13), by giving

The commander of the Lord's army appears before Joshua with a drawn sword. Warrior deities were common in the ancient Near East. This bronze figurine wields a sword and shield (fifteenth to thirteenth century BC, Megiddo).

him a specific task, as God did with Moses (Exod. 3:10).[1] However, 5:13–15 functions naturally as a transition to chapters 6–12, and the absence of a specific task in verses 14–15 suits the purpose of focusing on Joshua's obedience. The commander is the true leader who will accomplish on behalf of Israel the victories described in chapters 6–12. Moreover, the passage shows that Joshua is dependent on the Lord's presence for success. Joshua's question, "Are you for us or for our enemies?" (5:13), reveals what is of utmost importance to him. The Lord's revelation as the holy commander of the Lord's armies confirms Joshua's faith and Israel's victory.

Interpretive Insights

5:13 *near Jericho.* The scene shifts from Gilgal to Jericho (4:19), where Joshua may have been on a reconnaissance mission, viewing the enemy stronghold. Yet the important sighting is the revelation of the commander.

saw a man. "Behold, see" are the traditional renderings (e.g., ESV), but many English versions do not give a literal translation, preferring to rely on the nuance of "saw, looked" in the passage. "Behold" (hinneh) follows "saw" in the text; "behold" commonly introduces a vivid depiction of imminent, surprising events. The figure appears to be a man, and only at his answer to Joshua's question does Joshua realize he stands before the divine presence.

standing in front of him. The expression furthers the mystery of the stranger's identity since it often describes an inferior standing before a person of greater rank, such as royalty (e.g., Gen. 43:15 ESV), yet here the commander is described as the one standing in front of the inferior Joshua.

drawn sword. Military dress included a belt and side sheath. A sword was a common weapon for a champion combatant (1 Sam. 17:51); that it is drawn indicates he is positioned for battle (contrast Judg. 8:20). The idiom "those drawing the sword" means "armed troops" (e.g., 2 Sam. 24:9).

went up to him. Joshua's first action shows no sign of timidity, indicating that he thinks the man is an unidentified warrior.

for us or for our enemies? If he were an opponent, then a duel between warriors may have ensued (2 Sam. 2:14–15).

5:14 *Neither . . . commander of the army of the LORD.* The response is the explicit negative "No!" (*lo'*). Joshua's question is irrelevant since the commander is a different order of being altogether. The identity of the man is at the head of the verse, emphasizing his distinctiveness. The title occurs twice in Joshua (5:14, 15). "Commander of the army" (*sar hatsaba'*) describes human and divine leaders of armies (1 Sam. 17:55; Dan. 8:11). "Commander" (*sar*) often describes captains of military groups (Gen. 21:22) and is used of angels (Michael, Dan. 10:21; NIV: "prince"). "Army" (*tsaba'*) is also used of

Key Themes of Joshua 5:13–15

- The appearance of God as the commander of Israel's armies indicates that he fights Israel's battles.
- The Divine Warrior reveals his identity as the holy emissary of God.
- Joshua acknowledges the Divine Warrior and humbly submits to his instructions.

the "hosts" of angels (Ps. 148:2) and of the heavens (Deut. 4:19; see ESV). The divine title "the LORD Almighty" (or "LORD of hosts," *yhwh tsᵉba'ot*), indicates his sovereign rule over Israel's armies (1 Sam. 17:45). The commander is the Divine Warrior who defeats Israel's enemies (21:44; Exod. 15:3). The Lord promises Moses that he sends his angel ahead to conquer the nations (Exod. 23:20–23). The allusion in verse 15 to the burning bush revelation suggests that the commander is the same "angel of the LORD" who speaks to Moses, identified as "the LORD" (Exod. 3:2–6; see the sidebar). The verse alludes to "the angel of the LORD" with drawn sword who appears to Balaam (Num. 22:22, 31). Joshua bows subserviently, indicating that the commander is Joshua's superior. Some believe that the angel is a special representative (Michael, Dan. 12:1) but not God himself. But the exhortation for Joshua to remove his shoes because of holy ground means that the identity of the "man" is the Lord God (5:15). That the stranger accepts worship suggests that he is worthy of worship (cf. Acts 14:12–15; Rev. 19:10).

fell facedown . . . in reverence. Joshua expresses ultimate humility before a superior (2 Sam. 14:22). "Fell facedown" occurs once more in the book, when at Israel's defeat Joshua collapses in grief before the ark (7:6). "Reverence" translates

The Angle of the Lord

The title "the angel of the Lord," employing the divine name Yahweh, is a distinctive name that occurs forty-eight times in the Old Testament.[a] It appears eleven times in the New Testament but importantly without the definite article ("an angel of the Lord," *angelos kyriou*). The exception is Matthew 1:24, but there the article refers back to 1:20, where it is indefinite, "an angel of the Lord" (*angelos kyriou*). The relationship of the angel and the Lord himself is perplexing since the two can be differentiated but also equated (Zech. 1:12; 12:8). He is identified as God (Gen. 22:15–18; Exod. 3:2–6, 14). To see "the angel of the Lord" means death, as when one sees God (Judg. 6:22–23; 13:21–22). Christian tradition identifies the mysterious "angel of the Lord" as the preincarnate Jesus Christ, due in part to the fact that an angel by this title ceases to appear after the incarnation of Jesus. This identity, however, cannot be established with certainty. What is certain is that in the Old Testament God at times reveals himself as an angel who instructs his people.

[a] See further MacDonald, "Christology and the Angel of the Lord."

hawah, indicating obeisance (Ruth 2:10; NIV: "bowed down") or worship (2 Chron. 20:18). Many English versions translate the word "worship" in this verse, interpreting the commander to be deity. The incident recalls the response of Abraham, whose three visitors are identified variously as "men" (Gen. 18:2), "the Lord" (18:22), and "angels" (19:1).

my Lord . . . his servant. Joshua matches his act of reverence with submission to the commander's will. "My Lord" (*'adoni*) is the general word for "lord" (*'adon*), referring to a human of superior position (Gen. 23:6; NIV: "sir") or to God (Exod. 34:9). It is *not* the divine name Yahweh, which is always spelled "Lord," in small capital letters, in English versions. By using the ambiguous term "lord" the text maintains the reader's concentration on the commander's identity.

5:15 *Take off your sandals*. This directive clarifies that the identity of the commander is God. It recalls the burning bush (Exod. 3:1–12) that confirms the role of Joshua as Moses's successor and encourages his confidence in the Lord's directive. "Sandals" represents a person's power or authority (Deut. 25:9; Ruth 4:7–8), indicating Joshua's submission. Also, sandals are soiled by refuse and are not worn on sacred ground. The description of priestly garments does not mention shoes (Lev. 8).

the place . . . is holy. The place is "holy" (*qodesh*) because of the Lord's presence. This particular term occurs once more, to describe the booty retrieved from Jericho that is dedicated to the Lord's service (6:19). Related terms in the word group "holy / sanctified / consecrated / holy place" (*qdsh*) appear also in 3:5; 5:15; 6:19; 7:13; 24:19, 26. The essential meaning of what is "holy" is defined by God himself and his character, since he alone is inherently holy (24:19). Etymologically the term means "wholly other, sacred" in the sense of being apart from what is human and what is ordinary. It also has the related meaning "possessing moral purity," for God is ethically perfect, having no sin.

Theological Insights

God is the essential actor in the destiny of Israel. It is God's will and power that secure for Israel a place in the land. As with Isaiah, who sees in a vision the true "King, the Lord Almighty [*yhwh tsᵉba'ot*]" (Isa. 6:5), Joshua meets the true commander of Israel. The concreteness of this event is greater since Joshua's experience is not a vision but a meeting with the Lord as though he is a man (theophany). That the event echoes the burning bush revelation shows that whether it is Moses or Joshua in leadership, the determining factor for success is the Lord. Human leaders come and go, but the Lord's faithful commitment does not wane (Prov. 19:21).

The theology of holiness, although not explicitly prominent in Joshua as a whole, is a fundamental principle underlying the book. In the present passage, holiness is overtly important to understanding what is transpiring when the commander encounters Joshua. Consecration of the people has occurred (3:5; 5:1–12), and the people are now fit to move forward as holy vessels to achieve a task that is a necessary expression of the Lord's character. That the Lord is intrinsically holy and humans are intrinsically sinful (Ps. 143:2) creates a "problem" that must be addressed by God when he relates to his creation (Ps. 99). Divine holiness demands his response to sin and sinful people by judgment (Ps. 9). The whole world collapses in moral chaos otherwise.

Indeed, humans recognize the "rightness" of justice (Gen. 18:25; Job 34:10). That "there is no honor among thieves" is true, but even thieves expect loyalty—granted that they do not practice it! Joshua and the people must never lose sight of the purpose for their campaigns, which include horrendous violence. The explicit appearance of the commander who reminds Joshua of his holiness reinforces the cause of empowering the people.

Moreover, the response of God to Joshua's question shows that God is not partisan (Deut. 32:4). His purposes are not

Joshua bows before the true commander of Israel, the Divine Warrior who will deliver Jericho into the hands of the Israelites. Other cultures in the ancient Near East also believed that the gods fought on behalf of their people and that defeat or victory depended on the strength or will of the gods. This Assyrian relief shows an Assyrian god flying in front of the charioteers with bow drawn, fighting alongside Ashurnasirpal (Nimrud, 865–860 BC).

Joshua 5:13–15

subject to human agendas. He does not choose Israel for ethnic reasons or for Israel's worth. If Israel fails to live in holy obedience, it too faces God's wrath. This is shown at Ai when Israel suffers for Achan's disobedience (chap. 7).

Teaching the Text

The most important teaching point is what the passage says about the Lord. First, it shows that God closely superintends the lives of his people. His surprising appearance shows that the Lord, although not always seen or evident, is present with Joshua as he has promised. Second, the Lord gives his people assurances through dramatic miracles (Jordan River) but also through encounters of the spoken word. The special assignment and times require the miraculous events of the conquest. The Lord grants Joshua this meeting to encourage him to move forward in faithful obedience. Christians, however, have the full incarnational revelation of God in Jesus, the empowerment of the Holy Spirit, and the fully truthful inscripturated word (Eph. 1:7–9; 2 Tim. 3:16). Before Christians act, their decisions must be soberly undertaken, requiring them to know the clear commands of Scripture and to enter into seasons of prayer, seeking the Lord's guidance (Ps. 40:8; Col. 1:9).

The concept of the holiness of God especially stands out in this passage. Confusion reigns today as to what "holy" means. Yet understanding the meaning of holiness is critically important to understanding God's character since he alone by nature is holy. The Lord stands in stark contrast to humans in their very nature. The Lord is

not simply greater in degree than Joshua but is of an entirely different order, as his holiness demonstrates. Holy living encompasses every aspect of Israel's life (see "Holiness" in the introduction). For Christian readers God's holiness is revealed in Christ and received by the vicarious death of Christ (2 Tim. 1:9; Heb. 10:10). Bray comments, "For us to be holy is to know what God likes and to learn to like it ourselves" (1 Cor. 2:16; Phil 2:5).[2]

Also essential to Israel's success is the response of Joshua, who humbly accepts his subservient role. Joshua recognizes that he has no station apart from God's grace. The commander's refusal to answer Joshua's question as to whose side of the conflict he stands for testifies to God's independence and freedom from human manipulation. Unlike pagan nations, whose deities' affection was won by ritual means, the Lord's people must be subject to his will (Ps. 143:10; Rom. 12:2). Historically, there are always rulers and political parties who seek to justify their causes by claiming to represent the Lord by divine right. The issue is not "Is God on my side?" but "Am I on God's side?" Christians must avoid cavalierly claiming that God is in their camp to the exclusion of another (cf. Mark 9:38–41), based on a perceived sense of self-righteousness, rather than relying on the victory won by Jesus at the cross (Col. 1:13–23).

Illustrating the Text

God is involved in the lives of his people.

Lyrics: "From a Distance," by Julie Gold. In 1990 singer Bette Midler released this song written by Julie Gold. The popular song proclaims, "God is watching us from a distance."[3] The good news is that this song is wrong. God is not watching us from a distance but is intimately and compassionately involved in the lives of his people. This is the proclamation of the Bible not only in Joshua 5 but from Genesis to Revelation. The Lord did not create us and then walk away. Rather, he is present. The implication of this reality is that we can look to the Lord each and every day. God hears our prayers and responds to our needs.

There is danger in claiming that God is on any particular nation's side.

History: In his eulogy for Abraham Lincoln, Reverend Matthew Simpson remarked,

> To a minister who hoped the Lord was on our [the Union's] side, he [Lincoln] replied that it gave him no concern whether the Lord was on our side or not. "For," he [Lincoln] added, "I know the Lord is always on the side of the right," and with deep feeling he added, "But God is my witness that it is my constant anxiety and prayer that both myself and this nation should be the Lord's side."[4]

We must avoid the trap of nationalism, which gives people a false sense of security, assuming that the Lord is on "our" side. Rather, the Lord wants us to be on his side.

Godly leadership is marked by humility.

Children's Book: *Charlotte's Web*, by E. B. White. This children's story is about a spider named Charlotte who lives in a barn, just above the stall of a pig named Wilbur. Wilbur is concerned that one day, when he is fat enough, the farmer will turn him into bacon. Charlotte uses all her resources to try to rescue Wilbur. In his book *Xealots: Defying the Gravity of Normality*, Dave Gibbons writes: "As the story draws to a close, Charlotte the spider is in the barn dying, and she can hear the roar of applause for Wilbur [as he wins a prize and his life is saved]. Charlotte finds great joy in knowing that her life has meant the success of another, her close friend, Wilbur. Though no one will remember her, the things she has done, and the sacrifices she has made, she is satisfied, having loved her friend in life and in death." Leadership is about serving the Lord so that there is less of us and more of God. As Gibbons writes, "It's about fading. The great ones willingly move into irrelevance. 'He must become greater . . . I must become less.'"[5]

Jericho Falls

Big Idea *By the power of God's presence and by their own obedience, God's people experience his blessing.*

Understanding the Text

The Text in Context

After the preparations for conquest are complete (chaps. 1–5), the Lord instructs Joshua to possess the land (chaps. 6–12). Chapters 6–12 narrate the conquest under the leadership of the Divine Warrior, who fights Israel's battles. Chapter 6 introduces the battles, and chapter 12 summarizes the victories by a selective catalog of captured kings. Chapters 6–11 describe three campaigns: (1) the central highlands (chaps. 6–9); (2) the five kings in the south (chap. 10); and (3) the coalition of kings led by Hazor in the north (11:1–11). A summary of Joshua's military policies follows in 11:12–23.

Two recurring features bind chapters 6–12 to the preceding chapters 1–5. (1) The first feature is the leadership of Joshua. In chapters 1–5 he is a surrogate Moses, and in chapters 6–9 he is the appointed leader, as Moses was east of the Jordan (12:1–6). In particular, Joshua encounters the mysterious "commander" near Jericho (5:13–14), and the setting of chapter 6 is also Jericho. For the relationship of 6:1–5 to 5:13–15, see the discussion in "The Text in Context"

in the unit on 5:13–15. (2) The ark of the covenant is the second feature, occurring seventeen times in chapters 3–4. The ark represents the presence of God but also the power of God, "the Lord of all the earth" (3:11). The crossing on dry ground is the Red Sea déjà vu event. In chapters 6–9 the word "ark" (*'aron*) appears twelve times, but ten of these are in chapter 6. By the presence and power of God, the Israelites successfully cross the walls, so to speak, and capture the city.

Chapters 6 and 7 describe polar opposite results. Israel's defeat at Ai (chap. 7) contrasts with the positive picture of Israel's obedience (chap. 6). The theft of devoted things by Achan results in defeat, showing that Israel's victories are not automatic and are ultimately in the Lord's hands.

Chapter 6 includes three literary patterns. (1) First is the prediction/fulfillment pattern. The Lord predicts "the wall . . . will collapse" (6:5), and the prediction is fulfilled when "the wall collapsed" (6:20). (2) Second is the familiar command/obedience pattern. The Lord instructs Joshua (6:2–5), and Joshua relates the instructions to the people, who obey (6:6–14), resulting in the destruction of the city (6:15–27). (3) Last is the six-plus-one pattern. The number "seven" occurs eleven times. The pattern recalls creation's seventh day—the day of consecration. For six days the Hebrews circle the city once a day (6:11–14); on the seventh day they circle seven times; and on the seventh trip the trumpets blast and the people shout (6:15–21). The imitation of God's creation shows the power and authority of the Lord. The Jericho moment is a new beginning for Israel. The land is the new Eden. The number "seven" and the prominence of the ark and the priests suggest a religious ritual. In its destruction, Jericho is "devoted" (*herem*) to God (6:17–18, 21). The vocabulary and the pattern of the procession indicate that the event is both cultic and military in character—for example, the trumpets of rams' horns and the shouting.[1]

Interpretive Insights

6:1 *securely barred.* The Hebrew text repeats the word "shut" (*sogeret um⁰suggeret*), and this redundance emphasizes the emergency closure of the city. It echoes the same measure taken in the story of the spies (2:7, 15). This is to no avail, since the walls collapse and the surrounding warriors march straight ahead (6:5, 20).

6:2 *I have delivered.* The Lord speaks as though it is an assured fact.

6:5 *everyone straight in.* The walls' collapse means that the city loses its primary defense and its advantage of the high ground. The inhabitants will be in a panic and surrounded by the enemy with no avenue of escape.

6:6 *ark of the covenant.* (See the sidebar "Ark of the Covenant" in the unit on 3:1–17.)

God—not Joshua's genius or Israel's military advantage—is the source of Israel's success.

6:8–9 *priests . . . ark . . . armed guard.* At the Jordan the ark leads the way (3:14, 17), remaining on the dry riverbed until the congregation passes over. At Jericho the order of the procession is the soldiers, the priests with trumpets, the ark, the rear guard, and last the people. This arrangement positions the ark in the center of the procession. Both arrangements place emphasis on the ark's role.

6:10 *do not say a word.* In contrast to the trumpets' blast, the congregation is deathly silent.

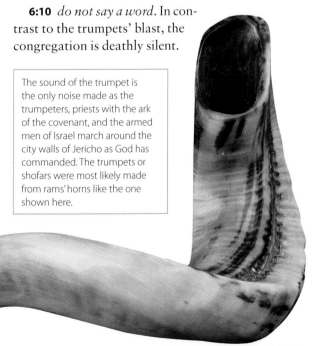

The sound of the trumpet is the only noise made as the trumpeters, priests with the ark of the covenant, and the armed men of Israel march around the city walls of Jericho as God has commanded. The trumpets or shofars were most likely made from rams' horns like the one shown here.

The effect is psychologically disturbing and solemn.

6:18 *devoted things . . . destruction.* "Devoted" and "destruction" are from the same word (*herem*; see "Christian Interpretation" in the introduction, and cf. the comments on 2:10). The cultic terms "sacred" and "treasury" indicate that Jericho is an offering to the Lord (6:19, 24; 1 Kings 7:51).

bring trouble. "Trouble" (*'akar*) is a play on the sound of the name "Achan" (*'akan*), who steals from the city (7:1). It occurs twice more, describing Achan's sin (7:25 [2x]), and plays on the name Valley of Achor, meaning "Valley of Trouble" (7:24, 26).

6:25 *spared Rahab.* Verse 25's description of Rahab's deliverance contrasts with the destruction in the preceding verses.

6:26 *Cursed . . . firstborn son . . . youngest.* The imprecation is reminiscent of the tenth plague in Pharaoh's household (Exod. 12:29). References to the "firstborn" and the "youngest" (i.e., last born) form a merism, meaning no descendant will survive. Merism is a literary device using opposite terms to express totality (e.g., he searched high and low). The offender's heritage will be completely cut off. Rebuilding the city means benefiting from what is designated for the Lord. That the curse falls on Hiel of Bethel (1 Kings 16:34) shows that God has acknowledged Joshua's faithfulness (Josh. 6:27). Deuteronomy 13:16 gives the rationale for Jericho's permanent ruins.[2] The Israelites were permitted to live there provided they did not build it into a fortress (18:21; Judg. 3:13; 2 Sam. 10:5).[3]

6:27 *the Lord was with Joshua.* A similar expression describes Moses (1:5, 17; 3:7; Deut. 31:8, 23).

Theological Insights

The destruction of Jericho is a work *by* God and *for* God. The passage reiterates that God alone is the champion of the battle, not Joshua or any other person. Also, the nuances of ritual and holy offering confirm that the city's destruction is motivated by God alone. This excludes economic gain as a motivation by the Israelites. If the Israelites plunder the city, they steal from God and are liable to destruction themselves. The story testifies to God's judgment against sin but also to his salvation for those who acknowledge him regardless of their ethnicity. Rahab's deliverance evidences God's mercy in contrast to the judgment rendered against the city.

The silence of the people speaks to the solemnity of the event. There is no pleasure in the judgment that is to take place. The idea of silence may describe God's judgment against the wicked, who are silenced in death (Ps. 31:17), or trust in the Lord when the pious meditate before him and wait patiently for his deliverance (Pss. 4:4; 62:5). The Jericho incident shows that the Lord demands a just accounting for moral corruption in society (Ps. 9; Jer. 25:15–16). Yet he is merciful toward nations that repent (Jon. 4:11).

Coupled with the text's focus on God is its focus on human instrumentality. God utilizes Joshua, the priests, warriors, and the congregation, making both the divine and human involvement essential to Israel's entering the blessing. He also uses Rahab, an unexpected ally of the Israelites. Each person has a part. As in cases of capital punishment in Israel, all the community participates in the battle, evidencing individual and collective responsibility for the action (e.g., Lev. 24:14, 16; Num. 15:35–36). The law requires death for those who practice the idolatry of the Canaanites (Lev. 20:2).

The passage portrays the holiness of God. Only valuables devoted to the Lord's treasury survive the holocaust (6:19). The allusion to the year of Jubilee (*yobel*) by the rams' horns (*yobel*) blown by the priests indicates the divine origin of the judgment (6:4). A ram's horn is blown to announce the year of Jubilee, a sacred year every fiftieth year, in which debts are forgiven and land restored (Lev. 25:10–13). The rams' horns connect the ideas of holiness and

God is the one responsible for the destruction of Jericho. The battle plan for conquering Jericho is unusual, but the people follow God's instructions and Jericho's walls fall. Excavations at ancient Jericho have uncovered this Middle Bronze revetment (retaining) wall that supported a higher mud-brick wall. Collapsed portions of this mud-brick wall have also been found, but the date of its destruction is much earlier than the customary dating of Joshua.

the themes of justice and freedom.[4] The restoration of the land to the Israelites by virtue of the promise to their ancestors is a new beginning, a season of Jubilee.

Teaching the Text

The primary lesson is the centrality of God, who has guaranteed his purposes and promises for his people. Yet the Lord requires faithful obedience to actuate the working out of the promises. This is especially shown by the faithful and courageous responses of Joshua and Rahab. She and her household receive mercy because God honors her faith and righteous deed. She is referred to as "Rahab the prostitute" in Joshua (6:17, 25; cf. Heb. 11:31; James 2:25). The text does not wipe clean her sinful past and has the effect of trumpeting

the grace that God shows her. God uses Rahab at a strategic moment in his plan for the Israelites and for the ages (cf. Matt. 1:5). For Christian readers, the message is good news because no one's past precludes a person from salvation (Col. 3:5–7; 1 Tim. 1:15). This is good news for each one of us but also ought to remind us that this is good news for others. Our passage is a reminder to trust in the power of the gospel to save those whom we are tempted to consider hopeless in their sins.

A popular interpretation of the Jericho narrative is transforming it into an allegory about the Christian's victories over the spiritual "walls of Jericho," such as "the Jericho of sin," "the Jericho of materialism," and "the Jericho within the church."[5] Joshua's narrative refers to the walls as literal walls, not as signs for spiritual lessons. Such interpretations diminish the historical reality of what occurs at Jericho. Allegorical interpretations are subject to speculative imaginations and attempt to legitimize interpretations that erroneously correlate Old Testament stories and spiritual realities. There is sufficient spiritual truth in the text as it stands for effective teaching without resorting to mystical interpretations.

Illustrating the Text

Learn to respond to the Master with obedience and commitment.

Human Experience: In 1994, singer Rich Mullins wrote an article in which he compared his response to the Lord with the response of his golden retriever, Bear, to him as his master. Mullins begins, "If I loved my Master like my dog loves his, I would be more saintly than John the Divine . . . more radical than John the Baptizer . . . more deeply devoted than St. John of the Cross." He shares Bear's response to a storm, when he runs between his master's legs, which is a reminder to Mullins that he would do better to crawl between his Master's legs in times of storms than to act courageous or to seek inferior shelter. In a right relationship between a dog owner and a properly trained dog, we see obedience and commitment to the commands of the master.[6] What a reminder to all of us that we need to learn to respond in prompt obedience to the Word and commands of our Lord.

Obey even when God's commands seem irrational or unusual.

Statistics: In a 2014 study conducted by the dating website ChristianMingle.com, Christian singles between the ages of eighteen and fifty-nine were asked this question: "Would you have sex before marriage?" The response was surprising, as 63 percent of the Christian single respondents indicated yes. In analyzing this data, author Kenny Luck wrote, "It is equally honest to say that nearly nine out of 10 self-proclaimed single Christians are, *in practice*, sexual atheists. . . . God has nothing to say to them on that subject . . . to dissuade them from following their own course of conduct."[7] Too often Christians more closely reflect current cultural norms than they do biblical standards. To some, many of the commands of Scripture may seem out-of-date or out-of-touch in light of current culture, but the question is one of authority. Who is really in charge of my life? To whom am I really accountable? Whom will I obey?

Kingdom victory comes through complete obedience and surrender.

History: Corrie ten Boom tells of the beginnings of her family's efforts to protect Jews from the Nazi madness sweeping across Holland during the Second World War. One night while delivering a watch to a Jewish family and visiting with them, she prayed, "Lord Jesus, I offer myself for Your people. In any way. Any place. Any time."[8] She later tells us that her main "job" in the resistance movement was "to follow [God's] leading one step at a time, holding every decision up to him in prayer."[9] Many Jews were saved from certain death by that surrender to the Lord, although four members of the ten Boom family died for it. After surviving the Ravensbruck concentration camp, Corrie spent the rest of her life telling her story and proclaiming the gospel around the world.

Joshua's Jihad?

The Muslim terrorist movement has raised in the West an acute awareness of the growing global influence of Islam. The Arabic term "jihad" has become a popular synonym in the West for war by Muslims against non-Muslims, coercing them to submit to Islam's Allah ("God"). Islamic militants, it is thought by many, take this ideology to the extreme by murdering innocent (noncombatant) non-Muslims, even practicing suicide bombing. Government officials and media outlets in the West forcefully affirm that terrorism is not a legitimate view among Muslims themselves and that only a small minority interpret "jihad" to mean armed conflict. When it is pointed out that the early centuries of Islamic expansion were achieved often through aggression, not persuasion, a popular response—especially by academics and media—is the charge that Christianity too had its medieval crusades and the Bible has wars carried out in the name of God.

In the introduction ("Christian Interpretation"), I have addressed the issue of Israel's wars in general. Now, I focus on the specific issue of Joshua's wars and the Islamic idea of jihad. There are two aspects of the discussion that are often misunderstood and must be pursued. First, jihad has different meanings among those of the Islamic faith. What does "jihad" mean? Second, confusion reigns today because people wrongly make a moral equation between Israel's conquest and the Islamic doctrine of jihad. What is the difference?

First, the Arabic term "jihad" means "struggling," which in the Qur'an (Islam's scriptures) can refer to inner spiritual resistance to evil ("greater jihad") or to armed conflict ("lesser jihad"). Peaceful ways of striving for the faith are explicit in the Qur'an, such as conversion by the "pen" and the "tongue." Among Muslim scholars there is dispute as to what "jihad" means for Muslims today since the Qur'an has conflicting ideas, some verses calling for armed aggression and territorial expansion and others rejecting any form of coercion (e.g., Qur'an 2:256). In the case of armed conflict, some passages set rules of warfare, such as fighting only defensive battles (e.g., Qur'an 22:39–40). Still other verses that address warfare have no boundaries limiting the engagement (e.g., Qur'an 2:216; 9:5, 29). Scholars argue about which ideology better represents the ethics of the Qur'an. Classical Islam contends that the militaristic verses are later and have cancelled out the tolerant verses. Regardless of a final resolution to the meaning of jihad in the inner-Muslim debate, it is clear that unrestricted territorial expansion is called for in the Qur'an, and classical Islam (seventh–thirteenth centuries) had its greatest expansion as a consequence of warfare against non-Muslims, from Spain to India, including North Africa.

Second, what differences occur between the battles in the Bible and in Islamic history?[1] Before we begin this discussion, there are two important principles of interpretation that must be remembered. (1) Biblical narratives are largely descriptive, simply telling what occurred, not prescriptive, calling readers to the same action. That the Bible reports that the Israelites engaged in wars does not always mean that battles had divine sanction. The Qur'an, on the other hand, is prescriptive. Nevertheless, there are specific passages in Joshua where God explicitly directs his people to do battle. Here, similarities between Yahweh's wars and jihad may mislead. (2) Counting up similarities versus differences does not necessarily determine whether an analogy between entities is legitimate. The matter of parallels is more complex than simply counting. More likenesses or more differences do not reveal the inherent nature of the items under comparison. The point of comparison must be at the most fundamental level—the substance of the two systems.

The most fundamental difference between the two understandings of war is the extent of the action that God calls for. Classical Islam requires Muslims to subject all nations to Muslim rule. It is a global program of establishing Islamic law. In Islamic thought there is envisioned a global religious and political community. Islamic identity supersedes national boundaries. Since the mission is to achieve a worldwide institution of Islamic religion, there is no restriction on the time required to achieve the goal. There is no end in sight until all peoples live under Islamic rule and faith. Until this time, Islamic jihad has no space or time boundaries; there is a perpetual "struggle."

Israel's conquest of Canaan, however, had limitations of both geography and time. Its purpose was to establish a safe haven, a community of related tribes that would eventually establish a geopolitical state. Israel's mission was to pacify the land of promise, Canaan. During the Late Bronze Age, Canaan was in constant turmoil, as the Amarna documents reflect. Israel's mission was not a global mission. The boundaries of other peoples were respected. For example, the Israelites were specifically prohibited from displacing neighboring Edomites and Moabites (Deut. 2:4–5, 9–12). Only those people groups living in the land of Canaan were potential opponents in war. Also, there was necessarily a time factor involved, because the purpose of controlling the land did not require unlimited domination by the Israelites. Israel's victories were limited and were temporary. Israel did not engage in perpetual warfare against towns once their threat had been downgraded and their influence in the region diminished.

Moreover, the conquest was deemed an act of God's judgment against a specific people—the Canaanites—because of their heinous (Lev. 18:6–23) and long-standing (Gen. 15:16) moral failings, not because they were non-Israelites or because they did not worship Yahweh. Thus, as judgment, utter destruction was called for (compare Josh. 6:17–21 with Deut. 20:10–18). Whereas jihad is one of the central means of extending the Islamic faith, the means of extending the kingdom of Yahweh was not militaristic but primarily through proclamation (e.g., Jon. 3:4–10).

Defeat at Ai

Big Idea *Divine discipline calls for renewed consecration to God.*

Understanding the Text

The Text in Context

The defeat of Israel at Ai occurs between two episodes of Israel's victories over their enemies—Jericho (chap. 6) and the second attack at Ai (chap. 8). Chapters 6–8 are a cohesive unit, reporting the capture of two critical sites in the central region. Jericho and Ai give a contrasting picture—obedience versus disobedience. The delegation of spies (7:2) echoes the Jericho narrative (2:1; 6:22, 23, 25). References to "devoted things / destruction / destroy" (*herem/haram*; 6:17, 18 [4x], 21; 7:1 [2x], 11, 12 [2x], 13 [2x],

15), the word "trouble" (*'akar*; 6:18; 7:25 [2x]), and its wordplay "Valley of Achor/ Trouble" (*'akor*; 7:24, 26) tie chapters 6 and 7 together.

Chapter 7 divides into two parts: (1) the occasion of the crime (7:1–15) and (2) the outcome of the criminal's discovery (7:16–26). Verses 1–15 describe Israel's abortive attempt to capture Ai by acting independently of God's direction, which results in Joshua's perplexed appeal to God. The Lord reveals that Israel has sinned and instructs Joshua to prepare the people for discovering the culprit. Verses 16–26 describe the process of discovery by the casting of lots and the subsequent execution of the offender and his family. The chapter begins with God's "burning anger" (7:1; NIV: "anger burned") and concludes with the

> The city of Ai is small, but Israel is unsuccessful in battle because of Achan's sin against the Lord. The exact location of ancient Ai is intensely debated by scholars. The traditional opinion identifies Ai with et-Tell, shown here.

notice that God has turned from his "burning anger" (7:26; NIV: "fierce anger"). For lexical connections between the two parts, see "The Text in Context" in the unit on 7:16–26. Joshua 7:1–15 has four elements: Achan's theft (7:1), Israel's defeat (7:2–6), Joshua's prayer (7:7–9), and the Lord's indictment and instructions (7:10–15).

Historical and Cultural Background

Ai ("the ruin," *ha'ay*) was located east of Bethel (Gen. 12:7–8; Josh. 7:2; 12:9). The identification of Ai with modern et-Tell ("ruin," Arabic) is widely accepted. It is about twelve miles north of Jerusalem and two miles east of modern Beitin (biblical Bethel?). Problems with this proposal, however, have led to alternative suggestions for the location of Ai, and related cities such as Bethel have also been disputed. The problem with et-Tell is the absence of evidence for an occupation corresponding to the time of Joshua, whether one takes the early date (ca. 1400) or the late date (ca. 1200) for the conquest. Ai's specific location remains a mystery, but it is clear that Ai and Bethel were in the central highlands (Josh. 16:1), about a fifteen-mile march from Jericho. Ai and Bethel were strategically located, and their defeat broke the control of the Canaanites, giving the Israelites a hold in the region.

Interpretive Insights

7:1 *But . . . were unfaithful.* "But" contrasts the failure of Israel with the victory at Jericho. The first word in the text is "to act unfaithfully" (*ma'al*), emphasizing its importance (see the comments on 22:16; cf. 22:20). Here, the term may be used in its

cultic sense, a violation against God's holiness, by removing the sacred items into the realm of the profane/common (Lev. 5:15).[1] The entire community is liable and responsible for removing the offender.

devoted things. The *herem* belongs solely to God, meaning Achan steals from God (on *herem*, see "Christian Interpretation" in the introduction).

Achan son of Karmi. Identifying Achan's family lineage at the start anticipates the drama of detection (7:12–18).

7:2 *Ai . . . Bethel.* These two sites recall Abraham's travels (Gen. 12:8), connecting the promise of land and the conquest (Josh. 1:6; 21:43). Locating Ai near Beth Aven, which means "house of iniquity," may be a clever wordplay on Israel's disobedience (cf. Hosea 4:15).

7:3 *a few people.* Referring to "few" in number reflects Israel's preoccupation with troop strength rather than trust in God (Deut. 7:7, 22); that only three thousand attack differs sharply from the forty thousand at Jericho (4:13). On the word "thousand," see "Historical and Cultural Background" in the unit on 8:1–29. Unlike at Jericho the Israelites act presumptuously by not consulting the Lord. The sole reference to the "ark" (7:6) contrasts with its prominence at the Jordan and at Jericho (chaps. 3–4; 6).

7:5 *about thirty-six . . . hearts of the people melted . . . like water.* Although a small number dies, this loss is devastating since the mightier Jericho falls without Israelite loss. The people's fear signals another reversal of what happens at Jericho (2:11; 5:1).

7:6 *tore his clothes and fell facedown . . . till evening.* Tearing clothes expresses overwhelming grief over loss (Gen. 37:34). Bowing before the Lord expresses contrition and worship (5:14). That Joshua spends a daylong vigil expresses the depth of his contrition and the gravity of the situation (cf. Num. 14:6).

The elders . . . sprinkled dust. The elders' action indicates distress (Lam. 2:10).

7:7 *into the hands of the Amorites.* Joshua's despair recalls the spies' charge against God at Kadesh Barnea (Deut. 1:27), but ironically, Joshua believed God's promise then (Num. 14:6–9).

7:8 *has been routed.* Literally, "turned their backs" (*hapak 'orep*) (cf. 7:12), this reverses what God promises will happen to their enemies (Exod. 23:27).

7:9 *our name . . . your own great name.* By using "our" and "your," Joshua links Israel's well-being and the reputation of God (Deut. 9:14). Purging Israel is necessary for its witness as a holy people (4:24; Deut. 28:9–10).

7:10 *Stand up!* The exhortation (*qum*) plays on the inability of Israel to "stand" (*qum*) against its enemies (7:12, 13).

What . . . on your face? Israel, not the Lord, fails in covenant faithfulness. The question calls for Joshua to deal with the problem instead of grumbling (9:18; Num. 14:27).

7:11 *sinned . . . violated.* "Sinned" (*hata'*) is the general term for committing wrong, and "transgressed" (*'abar*; NIV:

"violated") conveys the idea of stepping over a boundary.

taken . . . stolen . . . lied . . . put. This verbal litany describes what will later be revealed as Achan's crime. Achan's sin is stealing, compounded by deception and furthered by putting the goods among his personal items. "Stolen" (*ganab*) is the word occurring in the Ten Commandments (Deut. 5:19), showing that the offense transgresses the heart of the covenant. "Lied" (*kahash*) indicates that Achan pretends to comply (cf. Lev. 19:11).

7:13 *Consecrate yourselves.* The appearance of the Lord requires consecration. This command echoes preparations for crossing the Jordan (cf. the comments on 3:5), but sadly here it is necessary because of their sin.

7:14 *present yourselves.* Although the text does not mention casting lots (cf. 18:6), it is probably assumed (see "Historical and Cultural Background" in the unit on 14:1–15). Casting lots is under the direction of the Lord (Prov. 16:33); it identifies the guilty (Jon. 1:7). Achan acknowledges his crime only after being discovered (7:20).

7:15 *destroyed by fire . . . outrageous thing.* Capital punishment by burning the criminal is not common in Israel, occurring only for violations against God's holiness (Lev. 20:14; 21:9). "Outrageous" (*nebalah*) describes morally foolish actions, including sexual perversions (Gen. 34:7).

Theological Insights

God's commands are not to be trifled with. Disobedience angers the Lord, and he sets in motion events that discipline. The nature and circumstances of that corrective are not uniform; what is constant is that

In response to the death of Israelite soldiers at the hands of the men of Ai, Joshua and the elders tear their clothes and sprinkle dust on their heads before the Lord. These were typical ways to publicly express grief and mourning in the ancient Near East. In this Egyptian tomb painting, a mourning woman puts dust on her head as a sign of her sorrow (Tomb of Nebamun, ca. 1350 BC).

offending the holy name of God, stealing, lying, and coveting. Yet the punishment at Ai has the benevolent end of restoring favor. The Lord also shows mercy by plainly revealing the crime (7:10–12) and the remedy (7:13–15) so that the people do not languish in darkness or doubt his commitment. Although the community suffers, he restrains punishment by not eradicating the whole nation (Exod. 32:9–14; Num. 14:11–24; Amos 7). The Lord shows his incomparable patience toward Israel. Only after centuries of disobedience does he eventually expel the people from the land (Deut. 28:36–37).

The passage also demonstrates the power of temptation and sin. No crime is solely one's own business, and it cannot be altogether held in secret, for the Lord knows and exposes our sin (Deut. 31:21; Jer. 17:9–10). But this passage teaches that sin is neither inevitable nor permanent. By far most of the community resist the temptation to take the plunder. Moreover, the people learn more perfectly the instruction of the Lord (Deut. 11:2; Prov. 3:11), so that in future battles they painstakingly obey. After the people acknowledge their sin, the Lord forgives and reinstates them (Deut. 30:6; Ps. 32:5).

The passage shows the necessity of humility to receive divine forgiveness and favor (7:6–9). Joshua's actions of contrition speak louder than his words. He recognizes that he is helpless without God's blessing, and he cannot explain what has happened to the benevolent presence of the Divine Warrior. Joshua's rationale for renewal relies on God's reputation, not Joshua's alone. The identities of Israel and of the Lord are intertwined—as Israel goes, so goes the Lord's reputation in the eyes of

he does not present commands as though they are options. He is not fickle, subject to humanlike passions. Rather, he forewarns the people, both by direct prohibition (6:18) and by historical memory (2:10; 5:1; Deut. 31:4). Since this is the first breach of his law upon the people entering the land, it is a critical moment that necessitates a quick and harsh response. Achan breaches several aspects of the Ten Commandments, the nations (7:9; Jer. 14:9; Dan. 9:19). For the nations' view of the Lord, see Numbers 14:16–17; Deuteronomy 4:6; Isaiah 52:10.

Although Joshua's interests correspond at points with the purposes of God's kingdom, he places the weightier theology of the kingdom above himself. Despite the Lord's adoption of Israel as his own unique people, their success is not automatic. God is free to act as it pleases him, achieving the higher goals of his own glory and justice. He may condemn, or he may save (Deut. 28:37; Joel 2:18).

Teaching the Text

Teaching the passage presents the difficulty of understanding divine judgment and divine discipline (7:6–8, 12). The ideas of judgment versus discipline convey different purposes for punishment. "Judgment" is condemnation, and "discipline" is correction motivated by love leading to faithfulness. Discipline benefits and should not be avoided (Job 5:17–18; Heb. 12:5–11 [with Prov. 3:11–12]). Israel is "liable to destruction" (*herem*, 7:12) because of the special circumstances that call for God's anger against Israel as a nation as well as his wrath against the individual culprit, Achan. The circumstances in Joshua's day are distinctive, not the norm for every generation of the Israelites. The immediacy and the extent of the punishment match the urgency of the situation. The confrontations with Israel's enemies who are determined to destroy God's people make it necessary for God to put an immediate stop to disobedience. In the application of this passage, the circumstances of Achan's sin and God's response should not be equated

with the way God responds to individual Christians today who sin against the Lord. That the Lord deals harshly with the sin of Achan does not mean that the Lord punishes Christians in the same way or to the same degree. Christians do not live under judgment as hopelessly condemned sinners; rather, they are freed from eternal condemnation (Rom. 8:1; 1 Cor. 11:32).

Also, the passage shows that sin is pervasive, insidiously impacting the lives of innocent people (7:4–5). The line between private and public behavior in Israel was nonexistent. What people do privately seeps into the culture. Sin and repentance are individual but also public. Yet the passage also shows that God exhibits grace. His wrath is restrained and appeased. He gives Joshua and even Achan (and family members) ample opportunity to confess, repent, and avert any further recriminations (7:13). The people as a whole learn from this setback and grow spiritually so that they achieve victory over Ai. For Christians, Paul likens sin to yeast that permeates the whole lump of dough (1 Cor. 5:6; Gal. 5:9), jeopardizing the reputation and viability of the community (1 Cor. 5:1–11; 1 Pet. 2:12).

The passage shows one kind of temptation in the land that the Lord has forewarned will occur. Achan's lust for enrichment at the expense of obedience leads to his death (7:1, 20–21). What occurs for Achan and his family illustrates what may befall the nation as a whole if it chooses to surrender to Canaanite culture. Joshua in his last speeches cautions the nation against betraying its allegiance to the Lord by embracing Canaan's gods (23:6–8, 14–16; 24:19–20). Similarly, we must stand on guard against those temptations that are especially pernicious to us, "the sin that so easily entangles" (Heb. 12:1). Christians face temptations, but they please God through yielding to the Spirit in obedience (Rom. 6:6–7, 19; 8:14; 1 Cor. 10:13; 2 Pet. 2:9).

Illustrating the Text

The disobedience of one person affects the entire community.

Children's Book: *The Lion, the Witch and the Wardrobe,* by C. S. Lewis. In this book, one of the children, Edmund, succumbs to the temptation of the White Witch, who brings him under her spell. The results are catastrophic for the four children, Aslan, and all of Narnia. Although Aslan, who represents Jesus Christ, is victorious in the end, everyone must endure suffering in the meantime. There are many cultures in the world that emphasize individuality over community responsibility. We must remember that our choices impact not only us but others as well. This is certainly true for genuine Christian community.

Take practical steps to stand firm against temptation.

Mythology: In the classic work *The Odyssey,* Homer provides an example of temptation through the story of the Song of the Sirens. The Sirens' song is so irresistible that none who hears it can escape. There is peril for the voyagers, because sailing toward the Sirens would result in the entire ship crashing into dangerous rocks. Odysseus is determined to hear the song for himself, despite the danger, and devises a plan to ensure his survival. He plugs his men's ears with beeswax, and he ties himself to the mast. He makes his crew promise that

no matter how hard he pleads and begs to be released, they will not untie him. This is the only way Odysseus can resist the temptation of the Sirens' song. If Odysseus had given in to the temptation of the Sirens, the whole crew would have followed and surely been destroyed. What are the temptations you face in your life? What practical steps can you take to stand firm in obedience?

It is important to correct or discipline in love.

Quote: The Bible is clear that we are to be willing to challenge one another by speaking the truth in love (Gal. 6:1–2; Eph. 4:15). The purpose of this challenge is to encourage other people to make better choices in their lives. But this is difficult to do if they are unwilling to receive the truth, or if they do not want to be challenged, or even change. To keep others at bay, they may remind us that we are not to be "judgmental." As Maranda M. states on her blog, *Revealing Truth Today,*

> Many people won't take a stand against evil for fear of coming across as judgmental. In the name of "love" and "acceptance" and "tolerance," they remain spineless. This is not love, acceptance, nor tolerance; but it is cowardice and disregard for another's well-being. Such people will not take a stand against sexual immorality, moral decay, false religions, or deception found in much of today's "entertainment," all because it is politically correct, popular and accepted—and they wish to be popular and accepted.[2]

Do you love other Christians enough to be willing to speak the truth in love?

Achan's Punishment

Big Idea *Disobedience results in community guilt and punishment, but God still provides saving grace.*

Understanding the Text

The Text in Context

Joshua 7:16–26 describes the consequences of Achan's theft and Joshua's repentance depicted in verses 1–15. Whereas 7:1–15 mainly reflects the perspective of the Lord, 7:16–26 adds the human perspectives of Achan and Joshua. Details about the theft—the temptation, the items stolen, and the hiding place—are recounted. There are clear connections between the two halves of the chapter (e.g., 7:14, 16, the morning's assembly). (1) Verses 16–18 narrate the suspenseful countdown of casting lots by family group, which is already identified in verse 1. Lexical ties are evident: the verb *lakad* ("chooses/caught") in verses 14–15 (4x) appears in verses 16–18 ("chosen," 4x). (2) Verses 19–21 consist of the exchange between Joshua and Achan, who acknowledges his crime, "I have sinned" (7:20), and parallels the exchange between Joshua and the Lord when the Lord charges, "Israel has sinned" (7:11). (3) Verses 22–24 detail the discovery of the stolen items, and verses 25–26 describe Achan's execution, corresponding to the Lord's instruction in verse 15.

Interpretive Insights

7:16–18 *Early the next morning . . . Judah was chosen.* Joshua's immediate compliance (7:13–14) signals a repentant Joshua (the same language in his victories, 3:1; 6:12; 8:10). "Judah" brackets verses 16–18. It is the largest tribe, the tribe of Caleb and David. "Chosen" (*lakad*, "taken") also means "captured," here in the sense of "selected."

tribes . . . clans . . . families . . . man. The order progresses from the largest unit to the smallest (see 7:14). Achan selfishly remains silent, while the people fearfully wait.

7:19 *My son.* Joshua addresses Achan with a surprising paternal spirit (Gen. 48:19), designed to elicit a confession (Gen. 3:13).

give glory . . . honor . . . Tell me what you have done; do not hide it. The four inquiries are two sets of parallel instructions.[1] Joshua implores Achan at last to grant God his due by confessing his crime. "Give glory" may suggest an oath, swearing to a truthful account. "Honor" (*todah*, "praise/thanksgiving") means in this context that by confessing his sin, Achan is giving glory to the Lord. Ironically, he would have brought glory to God by initially obeying. "Have done" and "hide" are reminiscent of Eden (Gen. 3:8, 13–14; cf. 4:10).

7:20 *I have sinned.* Achan's confession and his execution atone for Israel's collective guilt (7:11).

7:21 *saw . . . a beautiful robe from Babylonia . . . silver . . . gold.* The robe is "beautiful" (*tob*, "good, valuable") in appearance and costly, attracting Achan ("saw"). The toponym refers to the region of Babylonia (= "Shinar," Gen. 10:10) or all of Mesopotamia. The foreign garment reflects the international commerce of that time. The value of metals was determined by weight (shekel = ¹⁄₁₀ of an ounce). Gold and silver are common metals for creating idols (Deut. 7:25).

coveted . . . took . . . hidden. The temptation becomes action (cf. Eve's temptation, Gen. 3:6). "Coveted" (*hamad*) occurs in Genesis 3:6 ("desirable") and the Ten Commandments (Exod. 20:17). The idea of secrecy is prominent: Joshua and the elders are ignorant of the crime; "hidden" occurs twice (7:21, 22) and "underneath" twice (7:21, 22), which contrasts with setting the items for all to see and "before the LORD" (7:23). "Hidden" (*taman*) recalls Joshua's exhortation ("hide," *kahad*; 7:19).

Achan confesses to stealing a beautiful Babylonian robe from the spoils of Jericho. Puzur-Ishtar, the governor of Mari, wears an elaborate robe in this statue from the Old Babylonian period (ca. 1894–1594 BC).

7:22 *sent messengers . . . ran to the tent.* The messengers are unofficial witnesses to the stolen items, confirming Achan's account (7:21; cf. Deut. 17:6). That the messengers hurry reflects the situation's urgency and gravity.

7:23 *spread them out before the LORD.* The community as a whole suffers defeat and now collectively witnesses the reason for defeat. "Spread out" is also "poured out" (*yatsaq*), a term describing the pouring of oil for sacrifice (Lev. 2:1). The property is in the presence of the Lord (the ark or sacred tent?), suggesting a sacrificial act (Lev. 1:5).

7:24 *Achan . . . the silver, the robe, the gold bar . . . all that he had.* Achan and the items are named first, suggesting that Achan's personal crime is responsible for the calamity of others. Ironically, by his effort to gain more, Achan loses all. On the "Valley of Achor," see the comments on 6:18.

7:25 *trouble on us . . . trouble on you.* The balanced response of "trouble" for "trouble" indicates a just reprisal.

stoned . . . burned.
Stoning was the common
means of capital punish-
ment (Lev. 20:2), but
burning (purging
evil) was for viola-
tions against holiness
(Lev. 10:1–3, 6; 20:14;
Num. 16:35). Burning the
remains of a person was
a humiliation (Amos 2:1).
Burning up the family and possessions
corresponds to burning the cities devoted
to the Lord (e.g., Jericho, 6:24).

stoned the rest. The stoning reflects the
measure of guilt, beginning with Achan.
The Hebrew text's order is difficult: "they
stoned [*ragam*] him . . . they burned them
. . . they stoned [*saqal*] them" (cf. ESV);
probably the burning occurs after the
stoning (cf. 7:15). The word *ragam* may
refer to piling on rocks (cf. 7:26), whereas
saqal means stoning to death.[2] The family's guilt may be related to concepts of
community solidarity (see the comments
on 1:18; 2:12) or violation of holiness by
ritual contamination.[3] Possibly the judgment also includes the eradication of his
"name," meaning his progeny.[4] Perhaps
family members know and are complicit
by silence.

7:26 *pile of rocks.* In contrast to the
memorial stones testifying to God's grace
(4:7, 9), the gravestones perpetually testify
to the consequence of disobedience.

turned from . . . anger. God's anger initially is against all "Israel" (7:1) but now is
satisfied by Israel's action.

Valley of Achor. "Achor" is the Hebrew
word "trouble," which is the punishment
forewarned by God at Jericho (6:18).

All the gold, silver, bronze, and iron from Jericho
are declared sacred to the Lord and placed in the
tabernacle treasury. When Achan takes the gold
and silver pieces, he brings God's punishment on
himself and his family. The precious metal pieces
shown here are part of a hoard found at el-Amarna
(1350–1300 BC) that contained twenty-three bars
of gold in addition to bars and rings of silver.

Theological Insights

God is zealous for his holiness and reputation. He does not tolerate egregious
disobedience in his people. The severity
of the offense is shown by the severity of
the punishment against Achan and those
impacted by his selfishness. Although the
stolen items are few, expectations of compliance are not relative to the number or
value of the items taken. All Israel carries
out the penalty, but it is at God's command
(7:15, 25b). In effect Achan robs God's
"home" ("treasury," 6:18–19, 24) to adorn
his own. Achan challenges the Lord's reign.
He acknowledges that his sin is "against
the Lord" (7:20; cf. Ps. 51:4[6]). But it also
injures Israel ("on us," 7:25a). His confession and death show that God is truthful
and faithful to his forewarning.

That God gives fair warning (6:18) and
ample opportunity for repentance shows
that the Lord is not intractably angry. Achan

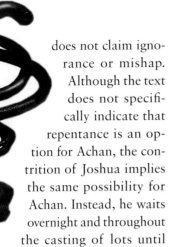

does not claim ignorance or mishap. Although the text does not specifically indicate that repentance is an option for Achan, the contrition of Joshua implies the same possibility for Achan. Instead, he waits overnight and throughout the casting of lots until he must confess (7:16–18). What Achan thinks he can conceal becomes known to everyone (7:23). Sadly, Achan fails to recognize the lavish provision of God (24:13). The restrictions on plunder are uncommon (cf. 11:14; 22:8) and actually lifted in the subsequent battle against Ai (8:2, 27). Nothing is left of Achan's legacy, only a pile of stones shaming his memory. Moreover, declarations of impending doom presuppose the possibility of averting God's judgment (e.g., Nineveh, Jon. 3:10; 4:2; cf. Exod. 34:6). Whereas repentance may have led to a mitigation of the punishment, the failure of Achan to confess his sin early and restore the stolen items means that only through his death will the anger of God be appeased. The psalmist learns that refusal to repent only means more personal anguish (Ps. 32:5–7).

But is there evidence of grace in the passage? First, the Lord does not threaten to exterminate the whole nation (Exod. 32:9–11). He restrains his anger ("on you," 7:25a). Second, he reveals the crime so that the people might deal with the matter, leading to their forgiveness ("turned from his fierce anger," 7:26). Third, they evidently learn from the chastening, since they exhibit careful obedience in subsequent wars. Fourth, despite their failure, the blessing and hope of life in the land continue ("remains to this day," 7:26).

Teaching the Text

The principal message of the passage is the perverseness of human sin in the eyes of God. The destructive power of sin is pervasive and persistent, corrupting individuals and harming others. Achan's act impacts the whole community. He has lusted after the valuables at Jericho; he "coveted them and took them" (7:21). He has transgressed commandments prohibiting theft, lying, and covetousness (Lev. 19:11; Deut. 5:19, 21). By taking what belongs to God, he has committed the theft of holy things. By his silence he lies, refusing to confess his sin until he is found out by the community. The Ten Commandments were the "charter" for the nation of Israel. They were the stipulations required of Israel as a holy people in covenant with a holy God. Creach comments, "The story *is* about the values of two worlds, the choice of holiness in covenant with God and prosperity obtained through secular greed."[5] The New Testament comments too on the power of human selfishness that leads to spiritual death (1 John 2:16). Sadly, it is Judas's crime of lust for money that leads to Jesus's arrest and ultimately to Judas's regret and suicide (Matt. 26:14–16; 27:1–10). People today face the choice of serving God or obsessing over material gain (Matt. 6:24).

Teachers must avoid using Achan's experience as a paradigm for punishment. The punishment that the Lord inflicts is not the norm in Israel, and Achan's situation is a rare circumstance. Achan's family is horribly executed too. This is difficult to understand because of today's emphasis on individual accountability. The Bible too acknowledges that individuals should suffer for their own sins, not the sins of others (Jer. 31:29–30; Ezek. 18:1–32). The principle of corporate solidarity, however, takes precedence in this case since the objective of entirely destroying the city is to cut off pagan influence. Achan's action places him and his family under the same judgment of death, as the Lord has forewarned.[6] Rahab, the Canaanite "outsider," is responsive and is treated as an Israelite when she recognizes the power of Yahweh and acts accordingly (Josh. 2). Achan, the Israelite "insider," places himself by his disobedience among the Canaanites and is treated as one of them. Both situations have corporate overtones: Rahab's family and Achan's family each share the results. For Christian readers,

a similar corollary is the accountability that people have for actions before the Lord and before others (2 Pet. 1:10). Christians live in community, and their choices contribute to the welfare or to the detriment of others. For this reason the church must practice discipline, albeit in a most cautious way (Matt. 18:15–20; 1 Cor. 5:1–13).

Illustrating the Text

Beware the danger of compromise and mission drift.

History: When Harvard University was founded in 1636, one of its guiding rules was, "Let every student be plainly instructed and earnestly pressed to consider well, that the main end of his life and studies is to know God and Jesus Christ . . . and therefore to lay Christ in the bottom, as the only foundation of all sound knowledge and learning." The university began with Christian professors and emphasized character formation in its students.[7] What is the spiritual state of Harvard University today? At the 350th anniversary celebration of Harvard, Steven Muller, former president of Johns Hopkins University, stated, "The bad news is that the university has become godless."[8] Churches, organizations, and individuals all have a tendency, if not careful, to drift to conform more to cultural norms than to the standards of the Bible. We must be willing to speak the truth to one another whenever we see examples of mission drift.

Are you a "culture-conformer" or a "culture-transformer"?

Applying the Text: There is a significant difference between a thermometer and a thermostat. A thermometer

Achan and his family are stoned, and the bodies and all his possessions are burned as commanded by the Lord. This illumination from the Queen Mary Psalter (fourteenth century AD) depicts the stoning of Achan.

merely adjusts to the temperature of the environment, while a thermostat actually sets the temperature. As Christians, we must choose whether we are going to be a thermometer or a thermostat as we live in this world. That is, are we going to merely conform to the values of our culture, or are we going to transform our culture? The Israelites faced the question of adopting or rejecting the values of Canaanite culture. Christians today face a similar challenge. The apostle Paul said, "Do not conform to the pattern of this world, but be transformed by the renewing of your mind. Then you will be able to test and approve what God's will is—his good, pleasing and perfect will" (Rom. 12:2).

The choices we make impact others.

Quote: Oliver Wendell Holmes Jr. wrote, "The right to swing my fist ends where the other man's nose begins."[9] This quote has often been used to describe the limitation of human rights. But what is often missed is that even so-called victimless crimes impact others. For example, would it not be a crime to even threaten to swing at another person? "Victimless crime" has been defined as "an infraction of criminal law without any identifiable evidence of an individual that has suffered damage in the infraction." No harm is imposed on another person through the crime. Examples of "victimless crimes" include violations and laws concerning the sale/possession/use of illicit drugs, prostitution, suicide, and gambling.[10] The question becomes, are the victims of these crimes really limited to the individual committing the infraction, or is society at large also impacted by the decisions of these individuals? When an addicted gambler loses his or her wealth and is in need of assistance from the government, is not society impacted? Achan's sin might seem like a "victimless crime" in that it does not impact another individual, but his sin of disobedience impacts the community's view on sin and their view of the Lord's tolerance of sin. Christians must remember that their choices do impact the community.

Victory at Ai

Big Idea *The Lord forgives his people and assures them of victory over opposition.*

Understanding the Text

The Text in Context

Chapters 6–9 tell of the campaigns in the central highlands: the defeat of Jericho (chap. 6) and Ai (chaps. 7–8) and the surrender of Gibeon (chap. 9). Chapters 7 and 8, which report the battle at Ai, are tightly connected, reporting two distinct phases of the same campaign. Similar settings and participants link these two chapters but also highlight their differences. These contrasts are most significant: disobedience/obedience and failure/success. Another contrast is the human/divine emphasis. Human initiative and *independence* of God dominate chapter 7, and divine initiative and human *dependence* on God characterize chapter 8. The importance of chapter 8 for the larger context is seen in the reaction of the nations at hearing of Ai's defeat (9:1–5). Unlike the majority of the nations that plan to attack Israel, the Gibeonites seek peace, although by deception. The idea of deception runs through chapters 7 through 9. Achan deceives Israel by theft (chap. 7), the Israelites ambush Ai (chap. 8), and the Gibeonites trick Joshua (chap. 9). Sandwiched between the deception by Achan (7:1–26) and by the Gibeonites (9:1–27) is the success at Ai (8:1–29). The chief difference in the failure and success of the two campaigns against Ai is the patience of Joshua, who waits on the Lord's directives in chapter 8. The subsequent failure to consult the Lord when approached by the Gibeonites results in the deception of Israel.

Chapter 8 divides conveniently into two parts: the battle at Ai (8:1–29) and the reading of the law (8:30–35). The relationship of these sections is not necessarily chronological; if topical, this arrangement emphasizes the common idea of obedience and trust in God's word (see the unit on 8:30–35). Joshua 8:1–29 consists of five elements: (1) the Lord instructs Joshua to attack (8:1–2); (2) Joshua provides his army with the plan for attack (8:3–8); (3) Joshua positions his army (8:9–13); (4) Israel defeats Ai's army (8:14–23); and (5) Israel destroys Ai's army and city (8:24–29).

Historical and Cultural Background

Ancient nations went to war to extend their power, exact revenge, and terrorize their enemies. Royal inscriptions boast of kings' victories and never mention any defeat, unlike the Bible, which reports on Israel's defeats (e.g., setback at Ai, Josh. 7).

The Egyptian account of the war against the Hittites at Kadesh on the Orontes (thirteenth century BC), for example, indicates a victory, whereas the Hittite version presents a different picture.[1] The truth is probably a stalemate that led to a peace treaty. Although ancient sources provide details of the battles, such as we have in Joshua 8, they do not regularly give the strength of forces in campaigns. Where they do, they can be inflated numbers for propaganda, glorifying the king and intimidating any would-be opponents.

Even the inscriptions' troop figures, however, are much less in number than what the Bible reports for Israel's population. The large numbers in Joshua 8 are difficult to square with the military campaigns in royal inscriptions. In the Assyrian war at Qarqar against a Syrian coalition of troops, King Shalmaneser III (858–824 BC) reports the numbers of each nation's troops that he vanquished. Among these is Israel's King Ahab, who produced a significant contingent of two thousand chariots and ten thousand soldiers.[2] Israel's male population is about six hundred thousand (Num. 1:32, 46; 11:21; 26:51). Joshua 4:13 reports the staggering number of forty thousand soldiers for only the two and a half Transjordan tribes. Also, if the ambush in 8:3 was thirty thousand, it is difficult to see how it could remain undetected. Although there are several proposals to explain the biblical

Key Themes of Joshua 8:1–29

- The Lord accepts the repentance of the people.
- God directs Joshua to destroy Ai, and the people carefully fulfill the command.
- Joshua and the people fearlessly trust the Lord's instructions.

numbers, there is none without its problems. The word for "thousand" (*'elep*) can also mean "unit, clan" (Num. 31:4; Josh. 22:14, 21, 30),[3] which would mean the ambush consisted of "thirty units."

Interpretive Insights

8:1 *Do not be afraid.* See comments on 1:9; 10:25.

whole army. By mustering the "whole army," in contrast to the "few" (three thousand, 7:4) at the first Ai attack, the people do not act presumptuously.

I have delivered. The tense "have delivered" (*natan*, "give") expresses certainty of victory, indicating that the task is completed in the mind of God (6:2; 7:7; 8:7,

Following God's commands, all the inhabitants of Ai are killed, and the city is burned. God permits the Israelites to keep the plunder and the livestock. This Assyrian relief shows the captured city of Hamanu in flames and soldiers demolishing the walls. Other soldiers leave the city with their arms full of the spoils of war (from the North Palace at Nineveh, 645–635 BC).

18). "Hand" indicates the idea of power (cf. Deut. 2:7; Ps. 89:13).

8:2 *plunder and livestock.* The people share in the spoil, but as at Jericho they must destroy the inhabitants and the city (8:8, 27).

Set an ambush. The instructions vary significantly from Jericho, showing that the victory is secured not by ritual but by God's will. Either Joshua receives unrecorded detail from God or he is free to develop the plan (8:4–8).

8:3 *night.* Although travel is hazardous at night, the surprise requires concealment (10:9; Judg. 9:32; 16:2).

8:4 *on the alert.* Precise timing is necessary for success.

8:8 *set it on fire.* By burning the city immediately, Israel eliminates its enemies' refuge, exposing the Ai troops to Israel.

See to it . . . my orders. Joshua speaks authoritatively since he conveys God's instruction.

8:9–13 Verses 11–13 further detail the general description of verse 9; verse 10 describes the initial attack.

8:9 *west of Ai . . . Joshua . . . with the people.* Ai does not expect attack from the direction of Bethel ("behind," 8:2). Unlike the first attack at Ai, Joshua leads the frontal attack.

8:11 *north of Ai . . . valley.* Ai's troops are trapped between the burning city and the ravine.

8:12 *five thousand men.* These warriors are the lead members of the ambush party (8:3).

8:14 *the king . . . hurried.* Self-assured, Ai's king acts rashly by leaving the city undefended, assuming that the battle will go as the first encounter did (8:16–17).

8:15 *let themselves be driven back.* The deception depends on the effective ruse of the main body.

8:18 *held out . . . javelin.* As at Jericho, Joshua waits on the Lord's directive to attack. The outstretched hand is reminiscent of Moses's staff that parts the Red Sea (Exod. 14:16; cf. Exod. 15:12). Javelin (*kidon*) is not the common word for sword (*hereb*) or spear (*hanit*) but a short or curved sword used in battle (cf. Goliath's weapons, 1 Sam. 17:45).

8:19 *quickly . . . rushed forward.* "Quickly" (*mᵉherah/mahar*) occurs twice, indicating a brave but disciplined action. This echoes the presumption of Ai's king, whose troops "hurried" (*mahar*, 8:14).

8:22 *neither survivors nor fugitives.* The narrative repeatedly describes the total destruction of Ai's inhabitants (8:22, 24 [3x], 25b, 26), showing the faithful response of the Israelites to the Lord's command.

8:23 *But they took the king of Ai.* The capture, shameful hanging, and burial of the king (8:29) carry out the Lord's command (8:2) and announce the just end for anyone who attacks Israel. Upon learning of these events, the kings form coalitions to assault Israel (9:1–2; 10:1–3).

8:25 *all the people of Ai.* The text details the identity and the number of the slain (twelve thousand), demonstrating the severity of the defeat and the complete adherence of Israel to the Lord's command. Eliminating women and children effectively cuts off future influence.

8:26 *For Joshua.* This verse is supplementary, specifying Joshua's part. This echoes Moses's role in defeating the Amalekites (Exod. 17:11–16), demonstrating that the Lord has favored Joshua as he did Moses (Josh. 1:17; 4:14).

Joshua "impale[s] the body of the king of Ai on a pole" (8:29) and places it on display by the ruins of Ai until evening. The impalement scene shown here is from the larger Assyrian relief depicting the defeat of the Israelite city of Lachish (700–692 BC).

lest they ceremonially defile the land (Deut. 21:22–23; cf. Gal. 3:13).

entrance of the city gate. The location of the corpse is symbolic since the king is the city's chief representative (10:27; 2 Kings 9:25).

large pile of rocks. As in the case with Achan (7:26), the stone memorial bears a perpetual witness.

Theological Insights

Contrast and diversity contribute to the theology of this chapter. One contrast is the failure and the success at Ai, and another is the means by which Jericho and Ai fall. God achieves his promises in diverse ways. The Jericho narrative makes the Divine Warrior and his supernatural power foremost. Human involvement, on the other hand, dominates the telling of Ai's demise, although it assumes that the Lord ultimately wins the battle. Joshua, for example, receives God's directive to set an ambush, but Joshua appears to have developed the plan with specifics not given directly by the Lord in the text. Another example of the interplay between divine and human agency is the crossing of the Red Sea; whereas the narrative in Exodus 14 emphasizes Moses, the poetic version in Exodus 15 does not mention Moses and declares that God's powerful arm delivers Israel. The differences between the conquest narratives in Joshua indicate that diverse circumstances and purposes dictate how the Lord gives Canaan to his people.

8:27 *livestock and plunder.* The language recalls the divine directive in 8:2.

8:28 *permanent heap of ruins.* "Heap of ruins" translates *tel*, an earthen mound that covers the remains of an occupation site. "Tel" (or "Tell") refers to ancient sites and may occur in names, such as Tell Hazor. Leaving the city in ruins fulfills divine judgment (Deut. 13:16). "Ai," meaning "ruin," probably was a second name given to memorialize its exceptional destruction. (See "Historical and Cultural Background" in the unit on 7:1–15.)

8:29 *impaled the body.* Public hanging was humiliating for kings (10:26; 1 Sam. 31:10); the law required hanging for murderers, who were viewed as accursed; however, they had to be taken down by nightfall

The event at Ai in light of the Jericho victory also shows that God holds the covenant people accountable and may impose penalties: "They had to learn how to react to a punishing God as well as a promising God."[4] He is not unpredictable, however.

He acts in accord with his character and his covenant warnings.

Also, the Ai story points to the effectiveness of Israel's repentance. Although the Lord brings a harsh judgment, he is not a robot that is indifferent to the suffering of his people. He is a personal being who exhibits caring mercy for his subjects (Exod. 3:7; Ps. 34:17). His chastening seeks repentance and restoration. Joshua and the elders acknowledge their failure to obey God, and the Lord accepts their repentance—giving them a second chance. They carefully obey when carrying out the judgment against Achan. God grants them forgiveness, as shown by his calling for Joshua to renew the attack on Ai. Moreover, he does not withhold the plunder of the city, sharing with them the reward that rightly belongs to God. This is one of many examples of how the Lord is long-suffering with his people (Exod. 34:6–7; Deut. 4:30–31).

Teaching the Text

Obedience, faith, and the authority of God's written word are values from this chapter appropriate for teaching. Chapters 7 and 8 demonstrate the centrality of obedience and faith in the life of Israel. The collapse of the walls at Jericho (chap. 6) was dramatic, but the people failed to learn the lesson it provided. More attention is given to the battles at Ai in chapters 7–8 because the events profoundly show what Israel must learn from them.[5] Disobedience means defeat and death, as shown in the Achan event. Obedience results in the opposite outcome, victory and life. Joshua, the elders, and the people strictly obey without challenging the Lord, and God gives the victory: "For I [the Lord] have delivered into your hands" (8:1); "The LORD your God will give it into your hand" (8:7b); "Do what the LORD has commanded" (8:8b); and "as the LORD had instructed Joshua" (8:27b). Faith spurs them on to fulfill God's directive, for they go forward despite the defeat that they previously experienced. They realize that defeat is only temporary, brought on by their sin, not by a fickle God. Ultimate victory is theirs if they rekindle their trust in the Lord. Christians experience spiritual setbacks at times because of their sin or because of discouraging circumstances. However, this text provides an opportunity for believers to reflect on their measure of devotion to the Lord (Gal. 6:1–5; Phil. 1:27–2:2).

The passage also illustrates that God fulfills his promises in different ways in different situations. The differences between the battles in the book of Joshua illustrate that God does not have a step-by-step procedure to be followed at all places and at all times. Biblical narrative is inspired literature conveying important theological revelation about God and his people, not a collection of blueprints. For example, there are no miracles here, as evident in the battles at Jericho, Gibeon, and Hazor (Josh. 6; 10; 11:1–15). For the battle at Jericho God gives Joshua a detailed plan—a rather bizarre one—whereas in chapter 8 the plan that Joshua describes is a very sound military strategy. That the Lord has revealed the plan to Joshua for the battle against Ai is not clear, only implied at best (8:8). Joshua prays at the battle at Gibeon (10:12b), but there is no report of prayer in chapter 8 leading to the victory. Every part of the Old Testament instructs disciples in godly service (1 Cor. 10:6; 2 Tim. 3:16–17), but there is no uniform formula of action intended by the Old Testament battle stories for Christian discipleship. For Christian readers, the passage shows that faith, perseverance, and godly living, for example, are admonitions that call for imitation—such as pursuing prayer, reading Scripture, practicing ethical behavior, and taking up godly obedience (e.g., Eph. 5:1; Heb. 6:11–12; 12:4).

Illustrating the Text

Do not give up if the Lord is calling you to persevere.

Biography: Colonel Sanders. Colonel Harland Sanders was the founder of Kentucky Fried Chicken, which in 2014 had more than twenty thousand restaurants in 109 countries around the world. But Colonel Sanders had to experience rejection before he realized success. In fact, at age sixty-five, he took his pressure cooker and secret recipe and hit the road to sell his method of frying chicken to restaurants. He received over three hundred rejections before he found someone who was willing to use his recipe and cooking method.[6] Imagine if the colonel had allowed the rejection to cause him to give up on his dream! Having already suffered defeat at the hands of the Ai warriors, in this instance as a result of their own rebellion, Joshua and the Israelites could have given up. But they persevered and were victorious. There are times when we will experience defeat and rejection (sometimes as a result of our own sin and other times not). In these times we must continue to seek the Lord while persevering to follow his plan.

The Lord's instructions are to be obeyed.

Humor: Consumer products sometimes include very strange instructions. On a hair dryer: "Do not use while sleeping." On a bag of chips: "You could be a winner! No purchase necessary. 'Details inside.'" On a bar of soap: "Directions: Use like regular soap."[7] Because of the often convoluted nature of instructions and the presence of directions obviously meant more to head off lawsuits than be of practical aid to most users, many people ignore product instructions and simply use the product as they see fit. Also, many people will ignore instructions because they believe they know better. We need to be careful about taking that attitude toward the Bible. The Lord's counsel and instructions are clear, and we are to both know and apply those teachings to our lives.

Beware of looking for specific patterns in how God deals with your life.

Television: *King of Queens.* This show aired an episode that depicts a common misunderstanding about God and prayer. In this particular episode, titled "Holy Mackerel," Carrie prays for a raise, which she subsequently receives. Her husband, Doug, is frustrated that his wife would pray for something so frivolous. But Carrie's not going to stop, because this prayer thing really works. She prays for her favorite shoes to go on sale, which they do. Seeing Carrie getting what she wants through prayer, Doug goes to his knees and prays for a New York Jets football win. All of this unravels in the end as things don't work out as planned.[8] It is our human tendency to try to find a pattern, something that manipulates God to give us what we want. So if we get what we want by praying with our eyes open, we keep them open the next time we pray, believing we've found the secret code. God is not to be treated as a computer to be figured out but is a Holy God who requires us to be committed to his purposes and his will in the world.

God's Covenant Word in the Land

Big Idea *God's people worship and honor the Lord through reciting and obeying his word.*

Understanding the Text

The Text in Context

The setting for the reading of the law shifts from Gilgal (5:10) to the two mounts, Ebal and Gerizim, which overlook the town of Shechem. In the flow of chapters 6–9, the episode may at first appear out of place since the attention to Israel's wars is interrupted. Joshua 8:30–35 can be read as a distinct unit, and scholars have suggested various places in the book where it originally might have appeared.[1] Its canonical

place, however, fits the preceding episodes at Jericho and Ai (6:1–8:29) by reaffirming Israel's commitment to obey Moses's commands (see the unit on 24:1–18). The name "Moses" occurs five times in the passage (8:31 [2x], 32, 33, 35), and the expression "Moses . . . commanded" appears three

The people of Israel assemble together for the reading of the Book of the Law. Half stand in front of Mount Gerizim, and half stand in front of Mount Ebal. In this photograph Mount Gerizim is on the left and Mount Ebal is on the right with the modern town of Nablus (the site of ancient Shechem) in the valley between them.

times (8:31, 33, 35). The people experience victory (Jericho) and defeat (Ai) and then victory again (Ai), teaching them that obedience is vital to success. By reaffirming the law in accord with Moses's instructions (Deut. 11:29; 27:2–13; 31:9–13), they express faith and faithfulness. This renewed allegiance prepares them for the coming wars (chaps. 9–11). The sequence of events is (1) building an altar (8:30–31a), (2) offering sacrifices (8:31b), (3) writing the law on stones (8:32), (4) positioning the twelve tribes (8:33), and (5) reading the law publicly (8:34–35). Since Shechem was the site of Abraham's first altar of worship in Canaan (Gen. 12:6–7), the location was important in Israel's historical memory.

Historical and Cultural Background

Although the name Shechem does not occur in 8:30–35 (cf. 24:1), the naming of the mountains Gerizim and Ebal puts Israel near Shechem (Tell Balatah). Mount Gerizim to the south and Mount Ebal to the north are two facing mountains that overlook Shechem (in modern Nablus), creating a natural acoustical amphitheater. The tell has a layer with evidence of a Middle Bronze I occupation, which some scholars believe correlates with Abraham's building an altar of worship in the area (Gen. 12:5–7). Located at a major crossroad in the central highlands, Shechem, a Canaanite city-state, held strategic importance politically. It was an important Canaanite city-state during the conquest and judges periods. In the mid-sixteenth century BC (ca. 1540) Shechem was destroyed by an Egyptian incursion and remained abandoned until its rebuilding in about 1450. But an imposing building on

> ### Key Themes of Joshua 8:30–35
>
> - Joshua, in accord with Moses's instructions, leads Israel to offer worship.
> - Israel honors God's covenant by reciting it and submitting to it.
> - The people are reunited by embracing the covenant word.
> - The covenant re-creates the community by including foreigners and natural citizens.

the acropolis, dubbed the Temple Fortress, endured as the central feature of the city (cf. "tower," Judg. 9:46–49). The Amarna correspondence during the fourteenth century shows that Lab'ayu, who was a formidable force in the politics of the region, claimed control of Shechem. A major destruction layer dated to about 1150 perhaps corresponds to the rebellion against Abimelek in Judges 9:42–49. The history of Shechem's occupations is significant evidence for dating the exodus and conquest periods (see "Historical Background" in the introduction), although its history is disputed by archaeologists. The biblical record has no battle against Shechem by Joshua. Tell Balatah evidences no significant break in the occupations at the end of the fourteenth century, which would question Israel's invasion if dated in the thirteenth century. If the conquest is dated in the fifteenth century, it must be maintained that either Shechem was resettled in the early fourteenth century or Joshua temporarily coexisted with the Canaanite leader. At some time later the city became an Israelite possession (cf. 20:7; 21:21; 24:1).[2]

Interpretive Insights

8:30 *built on Mount Ebal an altar to the* LORD. The altar is for worship, precisely following Moses's instructions (Deut.

Altar

The term "altar" (*mizbeah*, 8:30–31) means the place of sacrifice ("to sacrifice," *zabah*), although altars may serve other purposes (memorials, 22:26–27). Israel's altars are (1) the earthen and fieldstone variety (Exod. 20:24–25) and (2) the tabernacle's bronze altar and altar of incense, each having four horn-shaped corners and made of wood and metal (Exod. 27:1–7; 30:1–10). Altars are primarily for animal sacrifice, and blood is sprinkled on them for expiation (Exod. 24:6; Lev. 17:6). The altar is sacred, exclusively belonging to the Lord ("my altar," Exod. 20:26). Natural stones ("whole," "complete," *shalem*), uncompromised by human hands (Deut. 27:2–8), symbolize the purity of worship (Exod. 20:25). Uncut stones distinguish Israel's altars from Canaanite ones, which typically have carvings.[a]

[a] See further Hawk, "Altars." For an altar discovered at Mount Ebal, see Pitkänen, *Joshua*, 192–204; for a brief assessment, see Hess, *Joshua*, 174. Excavators at Gath announced the finding of a Philistine two-horned altar in 2011; see the unofficial field report at http://gath.wordpress.com/2011/07/25/the-news-is-out-a-large-stone-altar-in-area-d/.

27:1–8). The altar on Ebal, the place of reading the curses, is a fitting reminder of the consequence for transgressing the covenant (e.g., Achan and Ai, chaps. 7–8). Sacrifices of atonement and reconciliation are presented in the ceremony of covenant renewal. "Lord" (Yahweh) is the covenant name for God (Exod. 6:1–4), stressing his historical and personal connection with Israel.

8:31 *as Moses . . . commanded.* The verb "commanded" (*tsawwah*) is common, especially in Deuteronomy (e.g., Deut. 1:3), meaning "to give an order." The related word "commandment" (*mitswah*) may refer to instructions or teachings generally (Deut. 5:31) or to the Ten Commandments (Exod. 24:12).

Book of the Law of Moses. The expression indicates that the inscribed word is equally authoritative as the mediator Moses himself. The commandments are collected in the "Book of the Law" (Deut. 30:10) and placed beside the ark (Deut. 31:26). The tablets of the Ten Commandments are in the ark (Exod. 40:20).

burnt offerings . . . fellowship offerings. Burnt and fellowship (peace) offerings are atoning and thanksgiving offerings (Lev. 1:4; 7:12, 16; cf. Exod. 20:24; 24:5). The burnt offering is wholly burned, indicating complete devotion. The fellowship offering occurs after atonement, and thus recognizing that the people have been reconciled to God.

8:32 *wrote on stones.* The stones are overlaid with lime-wash plaster for a hardened finishing surface (Deut. 27:2, 4). That the altar bears the "law of Moses" indicates that Moses's instructions are the very word of God.

8:33 *Levitical priests.* Identifying the priests as bearers of the ark connects the covenant reading with their victories at Jordan's crossing (chaps. 3–4) and the defeat of Jericho (chap. 6).

foreigners . . . native-born. A "foreigner" (*ger*, "resident alien") is an immigrant who is a permanent resident. God grants the *ger* certain privileges and obligations like citizens (e.g., Exod. 12:48–49; 20:10), but some distinctions are made (food laws, Deut. 14:21). Inclusion of foreigners anticipates many newcomers who will join Israel under the covenant.

to bless the people. The purpose of the convocation is for the people to receive divine blessing. This explains in part the presence of and reference to the "ark of the covenant." An example of a formal blessing by the priests occurs in Numbers 6:24–26. "To bless" (*barak*) or "blessing" (*berakah*) in the Pentateuch means God's favorable treatment, including prosperity and peace (Deut. 7:13).

8:34 *Joshua read all.* Joshua reads the law, according to the passage, but probably in concert with the people, following Moses's directions. That Joshua is named reflects his leadership. By reading the law, Joshua acknowledges that Israel lives under covenant law as a people uniquely related to their God.

the blessings and the curses. The expression appears only here in the book of Joshua (cf. Deut. 30:1). It represents the whole of the covenant since it names the consequences of Israel's behavior (Deut. 27:15–28:68). The Deuteronomy passages anticipate Israel's disobedience and expulsion from the land, but their eventual return is also forecasted (30:1–10).

Book of the Law. The expression "Book of the Law" in Deuteronomy probably refers to Deuteronomy or some portion (29:21; 30:10; 31:26). The phrase "Book of the Law" or the "Book of the Law of Moses" in Joshua refers generally to the Pentateuch (1:8; 23:6; cf. Ezra; Neh. 8:1). Joshua's recording of the covenant in the "Book of the Law of God" (24:26) probably

refers to a separate book since the covenant of Joshua 24 does not occur in the Pentateuch.

8:35 *not a word . . . all.* The inclusive language indicates the completeness of Joshua's obedience.

the whole assembly. "Whole" (*kol*, "all") and "assembly" (*qahal*) show the inclusion of the entire nation. "Assembly" describes religious gatherings, such as temple worship (1 Chron. 29:20). Ezra reads the law to the "assembly" when Israel returns to the land after the exile (Neh. 8:1–5).

Theological Insights

First, the passage underscores the importance of strict adherence to the commands of Moses. Disobedience, not Canaanite power, is the chief challenge that Israel faces. The recitation of the law following the mixed results at Ai shows that spiritual renewal is possible through recommitment to the divine word. The account in Joshua has additions to the original command in Deuteronomy (27:2–13). The Joshua narrative emphasizes the presence of the ark (presence of the Lord) and the commands of Moses, as in Joshua 1; 3–4.[3] Moreover, the first record of formal sacrifices in the land occurs here (8:31). The people acknowledge

Joshua builds an altar to the Lord on Mount Ebal. An open-air altar was found on one of the ridges of Mount Ebal by Israeli archaeologist Adam Zertal and can be seen in this photograph. While there is considerable agreement that this is an Israelite sacred site, evidence indicates that it is not Joshua's altar.

through burnt and peace sacrifices that the Lord has spared them. They are reconciled to the Lord, and hope for life in the land has returned. Noah's offering expresses the same idea of thanksgiving for deliverance and the Lord's renewed benevolence toward the earth (Gen. 8:20–21).

Second, the passage presupposes the divine origin of Moses's instructions. The repetitive references to Moses highlight his mediatory role. Israel's identity and future hope for living in the land rest on God's word as uniquely mediated through Moses. The reading of the law at Gerizim/Ebal reinforces the authority of God's word. Pausing to read the law in its entirety for the first time in the land announces new beginnings—a new start after death at Ai but also a new start for Israel's history.[4] They are the covenant people who become the people of the Book (Deut. 31:26). The ark, representing the presence of God, and the Book of the Law, representing his commands, are associated in the passage (8:31, 33).

Third, the passage reiterates the inclusiveness of the people of God. People of all social strata are present. Foreigners reflect the ethnic diversity of the community (Exod. 12:38; Num. 11:4), and there is gender and age inclusion. The whole of the community is under obligation but is also the beneficiary of covenant blessing. Israel is not a closed community but open and inviting to those who demonstrate their allegiance to the Lord and his word. By reading the law, the people understand that their community is based not on ethnicity or political-economic ties but on their common commitment to the Lord. Also, reading the law is the means of educating the people regarding the requirements of the law (Deut. 6:1–9) and the consequences of their response to it (Deut. 11:26–28).

Teaching the Text

The priority of the passage is showing the superiority of the eternal word of God over human leadership and ingenuity. The word that Israel receives has come by direct revelation given through the mediation of Moses and Joshua. By it they know what God expects of them and what their future is. They are not totally dependent on Moses or Joshua, however, for the *torah* ("law, teaching") is always with them (1:8). Comparing 8:30–35 and Moses's command to read the law (Deut. 11:29; 27:2–13; 31:9–13)[5] demonstrates that the people restore obedience to the law as the center of their community. The law is formally proclaimed at a national level every seven years in concert with the forgiveness of debts and celebration of Israel's harvest (Deut. 31:9–13). As the New Testament teaches, the authority of the written word is enduring (Heb. 4:12; 1 Pet. 1:24–25). Christians must know the teachings of Scripture before they can obey them (Acts 18:11). The teaching and public reading of Scripture must be an integral part of the Christian experience in worship (Lev. 10:10–11; 2 Chron. 34:29–32; Neh. 8:1–12; 1 Tim. 4:13).

This passage also develops the relationship between the authority of Scripture and the whole community's obligation to observe it. All the people are present for the covenant's reading (8:33, 35). The passage's emphasis on the inclusiveness of the community shows that no individuals are exempted. It is the revelation of the word that creates the interdependence of individuals, forming an assembly. To participate in the community and receive its benefits, God's people must observe the teachings of the covenant (Deut. 11:13–15; James 1:23). By all accepting Yahweh as Lord, the people forge a single body, having a unified purpose and a universal outlook. The word for "assembly" (*qahal*, 8:35; Deut. 4:9–10) in the Greek Old Testament is *ekklēsia* ("church"), and in the New Testament *ekklēsia* describes the assembled Christians. As the case of Achan illustrates (chap. 7), disobedience by one person creates a ripple effect throughout the congregation (1 Cor. 5; Col. 3:11–17).

Illustrating the Text

All believers are to live in light of God's commands.

Cultural Institution: According to the United States Constitution, each elected president is required to take the following oath: "I do solemnly swear (or affirm) that I will faithfully execute the office of President of the United States, and will to the best of my ability, preserve, protect and defend the Constitution of the United States."[6] Every president is required to work within the boundaries and the guidelines of the Constitution. For example, a president could not unilaterally decide, "I really don't like this article of the Constitution, so I'm not going to enforce it." In the same way, every Christian, regardless of his or her position, social or economic status, and so on, is required to live within the boundaries and guidelines of the Bible. And just as the Constitution defines the president's authority, our authority as Christians is established by the Word of God.

The Bible is superior to human leadership.

History: In 1956, Jim Jones founded his own church, which he called "The People's Temple." In the early years his sermons focused on tolerance, social responsibility, and community. But as the church grew, he began to focus on demands for personal loyalty and obedience. He also became increasingly flamboyant. At one point he was asked by a friend, "Jim, why the change?" To which Jones answered, "Max, when you reach the top, you've got to play the part."[7] Eventually Jones took his church and people to a remote location in Guyana. Then, on November 18, 1978, he led a mass suicide of 912 people, including 276 children.[8] There will always be talented, charismatic leaders, but their teachings and life must always be measured against the truth of God's Word. We are to pledge our allegiance not to human leaders but to the Lord and measure the teachings and lives of leaders against the Bible.

God's people must obey all of God's commands.

Metaphor: You have instructions for assembling and calibrating helicopter instrument panels. The procedure involves using complicated equipment and performing a carefully ordered series of tasks. You decide not to follow step three because it seems unnecessary. The finished product is assembled, and because you left out step three the instrument panel is lacking a key operation. The defect may not be readily apparent, but there is a possibility of endangering lives. In the same way, purposely disobeying the Lord is akin to saying that we know better than the Lord about how to live our lives.

Gibeonite Deception

Big Idea *The Lord and his people show mercy toward those who submit to Israel's God.*

Understanding the Text

The Text in Context

Joshua 9 completes the campaigns in the central highlands (chaps. 6–9), and Gilgal continues as the geographical setting (9:6). The fall of the highlands provides a strategic wedge dividing the Canaanite strongholds in the south and the north. The kings' alarm ("heard," 9:1–2) relates this chapter to the previous episodes. The relationship of Gibeon to the ensuing battle is explained in 10:1–2: Gibeon is a member of an alliance headed by King Adoni-Zedek of Jerusalem.

The recurring motif of deception in chapters 6–9 occurs again in this passage. The deception by the Gibeonites especially echoes Rahab's lie (chaps. 2; 6). By deception both Gibeon and Rahab are delivered, but by the same tactic Achan dooms himself and the Israelites. Rahab and Gibeon also exhibit fear of and zeal for God, in contrast to those who oppose Israel (king of Jericho / kings of Canaanites). Israel swears an oath to both Rahab and Gibeon; in both cases, Rahab and the Gibeonites are saved, even though Rahab dupes the king and the Gibeonites dupe Joshua and the elders. The theme of failure or success in chapters 6–8

reappears in chapter 9. As in the initial failure at Ai (chap. 7), Joshua and the elders do not seek the Lord's instructions. Once the failure to obey is discovered, the leadership negotiates how it might correct the mistake and at the same time maintain its integrity. For Ai the remedy is Achan's execution for stealing devoted things (*herem*), but for Gibeon the penalty of conscripted labor is sufficient. Although Israel disobeys Moses's instructions (Deut. 20:10–18), its crime is redeemable.

The Gibeonite episode provides a contrast with the nations that plotted to destroy Israel (9:1–2). Also, Gibeon's attention to the story of God's victories and his commandments to the Israelites contrasts with the Israelites' failure to consult the Lord. The word *shamaʿ* ("to hear") occurs four times (9:1, 3, 9, 16; also the noun *shomaʿ*, "report," 9:9), showing a chain of reactions: (1) the nations hear and plot to attack; (2) the Gibeonites hear and plot submission; and (3) the Israelites hear and admit their irrevocable oath. It is because of the Gibeonites' fear of the Lord that they concoct their plot, and it is because of Israel's neglect that the elders fall into the trap. Ironically, the Gibeonites acknowledge the power of God, whose name they revere

(9:9), but Israel's sworn oath "by the LORD" (9:18, 19) misuses his name.

The commentary unit consists of three parts: (1) the occasion for the episode (9:1–2), (2) the Gibeonites' trickery (9:3–15), and (3) Israel's treaty with Gibeon (9:16–27).[1]

Interpretive Insights

9:1 *all the kings west . . . heard.* God's reputation spreads to all regions west of the Jordan (10:40–42; 12:8).

Hittites, Amorites, Canaanites, Perizzites, Hivites and Jebusites. These specific groups are widely distributed geographically and are representative of Canaan's inhabitants (3:10; 11:3; 12:8; 24:11; Deut. 7:1).[2]

9:2 *came together.* Israel as their common enemy incites them to form a military alliance (cf. 10:3–5; 11:1–5).

Joshua and Israel. The narration often depicts Joshua in a better light than the elders (9:3, 6, 8, 15, 22, 24–25, 26–27).

9:3 *However . . . Gibeon heard.* Although a formidable city (10:2), Gibeon fears Joshua and Israel (9:24). The Gibeonite coalition of four cities, located in Benjamin's territory (18:25–28), apparently has no king but is ruled by a council of elders (9:11; cf. Philistine "lords" [NIV: "rulers"], 13:3). Gibeon (modern el-Jib) is about six miles northwest of Jerusalem and about six miles west of modern et-Tell (= Ai?).

9:4–5 *ruse.* The word *'ormah* ("crafty") indicates a ploy (Exod. 21:14; cf. NASB) or shrewdness (Prov. 1:4; NIV: "prudence"). The related *'arum,* "crafty," describes the serpent's scheme (Gen. 3:1). Coupled with

Some of the people groups that inhabited the land of Canaan were the Hittites, Amorites, Canaanites, Perizzites, Hivites, and Jebusites. These glazed plaques decorated the palaces of Egypt and represent peoples from the region of Syria and Palestine (twelfth century BC).

"curse" (9:23; cf. Gen. 3:14), this word describing the Gibeonite deception recalls the serpent's deceit of Eve.

donkeys were loaded . . . old clothes . . . dry and moldy. The plot is carefully thought out, centering on items typically used for a journey. Ironically, worn-out clothing and moldy bread are the opposite of God's provisions for Israel in the wilderness (Deut. 8:2–4; 29:5–6).

9:6 *they went to Joshua.* The Gibeonites prefer to deal with Joshua (9:8), who ultimately delivers them (9:26).

Israelites. Literally, "man of Israel," this term occurs in verses 6–7, treating the congregation as a unified voice.

from a distant country. A city from afar may receive an offer of peace (Deut. 20:10–15), but those nations indigenous to Canaan are destined for destruction (Deut. 20:16–18). The severity of the policy assumes that idolatry is irreversibly corrosive to Israel's faith.

9:7 *Hivites.* The Gibeonites are Hivites (11:19), who also inhabit regions north (11:3; Gen. 34:2; Judg. 3:3). The identity of the Hivites is difficult to determine since they are not known from extrabiblical sources, and the Greek Old Testament has "Horites" instead of Hivites. The Horites, who were perhaps the ancient Hurrians originating in Mesopotamia, resided in Mount Seir and were later absorbed by the Edomites (Deut. 2:12).

perhaps you live near us. The Israelites are immediately suspicious, and Joshua poses the right questions (9:8), but he accepts vague answers and deceptive appearances. He and the leaders fail to consult the Lord (9:14).

9:8 *We are your servants.* "Servant" (*'ebed*) typically describes an inferior party of a treaty. The Gibeonites, when pressed for answers, curry favor by their submissive spirit (9:9, 11, 24).

9:9–10 *in Egypt . . . Ashtaroth.* They name early victories rather than recent ones to maintain the scheme.

9:14 *did not inquire.* The leaders do not consult the Lord, perhaps meaning they do not cast lots (see the comments on 7:14; cf. 18:6).

9:15 *let them live.* Although the treaty is achieved through deception, the Israelite leaders do not renege on their oath spoken in God's name, believing it is irreversible (9:19; cf. Gen. 27:34–37).

9:18 *grumbled against the leaders.* "Grumbled" (*lun*) recalls opposition to Moses (Exod. 15:24), although in this case it is the reverse: the people are in the right and moreover do not oppose Joshua.[3]

9:20 *God's wrath will not.* If the leaders rescind the agreement, they transgress the third commandment (Exod. 20:7), subjecting the camp to judgment. Their compromise appeases the congregation (9:26).

9:21 *woodcutters and water carriers.* The penalty for the Gibeonites is subservience to the Israelite community (cf. 9:27); however, as resident aliens, they are accepted participants in the covenant (Deut. 29:11).

9:22 *deceive us.* Joshua acknowledges he has been hoodwinked, putting the community in jeopardy.

9:23 *under a curse.* "Curse" (*'arar*) recalls the curses of the covenant (Deut. 27–28); the Gibeonites become a part of Israel but only as servants.

house of my God. This is the tabernacle, wherever it may reside in the future.[4]

9:25 *in your hands.* "Your" is singular, referring to Joshua. By seeking mercy, they surrender to Israel's God. "Your hands" recalls the divine promise of victory, which ironically is fulfilled (8:1, 7; 10:19; Deut. 7:24).

9:26 *Joshua saved them.* The congregation is fearful of repeating Ai's tragedy, but Joshua intervenes.

9:27 *woodcutters and water carriers . . . altar of the* LORD. Although as Hivites the Gibeonites should be devoted to destruction (Deut. 20:17), they escape when Joshua devotes them to the sanctuary (cf. Lev. 27:18). Wood and water are essentials for the daily operations of the sacrifices (Lev. 1:7, 9).

Theological Insights

God exhibits mercy to those who honor his name and his word (Exod. 33:19). Both the Gibeonites and the Israelites sin, but the Lord does not inflict retribution. The invocation of a divine curse may imply the Lord's judgment, but there is no direct condemnation in the narrative. The narrative has no word spoken by the Lord directly. His silence suggests his absence, but Joshua appears to stand in for the divine voice, since his actions recall God's response to the serpent's deceit in the garden. Joshua interrogates the Gibeonites (9:22), as God does Adam and Eve (Gen. 3:9–13), and he inflicts a curse (9:23), as God does against the serpent (Gen. 3:14). The Mosaic command to destroy all the inhabitants is evidently not absolute

(Deut. 7:2), as the exceptions of Rahab and Gibeon show.

What differentiates Rahab and Gibeon from the rebellious nations is their humility toward Israel. The Canaanite kings are hostile enemies, seeking to destroy Israel. Furthermore, the Gibeonites ultimately exhibit in this incident the character required of Israel itself. The narratives compare the Gibeonites to the Israelites largely in a better light.[5] Although the Israelites reunited into one community at the recitation of the covenant (8:30–35), they now splinter between the leadership and the community (cf. 1:17). But the Gibeonites are united,

As a consequence of their deception of the Israelites, the Gibeonites are made woodcutters and water carriers for the sanctuary. This relief from the palace of Sargon II in Khorsabad shows workers carrying logs that have been cut.

Joshua 9:1–27

expressing the one mind of their four cities (9:11). The Gibeonites' deception results from their acceptance of Moses's words (9:24). The Gibeonites function more cohesively around God's word than do the Israelites themselves. Nevertheless, there are solemn consequences. The Gibeonites become slaves to the Israelites, and the Israelites because of their new covenant with Gibeon subsequently face a formidable coalition of enemies (10:1–5).

In this passage the reputation of God as the Divine Warrior is intensified. The testimony of God's mighty acts from the time of Moses convinces Gibeon to yield. The Gibeonites' perpetual service to the Lord is a tribute to God and a witness to his victories over the Canaanites (23:3). Fittingly, the concession of the Gibeonites proves the fulfilling of divine promise, since they become subject to the Israelites.

Teaching the Text

The focus of the passage is the mercy of God, who deals patiently with neglectful Israel and deceitful Gibeon. Israel's failure to consult the Lord in the process of making a covenant is reminiscent of the debacle at Ai due to the leadership's arrogance (8:1–29). In the Gibeonite case, Israel does not lose lives, but the leadership endangers its reputation in the eyes of the people. The idea of mercy is also exhibited by the responses of the leadership and the congregation. Joshua is lenient when he intervenes on behalf of the Gibeonites, saving them from the congregation. The elders too fulfill their oath to Gibeon rather than claiming foul and killing the deceivers. The congregation is angry with the elders,

but the people do not rebel as the wilderness generation did against Moses (Num. 14:27). Christians too receive the mercy of God; the Lord's mercy has no limit (Titus 3:3–5), although his patience does. Moreover, we must show mercy toward others by forgiving them and exercising patience.

Israel's mercy extended to Rahab and the Gibeonites explodes today's stereotype of bloodthirsty Israelites who butcher everything in sight. The command to destroy the inhabitants of Canaan evidently excludes those who have a newfound faith in Israel's God. The Gibeonites' confession demonstrates a right theology in the making. Interestingly, because of their service to the Lord at the tabernacle, they live at the centerpiece of Israel's unity and worship.[6] By grace those initially outside the covenant are brought near to God. For Christian readers, Jesus's atoning salvation for all peoples brings outsiders into the fellowship of the Lord and the community of faith (Eph. 2:11–13; 1 Pet. 2:10).

Also, the crisis of leadership presents a lesson, although the narrative does not present a point-by-point model of how Christians should lead. If anything, the actions of the leadership are regrettable. What the passage says about leadership is illustrative of what the book of Joshua has already noted (1:16–17). Joshua is the new Moses, and the people follow him only as long as he is in step with God's instructions. For readers of the narrative, both the subtle allusions to the serpent's sin in the garden and the decay of their provisions (9:4) suggest that the Gibeonites are a threat despite their benign appearance.[7] Christian leaders must be thoroughly committed to following God's will if they are to take the people on the proper path. The New Testament requires leaders to meet high standards of faith and morality (1 Tim. 3:1–13; 5:22; Heb. 13:7, 17; James 3:1). Decisions at the top have serious consequences for the congregation.

Illustrating the Text

Choose to be faithful to the oaths you make.

History: After the rest of his team was killed in a fierce battle in Afghanistan, Navy Seal Marcus Luttrell was rescued and protected by a small group of Pashtun villagers in Afghanistan, who protected him until he could be brought to safety by friendly forces. Luttrell's story is found both in his eyewitness account of the battle, *Lone Survivor*, and in a movie of the same name.[8] Because of their choice to help Luttrell, the people of this village have been the target of reprisals by the Taliban. The villagers saved and protected Luttrell out of obedience to the ethnic-Pashtun tradition known as Pashtunwali, an ancient code that obliges Pashtuns to help and protect anyone in need, friend or enemy. They recognized the danger this decision would bring to their village, but they have never regretted their decision.[9] Do we take our obligations and oaths as seriously? Are we living faithfully to the oaths we took on our wedding day? Are we living faithfully to the oaths with which we joined our church? Are we willing to lay our lives and possessions on the line in order to stand firm for our obligations and for the Lord?

Express the love of God by showing mercy to others.

Biography: **Louis Zamperini.** Zamperini served the United States military in World War II against the Japanese Empire. Zamperini, whose story is told in the book *Unbroken*, was captured and held as a prisoner of war by the Japanese. In his internment he was degraded and beaten, and after the war he came home a broken man. But after receiving Jesus as his Lord and Savior, Zamperini sought to forgive all the men who had abused him. When Zamperini learned that one particularly cruel guard had died, all he saw was "a lost person, a life now beyond redemption. He felt something that he had never felt for his captor before. With a shiver of amazement, he realized that it was compassion. At that moment, something shifted sweetly inside him. It was forgiveness, beautiful and effortless and complete."[10] By forgiving those who have hurt us or mistreated us, we have the opportunity to express the merciful heart of the Lord. Whom do you need to forgive?

Godly leaders lead the people as they follow the Lord.

Object Lesson: Show your listeners a Gumby-like figure (a clay-like character that can be stretched into different shapes). Explain that there is a great danger in leaders being too much like Gumby, adjusting and adapting too easily to the expectations and whims of the people. The role of a godly leader is to lead the people as they follow the Lord. At times this means that the leader may even be in conflict with the people, but only if the Lord is in conflict with them. Godly leaders are not to be autocratic and are to listen to the people, but their responsibility is to lead the people as together they follow the Lord. This would be a good opportunity to call your listeners to commit to praying for the leaders of your church.

The Sun Stood Still

Big Idea *The Lord gives his people victory over his enemies, showing that he alone is Almighty God.*

Understanding the Text

The Text in Context

Chapters 9–11 function as a unit, describing the southern (chap. 10) and northern (11:1–15) campaigns. The account of Israel's defeat of the southern kings assumes Israel's peace treaty made with the Gibeonites in chapter 9. Joshua remains stationed at Gilgal when he receives an "SOS" message from the Gibeonites. The word "heard" (*shama'*) is a key term in chapter 9, where the Hebrew root occurs five times (9:1, 3, 9 [2x], 16). It also binds together chapters 9–11. "Heard" begins chapter 10's events (10:1; cf. 10:14, "listened"), and the same language begins chapter 11's account (11:1). What the southern and northern kings hear is a report of Joshua's victories; unlike the Gibeonites, who have sought peace, the southern and northern coalitions muster troops.

Chapter 10 begins with the assembling of five kings to attack Gibeon (10:1–5), and the chapter concludes with a general report of Joshua's conquest of the whole land (10:40–43). In between, the narrative describes (1) two phases in the Gibeonite campaign (10:6–15), (2) the execution of the kings (10:16–27), and (3) an itinerary of six captured cities in the south (10:28–39). Verses 6–15 present two overlapping descriptions of the same battle. The translation "then" (*'az*) beginning verse 12 (cf. KJV, NKJV, NASB) does not mean a sequential event but rather specifies God's role at the time of the battle. In other words, verses 12–14 step back and add further divine color to the picture (see the comments on 10:15).

The Gibeonites send a message, requesting Joshua's help (10:6), and the Lord instructs Joshua to attack and gives him the victory (10:7–11). Embedded is a summary of the battle (10:7–10), followed by further recognition of God's intervention by casting hailstones (10:11). In the midst of the battle, God answers Joshua's petition, securing complete victory for Israel (10:12–15).

Interpretive Insights

10:1 *Adoni-Zedek.* The instigator's name means "my lord is righteous," or his name includes a deity's name, "my lord is Zedek." Unlike in former accounts, specific names of the coalition's kings are given

(10:3). The authentic ring of the names indicates that the narratives originated in the Late Bronze Age (ca. 1550–1200 BC).[1]

totally destroyed. Herem, meaning "devoted to [God]," occurs six times (10:1, 28, 35, 37, 39, 40; NIV: "totally destroyed"), describing Ai's annihilation (Deut. 7:2; see "Christian Interpretation" in the introduction). This contrasts with Gibeon's survival by its seeking a peace agreement.

10:2 *very much alarmed*. The acquiescence of the Gibeonites and Israel's control of the region adjacent to Jerusalem put the king under immediate threat.

royal cities. The expression describes the palace city of a king (1 Sam. 27:5). Gibeon, although not governed by a king, has its own lord (see the comments on 9:3).

10:3 *Hebron . . . Jarmuth . . . Lachish . . . Eglon*. These cities are between the central plateau and the coast—all within thirty miles of Jerusalem.

10:5 *Amorites*. They are one of the "seven nations" to be destroyed (Deut. 7:1; 20:17).

10:6 *hill country*. The Amorites are remembered for Kings Og and Sihon in Transjordan, whom Moses defeated (2:10; 9:10; cf. Deut. 3:2).

10:7 *all the best fighting men*. The most valiant warriors join

in the war, matching in fervor "all" the Amorite troops (10:5).

10:8 *Do not be afraid*. Ironically, this is the same encouragement Moses gives the Israelites in the wilderness (Deut. 1:21), but in that instance they fail to believe God.

Not one . . . able to withstand you. The language recalls God's promise to Joshua (1:5; cf. Deut. 7:24; 11:25).

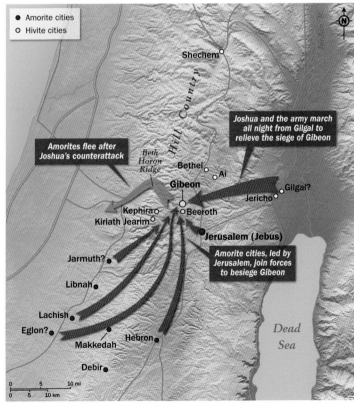

The king of Jerusalem persuades the kings of Hebron, Jarmuth, Lachish, and Eglon to attack Gibeon because of the treaty it has made with the Israelites. This map shows the troop movements as the armies prepare for battle.

10:9 *all-night march . . . by surprise.* Joshua responds to Gibeon's request for haste (10:6). Surprise attack is a tactic he also uses at Ai (8:3) and Hazor (11:7), probably contributing to the battlefield's chaos created by the Lord (10:10). Joshua's march by night is an arduous climb from Gilgal, about twenty miles, giving him the high ground.

10:10 *The LORD threw them into confusion.* The Lord, not Joshua, is responsible for the victory, emphasizing the role of the Divine Warrior (10:11).

Beth Horon . . . Makkedah. The enemy flees west/southwest, descending from their cities toward the Mediterranean coast along an east–west ascent/descent passageway via Beth Horon. Joshua may have traversed south of Gibeon, cutting off any retreat by the kings to Jerusalem.

10:11 *hurled large hailstones.* The timely hailstorm is due to the Lord, not coincidence. That more die from the storm than the sword shows the Divine Warrior is more responsible than Israel's soldiers for the victory.

10:12 *Joshua said to the LORD.* This clause begins the Hebrew verse and elevates Joshua, whose intercession at Gibeon is unique in all the conquest stories (10:14; cf. Moses, Exod. 33:12–34:8). Two verbs are conflated in the NIV (see rather ESV, NRSV); the Hebrew text also reads, "*and he said* in the sight of Israel," thus introducing the petition that follows. The antecedent of "he" is ambiguous; either Joshua or the Lord makes the entreaty (see "Additional Insights" following this unit).

Sun, stand still . . . and you, moon. The petition has the ABC//AB[C] parallelism (AT): "O Sun, over Gibeon, stand still // O Moon, over the valley of Aijalon[, stand still]."

10:13 *Book of Jashar.* Literally, "Book of the Upright One"—this is a noncanonical book known only from here and 2 Samuel 1:18. Apparently it included poetry and songs concerning heroic stories and major events. The author of Joshua assumes that it is available as another source confirming the miracle.

10:14 *listened to a human being.* The idiom "listened to" (*shama' . . . beqol*) means "obey," indicating in stunning language that God answers Joshua's prayer. As the celestial bodies obey the Lord, so the Lord "obeys" the words of a mortal man. "A man" (NIV: "a human being"), not naming a specific man, emphasizes human mortality.

10:15 *returned . . . at Gilgal.* The same statement occurs in 10:43, where it is more chronologically appropriate. Verse 15 may be a scribal dittography (accidental doubling) or used to set off the literary unit of 10:16–43.

Theological Insights

This chapter continues the theological message of the former conquest accounts and the book at large. The Lord is the all-powerful Sovereign who grants Israel victory as its Divine Warrior. The Lord accomplishes this through natural and human phenomena, showing that he is master over all things whose divine choreography merges events to achieve his purposes (10:9–11). Just as the Lord throws down hailstones and the sun answers the Lord's command to "stand," Joshua too obeys the Lord. Reciprocally, the Lord answers Joshua's prayer, for his petition agrees with

Joshua honors the treaty with the Gibeonites, bringing the Israelite army to their defense, but it is the Lord who provides the victory at Gibeon. The terraced tell shown here is the location of the ancient city of Gibeon.

the divine purpose (10:8). Joshua's obedience at Gibeon serves as the first step toward additional victories over many cities in the south (10:28–39), indicating that Joshua continues to advance the Lord's will. That God answers Joshua's plea is consistent with Scripture's teaching that the Lord hears the cries of his people for deliverance (24:7; Exod. 2:23–25). Since the march around Jericho (chap. 6) is depicted in the narrative as an act of ritual worship, perhaps the prayer of Joshua at Gibeon signifies the prayers that accompany worship.

The execution of the kings forewarns the nations against opposing God's people. The promissory blessing made to the fathers explains that hostilities against Israel result in God's curse against the nations (Gen. 12:3). The nations have no excuse, since they are aware of Israel's previous victories, and they can look to the Gibeonites as an example of survival (10:4). Yet

the nations' wickedness is full (Gen. 15:16; Deut. 9:5); they are unwilling to repent and surrender (11:20). Their sin is virulent, contagious, and threatening. Justice demands a corresponding measure of retribution. Their iniquity is reminiscent of Pharaoh's growing resistance to the Israelites and their God (Exod. 8:19; 14:17–18).

Teaching the Text

The focus of the narrative is not on the miracle per se but on the intervention of God, who performs mighty feats of victory on behalf of his people. This is the proper focus for the teacher. The lesson is that God, not human prowess, enables his people to carry out his purposes: "Surely the Lord was fighting for Israel!" (10:14b). Since this sometimes involves miracles, his people can thank God for his limitless power (see the sidebar "Miracles" in the unit on 4:1–24). Believing prayer, too, is central to the passage: "a day when the LORD listened to a human being" (10:14a). Joshua's prayer does not force God's gracious response, but Joshua does not hesitate to ask God to render aid. God's attention to Joshua, a mere man, encourages Israel that the Lord is with them in the battle and is attuned to each person's cry for deliverance. Unlike prayers and incantations to the gods among the nations, prayer by God's covenant people is not a manipulative tool to persuade their God to achieve victory. Joshua's petition furthers God's will, for the Lord has instructed Joshua to begin the battle. Christians too must pray in God's will and rest in knowing that God is merciful (John 9:31; 1 John 5:14–15). Christians are to trust; God is to perform.

That God uses a special day for the victory of Joshua serves as a memorial to his salvation. "There has never been a day like it before or since" (10:14a). Heaps of stones or ruins were testimonies to the Lord's victories over Israel's enemies (4:4–9, 20–24; 7:26; 8:28–29; 10:27). Special days in the life of Israel, such as Passover, celebrated by Israel upon entering the land (5:10–12), were memorials, known as "sacred assemblies" (e.g., Lev. 23:24–44). These special days remind the Christian community of the special days that believers celebrate as a community. Special days are memories of the Lord's death and resurrection, the beginning of a new creation (Acts 2:29–36).[2]

Illustrating the Text

Thank God for all things, for he is the one who provides.

Scenario: The wedding has been beautiful, and now the wedding party and guests are gathered for the reception at the country

Joshua prays for the moon to stand still over the Valley of Aijalon, shown here in an aerial view. Gibeon was east of the Aijalon Valley, so the moon would have been setting in the west.

club. The pastor is asked to come forward to provide a blessing for the meal, and as he prays he thanks the Lord for the provision of the meal they are about to eat. Following the prayer, one of the guests at the table comments, "I can't believe the pastor thanked God for the meal; he should have thanked the bride's parents!" Ask your listeners, "How would you have responded to this guest's comment?" This would be an opportunity to challenge your listeners to understand that all gifts come from the hand of God.

God hears our prayers and always answers them.

Testimony: It is important in the community of faith to encourage one another by sharing our stories of God's mercy and compassion as we reach out to him in prayer. Select persons in your congregation who have a story to tell about a time they looked to the Lord in prayer for a need and the Lord provided (even if not in the way they expected or intended). They can tell their story through video, through the teacher/preacher, or personally to the congregation.

The battle belongs to the Lord!

Quote: *Enter the Open Door,* **by Ann Conner.** In her daily devotional book, Conner reminds us that we must decide each day who will be in charge of our life battles. She writes, "If we are claiming the battle and trying to fight in our own strength, we will miss what only He can do. The battle is won according to His rules, not human effort and ingenuity." [3] Conner goes on to challenge her readers to align themselves with the Lord's commands and through obedience to let him lead the charge. Remind your listeners to look to the Bible for direction and to the Lord in prayer, and to humbly follow his leading.

Joshua 10:1–15

The Sun "Stood Still"

Among the prominent events reported in Joshua, the miracle at the battle of Gibeon in 10:12–14 is the most difficult to understand. Taken at face value, English translations indicate the sun and moon literally cease moving, creating a cosmos-wide, daylong change in the ordinary relationship of celestial entities. However, conscientious inquiry of the passage reveals difficulties at every level of exegesis, including the genre, syntax, and significance of the passage. Is the passage poetry or narrative or both? What is the precise nuance of the words "stand still" (*damam*, 10:12b, 13a) and "stopped" (*'amad*, 10:13a, c)? The word *damam* often means "stand, be motionless, rigid" or "be silent,"[1] and *'amad* means "stand, be motionless ['stopped']."[2] Who is the speaker in 10:12b (lit., "and he ['God' or 'Joshua'?] said in the presence of Israel")? Although scholars have offered many explanations for each of these exegetical complexities, I will group only the most prominent ones into two categories: literal and figurative interpretations.[3] I will explain each theory and comment on its merit. Before doing so, we must keep in mind that for the biblical author the fact that God responded to a human's prayer in a unique way was more important than the nature of the miraculous event itself (10:14).

Literal Interpretations

The literal interpretations believe the sun and moon in the passage are physical entities.

1. The traditional view is that the sun stopped (i.e., the earth's rotation ceased), thus prolonging the sunlight of the day. The overthrow of the fleeing Amorites can be thoroughly completed if they cannot escape into the night. The advantage of this view is the weight of historic interpretation, but it has two major complications that make it unlikely. First, the text itself does not support this view. Depiction of the sun "over Gibeon" and the moon "over the Valley of Aijalon" shows that the time of day must have been in the morning (10:12), not at midday, as this view assumes ("middle of the sky," 10:13). Gibeon and the Valley of Aijalon are on an east–west plane, meaning that with the naked eye the sun is seen in the eastern sky and the moon in the western sky. In astronomy this relationship is called "opposition." That the two celestial bodies appear in the sky at the same time indicates that the time of day is morning. Second, the traditional interpretation requires (in modern terms) a planetary disruption, which would result in cosmic and terrestrial chaos. This is not to question if God has the ability to achieve such a feat, but to note that it would be inconsistent with the miracles in the Bible that are usually (always?) local in range, not global.

2. The sun appeared to "stop shining" to the naked eye due to a solar eclipse or refraction (interference from the clouds and hailstorm, 10:11; cf. Hab. 3:11). In this theory, *damam* is understood as meaning

"to be inactive, motionless" in the sense of no longing shining, thus "darkened." One difficulty of this view is the lexical problem of defining the word *damam* as "dark," since this is a questionable inference. Another difficulty is that an eclipse would be too brief to have made a difference in the battle's outcome. The point the author makes is that the prayer of Joshua received an answer from the Lord that made a difference in the outcome.

3. The background to understanding the Joshua passage is the Assyro-Babylonian celestial omen texts, known in the second millennium but especially prominent in the late Neo-Assyrian period (eighth–seventh centuries).[4] By studying the positions and movements of celestial bodies, diviners discerned messages from the gods regarding human events. Diviners periodically provided the king a series of quoted omens and their predictions for disaster or blessing. For example, the celestial signs portended either good or ill for the king and the nation in battle.

A propitious sign was when the first day of the full moon fell on the fourteenth of the month, at which time "opposition" of the moon and sun briefly occurred in the morning. This sign was construed to mean that the month's days were accurately calculated and would have the appropriate length (thirty days). It was favorable, meaning social stability and prosperity, since harmony in the heavens meant correspondingly all is well on earth. On the other hand, if the opposition could not be viewed on the fourteenth because of interference (e.g., clouds), or the opposition appeared on another day (e.g., fifteenth day), the omen indicated disaster. This would be all-important in how the king viewed engaging in battle on these days. A positive omen would embolden the king, whereas an evil one would demoralize the army. Further evidence pointing in this direction is the celestial terminology used in the omen

One possible interpretation of Joshua's prayer is that he is asking God to provide a negative omen for the enemy. A large corpus of cuneiform texts known as Enuma Anu Enlil records omens connected to the motion of celestial bodies. The tablet shown here from the Seleucid period (third to first century BC) is one of several focusing on the movements of the stars and planets.

texts that have a possible conceptual correspondence to the terms "stand" and "stopped" in the Joshua text. That the "sun stopped in the middle of the sky and delayed going down about a full day" (10:13) comments on the further concerns of omen texts, which interpret the celestial opposition of sun and moon as a "full-length" day guaranteeing a month of "full-length" days. Since the event at Gibeon does not have a "full-length" day, it is a harmful omen in the eyes of the enemy. The prayer by Joshua therefore is a call for God to intervene by providing a celestial vision that occurs on a day other than the fourteenth, thus serving as a bad omen for the enemy. Thus, the passage says that God fights for Israel, enlisting sun and moon to carry out the divine plan.

Since throughout the ancient Near East the practices of astral worship and divination were commonplace, the theory provides a cultural background that makes sense of the passage. Theologically, it accords well with the point of Joshua's request, affirming it is the Lord who fights for Israel. Additionally, the "opposition" indicates a full moon the night before, and this would support the swift travel in the night by Israel's troops (10:9). Last, the observation that the prayer is spoken in the morning (during the time of opposition) suggests that it makes sense for Joshua to make his request at the start of the battle.

Although the practice of celestial divination was widespread in the Late Bronze Age (a notable exception is Egypt), there is uncertainty about the extent to which Joshua and the Canaanites knew the

The arrangement and movement of the celestial bodies were much studied in the ancient world. The heavily restored circular cuneiform tablet shown here is a planisphere that charts the heavens. It divides the night sky into eight sections and identifies stars in the constellations Gemini, Pegasus, and the Pleiades (eighth century BC). Omen literature relied on accurate recording of both mundane and spectacular celestial and life events.

technical art of celestial divination as conducted by trained scholars. Assyriologists are divided as to when and to what degree celestial omen calculation was current in Canaan during the Late Bronze Age. There is an assumption that star worship, which is specifically banned (Deut. 4:19; 17:3), also involved astral divination. However, there is no specific prohibition against *celestial* omens in Deuteronomy 18:10–11.

Figurative Interpretations

Although there are variations in figurative interpretations, they are not substantially different from one another and will be treated together. The figurative interpretations understand references to the sun and moon as figures of speech in poetic discourse, not a description of actual natural phenomena. There is agreement by these interpreters that verses 12b–13a are poetic verse, and others hold that verse 13c is also poetic. The poetic picture describes what the narrative explains. Other biblical accounts of battles have both narrative and poetic accounts of the same events, such as Exodus 14–15 and Judges 4–5. That the moon "stood still" and "stopped" refers to the night march by moonlight (10:13; cf. 10:9). The implication is that the moon was sufficiently full so that the soldiers could advance expeditiously, especially since a three days' march is reported in 9:17. The long day's battle in the sun's light ends at sunset in the narrative in 10:27. Verse 14 shows that the day's battle is not exceptional for its celestial abnormality but that the Lord accomplishes this victory (cf. 10:42). Importantly, the speaker of verse 12b, "Sun, stand still over Gibeon, // and you, moon, over the Valley of Aijalon," is best interpreted as the Lord, not Joshua. The Lord's call upon the celestial powers aligns with the biblical assertions that the Lord is sovereign over the heavenly hosts (e.g., Isa. 40:26; Jer. 31:35) and he can employ them to secure victory for Israel (e.g., Josh. 10:11; Exod. 15:10; Judg. 5:4–5, 20–21).

The conclusion I draw for verses 12–14, although it must be held tentatively, is the following: (1) Joshua prays to the Lord, requesting his help in the battle in verse 12b; (2) the Lord responds by calling upon the celestial powers to assist him in giving Israel the victory over the Amorites in verse 13a; (3) the author refers to the Book of Jashar in verse 13b, drawing on another witness to the amazing victory; and (4) verse 13c gives the conclusion of the battle by using the typical conquest language of hyperbole or possibly omen language showing a favorable day.

The Sun "Stood Still"

Victory over the Southern Kings

Big Idea *The Lord grants victory to Israel when they face formidable powers of resistance.*

Understanding the Text

The Text in Context

After the battle at Gibeon (10:1–15), the account continues, describing the outcome of the epic conflict (10:16–43). The passage divides into three parts: (1) the capture and execution of the five Canaanite kings who have formed a coalition (10:16–27); (2) the naming of six cities destroyed by Israel (10:28–39; a seventh city, Gezer, is named only by its king's ["Horam"] supporting role to Lachish [10:33]); and (3) a summary of the battle (10:40–43). That the list of cities does not match precisely the coalition of five kings shows that the five are only representative cities of a larger number of members. Although Jerusalem and Jarmuth are part of the coalition, they are not named as cities destroyed, suggesting that the two cities survive (on Jerusalem's fate, see Judg. 1:8; 15:63; 2 Sam. 5:5–16).

The description of the six cities that are destroyed includes formulaic phrases: for example, "put [the name of city] . . . to the sword"; "totally destroyed [*herem*; see "Christian Interpretation" in the introduction] everyone in it. He left no survivors"; and "did to the king of [name of city] as he had done to the king of [name of city]" (cf. 10:28). The recurring phrases may suggest that this section (10:28–39) is a prior composition wedded with the battle narrative. That the telling of the defeated cities,

Joshua summons his commanders and has them place their feet on the necks of the defeated, captured Canaanite kings, as a symbol of their victory and power over them. This Assyrian relief shows Tiglath-Pileser III with his foot on the neck of an enemy (Palace at Nimrud, 728 BC).

however, is not always the same suggests that the account is not invented or has not been standardized; rather, it reflects actual events.

Verses 40–43 are transitional, describing the victory of Joshua in general terms. Verses 15 (ending the first part of the chapter) and 43 (ending the second part) report the return of Israel to their base camp at Gilgal. The same arrangement occurs in the story of Hazor's demise (11:1–15). The battle narrative is followed by a territory report, summarizing the captured lands that Joshua controls (11:16–23). "Gibeon" in 10:41 echoes the beginning of the battle in 10:1, bringing the narrative to completion.

The biblical passage has historical and rhetorical features of ancient Near East conquest narratives. See "Inheritance of the Land" in the introduction, and "Historical and Cultural Background" in the unit on 11:16–12:24.

Historical and Cultural Background

Ceremonies symbolizing a victor's defeat of his enemies were widely practiced in the ancient Near East. Various methods signaled the submission and humiliation of a defeated foe. One such "victory lap" was the dismemberment of an enemy's body parts, designed to degrade the enemy and strike fear in potential adversaries (Judg. 1:5–7; 1 Sam. 17:51). Neo-Assyrian relief art notoriously portrays piles of severed heads, legs, and arms; impaled bodies; and flayed bodies. This demonstration was a statement of power. Another sign of submission was a defeated enemy groveling under the feet of the victor (figurative use, Ps. 110:1; Isa. 49:23). Joshua 10:24–25

Key Themes of Joshua 10:16–43

- The Lord gives Israel a far-reaching victory over a coalition of enemies led by Jerusalem.
- Joshua obeys the Lord's commands to destroy the Canaanites and wins the esteem of the people.
- Joshua's persistent campaign results in Israel breaking the hold of the southern kings.

describes Israel's commanders setting their feet on defeated kings' necks. The neck was associated with the ideas of strength and pride (Judg. 5:30). Egyptian art often depicts this solemn ritual. The ceremony in Joshua, however, is intended not merely to gloat over the fallen kings but to reassure the Israelites that total victory is theirs if they remain stalwart.

Interpretive Insights

10:16 *cave at Makkedah.* If the identification of the city as Khirbet el-Qom is accurate, it is about twenty-one miles west of Hebron (12:16). Caves were used as burial locations (Gen. 49:29–30), hideouts (1 Sam. 22:1), and dwellings (Gen. 19:30).

10:19 *has given them into your hand.* "Given [*natan*] into your hand" is a stereotypical phrase, meaning that God places Israel's enemies under its control. The tandem of human and divine dimensions is a recurring feature in the book's theology. God is credited with handing (*natan*) over the enemy to Israel five times in this chapter (10:8, 12, 19, 30, 32). It is Joshua's battle cry (10:19), which echoes the Lord's promise to Joshua (10:8).

10:21 *no one uttered a word.* The Hebrew is vivid: "No one sharpened a tongue." The figure of speech describes the extent of their enemies' submission. The Israelites' success on the field of battle breaks the spirit of the opposition. This overwhelming defeat motivates the kings of the north to mount a do-or-die effort (11:1–15). Fear of the Israelites fulfills the promise made to the people (e.g., 2:9; Exod. 15:14–16; 23:27).

10:24 *necks of these kings.* The symbolism indicates total humiliation and defeat, like a broken animal that submits to a plowman's yoke (Deut. 28:48).

10:25 *Do not be afraid . . . discouraged.* This language recalls earlier exhortations to stand firm in faith (1:9; 8:1; 10:8; see also 11:6). Rather than fear its enemies, Israel is to "fear the LORD" (4:24; 24:14).

10:26 *Joshua put the kings to death.* Joshua takes on the gory task himself, showing his courage. Joshua especially is highlighted in verses 26–42, culminating in the summary of verses 40–42.

10:27 *At sunset . . . into the cave.* Hanging the kings' corpses is further public scorn for their deed, but the law requires removing them at sunset lest they ceremonially pollute the land (8:29; Deut. 21:22–23).

10:32 *Lachish.* Lachish was significant in size and strategic location. It is the only city named that required two days to defeat. The narrative names it eight times, implying that it was an important site for the Israelites to capture in their campaign south.

10:40 *whole region . . . the hill country, the Negev, the western foothills.* The "whole region" refers to the southern regions: (1) "hill country" names Judah's mountains, traversing north–south; (2) "Negev" names the area southward; and (3) "western foothills" (lit., "lowlands," Shephelah) describes Judah's foothills, which slope toward the seacoast.

10:41 *Kadesh Barnea to Gaza . . . Goshen to Gibeon.* The author's point is the encompassing victory that the Lord gives. Kadesh Barnea and Gaza mark the southern border, along the east–west direction. Kadesh (Ain el-Qudeirat) is in north Sinai, the infamous site where Israel refuses to enter the land. Gaza (Tell Harube) sits in the southwest region in the coastal plain (Gen. 10:19). Gaza is a member of the Philistine pentapolis (five cities ruled by five "lords") during the settlement period and is one of the cities that has not been totally conquered (13:3), although it is temporarily controlled (11:22; Judg. 1:18–19). "Goshen to Gibeon" describes the south–north axis. Goshen is a city at the southern border toward the Negev (11:16; 15:51), not to be confused with the residence of the Israelites in the Egyptian delta (Gen. 47:27).

10:42 *in one campaign.* Joshua takes all the southern area in one war, a remarkable feat—one that could be achieved only because the Lord "fought for Israel."

10:43 *Joshua returned with all Israel.* That the Israelites abandon the defeated cities and return to their base camp at Gilgal explains why they can be reoccupied by Canaanites (cf. 10:15).

Theological Insights

The account of the wars against the southern coalition of kings conveys the core theological ideas of the whole book. "Because the LORD, the God of Israel, fought for Israel" (10:42) summarizes why Israel achieves remarkable victories against better-armed and better-trained armies. Although Joshua receives special attention in the narrative as Israel's leader, the presupposition underlying the passage becomes an explicit statement that it is the Lord who has assured the victory. Verse 42 essentially repeats the language of verse 14 but has the explicit identifier "the God of Israel." The recurring phrase "the LORD, the God of Israel" in the book of Joshua underscores the identity of Israel as the Lord's covenant people and designates Israel's God by the covenant name "LORD" (Yahweh) (10:40, 42; cf. 7:19; 13:14). This title differentiates the Israelites from the nations and Israel's God from their false gods, whom the Lord defeats. That these nations and their gods succumb is reminiscent of God's victory against Pharaoh and Egypt's gods (Exod. 12:12; 14:17–18).

Moreover, the passage shows that there are fruitful consequences when godly people repent and seek God's will in prayer. The people renew their unity and are forced by the threat of the Canaanites to consolidate around the Lord's appointed leader, Joshua. The inventory of seven captured cities that follows the battle story suggests that the victory affords Israel the beginning of better things to come, indicating that the defeat of the five southern kings has repercussions in the whole region. The Israelites fail through their compromise with the Gibeonites (chap. 9), but the Lord seizes this failure as a means of achieving his greater purpose of defeating the kings in the south (10:1–2). The effect of the victory subsequently impacts the northern kings, who form a formidable coalition (11:1–5), providing a future opportunity for the Lord to crush the hostile Canaanite armies.

Another theological purpose is to affirm the persevering faith of Joshua. The mention of "Kadesh" recalls the negative report presented by the spies, excepting Joshua and Caleb (Num. 13–14; Deut. 1:19–33). Both Joshua and Caleb receive their inheritance (14:6–15; 19:49–50; 21:12; 24:30). The attention to Kadesh serves as a criticism of the wilderness generation but also a commendation of Joshua and Caleb, who trust God.

Joshua conquers the cities of Makkedah, Libnah, Lachish, Eglon, Hebron, and Debir, subduing the southern region of Canaan. An aerial view of the ancient site of the city of Lachish is shown here.

Teaching the Text

The focus of this passage is the Lord's dependability in supporting Israel against dire hostilities by mounting opposition. Israel's victory is sure because the covenant Lord is trustworthy. The treatment of the kings (10:16–27) and the burning of the cities (10:28–29) are intended to give the Israelites confidence in the Lord's protection and their ultimate victory over their ruthless enemies. They also send a clear message to others that the wiser course of action is acceptance of the Israelites, not relentless hatred. Joshua's exhortation to the people in verses 25–26 reflects the Lord's persistent call to take heart and to press ahead in battle (1:9; 8:1; 10:8; 11:6). The widespread destruction that the story reports creates moral tension for readers today, especially in light of Jesus's teaching to "love your enemies" (Matt. 5:44; cf. 1 Pet. 3:8–9).

Here are three factors that might ease the moral tension. (1) The Israelites are attacked by a powerful alliance that seeks to annihilate them. The response of Israel is defensive in a life-or-death setting that is customary in the ethos of the ancient Near East. (2) It is necessary to note that individuals (Rahab) and nations (Gibeonites) who submit to Israel's God receive mercy. The objective is not wholesale slaughter on an ethnic basis but the preservation of Israel, whose ultimate task is to proclaim to the nations the worship of the Lord. (3) There are pockets of Canaanites who survive the wars (e.g., 13:1–8). The Lord uses these nations to test the future loyalty of the Israelites (Judg. 2:20–3:2). (4) These nations are characterized by idolatry, which is a threat to Israel's role as God's instrument of grace for the nations.[1]

Believers have the conviction that God has and will overcome evil, both in the world and in Christian discipleship (Col. 1:22). The forces mustered against Israel and the Lord's deliverance of his people can be set in the context of God's total victory over evil and those powers that would destroy his people (Eph. 6:12; Col. 2:15; 1 Pet. 3:22).[2] This too is a life-or-death struggle but one that the Lord has won on behalf of Christians (John 16:33).

Illustrating the Text

The Lord is our mighty fortress.

Hymn: "A Mighty Fortress Is Our God," by Martin Luther. This great hymn was written by Luther probably in October 1527, in response to an approaching plague.[3] In verse three we are reminded that we battle a spiritual enemy, the Prince of Darkness, who seeks to destroy us; but we do not fear him, for his "doom is sure" and "one little word shall fell him." Verse two reminds us that our confidence is in Jesus Christ, who stands with us. And verse four proclaims that God has given us his Spirit and gifts, which enable us to do battle in this world. Luther concludes his hymn with these words: "The body they may kill; God's truth abideth still; his kingdom is forever!"[4] Ask your listeners, "What are the temptations and the enemies you face in your life?" Tell them to remember that the Lord is our mighty fortress and that ultimate victory is already assured.

You too can experience victory in the battles you face.

Bible: Philippians 4:13. In the first ten chapters of Joshua we have read of the success of the Israelites against overwhelming odds. As we have seen, the secret to their success has been the faithfulness of God to fulfill his promises to his people. The application of this overarching biblical teaching is that we must put our confidence in the promises of God. In Philippians 4:13, Paul writes, "I can do all this through him who gives me strength." The "all this" refers to Paul's situation—whether our circumstances are good or bad, we can do the will of God, through the presence of the Lord, who provides all we need. Ask your congregants to reflect on this question: What is one challenge or battle you face in your life? Encourage your listeners to name the struggle or foe and then to ask the Lord for the strength to be victorious in that situation.

Repent, and receive God's mercy.

History: In Joshua, those, such as Rahab, who submit to the Lord's judgment of the people of Canaan receive God's mercy. Those who refuse to repent or to surrender to the Lord's leading receive just consequences. This is a reality that should be embraced by all people. On March 2, 1863, Senator James Harlan of Iowa introduced a resolution to call the nation to a day of prayer and fasting. The resolution was passed by the Senate and approved by President Abraham Lincoln. The resolution read in part:

> And, insomuch as we know that, by His divine law, nations like individuals are subjected to punishments and chastisements in this world, may we not justly fear that the awful calamity of civil war, which now desolates the land, may be but a punishment, inflicted upon us, for our presumptuous sins, to the needful end of our national reformation as a whole People? . . . It behooves us then, to humble ourselves before the offended Power, to confess our national sins, and to pray for clemency and forgiveness.[5]

This would be a good opportunity to lead your listeners in a prayer of confession and a prayer for your nation and your people (cf. Dan. 9:1–19).

Defeat of the Northern Kings

Big Idea *When the Lord's appointed servants and his people have courage, he fulfills his promise of victory.*

Understanding the Text

The Text in Context

The defeat of the northern kings, especially Jabin of Hazor, completes the conquest narratives that begin at Jericho (chap. 6). Chapters 6–8 describe the central campaign against Jericho and Ai. Chapters 9–10 show the peace made with Gibeon and the fall of the southern coalition of kings. Chapter 11, especially verses 1–15, focuses on the northern region. Together, these core narratives give the spectrum of Israel's victories. What follow in 11:16–12:24 are summary listings of conquered regions, peoples, cities, and kings, preparing the reader for the distribution of the land in chapters 13–19.

Chapters 10 and 11 have a general correspondence: both begin with a coalition of enemy kings (10:1–5; 11:1–5); both describe their respective battles (10:6–39; 11:6–11);

Jabin, king of Hazor, organizes the northern Canaanite kings to fight against Israel. Shown here is an aerial view of the very large and important ancient city of Hazor. The lower city is outlined by a now grass-covered rampart wall, and excavations of the upper city can be seen toward the middle left of the photo.

and both contain a summary of the fallen (10:40–43; 11:12–23). There are details that are similar, such as the Lord's explicit directive to engage the enemy and the author's attribution of the victory to the Lord (10:8, 14; 11:6, 8). The differences are significant too, such as the brief report in chapter 11 versus the longest battle description of the book in chapter 10. Also, there are no miraculous interventions specifically attributed to the Divine Warrior in chapter 11.

Joshua 11:1–15 gives a brief account of the battle because the reader can fill in the detail gathered from the similar battle in chapter 10 and because the narrative continues the same theological message already expounded in chapter 10. Chapter 11 targets the most fearsome army in the book, led by the most imposing city, Hazor. The point is, if Hazor falls, then no city can stand against the Lord's people. No more convincing on this point is necessary; therefore, the book subsequently plunges readers into the summary listings of the total capture. The subjugated land is truly "the land of Israel," as God has promised.

Commentators vary widely on where the narrative ends, concluding the section at verse 11, 15, 23, or even beyond.[1] Since the basic structure of 11:1–15 mirrors chapter 10, and because Hazor is mentioned again in 11:13, it is best to take 11:1–15 as a distinctive unit. The parts of the passage are (1) the setting and the naming of the kings (11:1–5), (2) the Lord's instructions (11:6), (3) the description of the battle (11:7–11), and (4) the summary (11:12–15).

Historical and Cultural Background

Hazor (Tell el-Qedah) was a major player internationally, known from Egyptian

Key Themes of Joshua 11:1–15

- Israel's enemies band together one last time to destroy the people of God.
- God instructs Joshua to attack, promising him total victory.
- Joshua obeys the Lord in every detail, showing that the victory is God's.
- Israel's leaders, Moses and Joshua, succeed because they fulfill God's commands.

(nineteenth century), Mari (eighteenth century), and Amarna (fourteenth century) records. It is also well documented in the Bible (e.g., 15:23, 25; Judg. 4:2; 1 Kings 9:15). Two critical battles occur at Hazor during the conquest and settlement periods (Judg. 4). The site has an upper (eighteen acres) and lower (two hundred acres) city, dwarfing all ancient ruins in Israel. It has been intermittently excavated from the 1920s to the present. It is nine miles north of the Sea of Galilee. Its size, commercial connections, and strategic location made it an important site throughout antiquity.[2]

Interpretive Insights

11:1 *Jabin*. This is a dynastic name (cf. Judg. 4:2), like Egypt's "Pharaoh." His powerful city makes him "head" of the coalition (11:10), indicating control of the region. That the narrative does not include his plea for help (contrast 10:4) may intimate that he has authority over the other kings.

Jobab . . . Shimron and Akshaph. Jobab is the only other king named, which may indicate that he is influential. The cities' locations are uncertain but in the general region of the Upper Galilee, stretching from the Sea of Galilee west to the Mediterranean coast (cf. 12:19–20). The Greek Old Testament has "Meron" instead of

"Madon," reflecting the battle site "Waters of Merom" (11:5, 7).

11:2 *in the mountains . . . Naphoth Dor.* The geographical breadth pictures the coalition's strength: far north to Mount Hermon; the northern portion of the Jordan Valley ("Arabah"); the northwest shore of the Sea of Galilee ("Kinnereth" may refer to the general area, 12:3; 13:27; 19:35 [see NIV notes]); the slopes toward the coast ("western foothills"; cf. 10:40); and the region on the coast north of Caesarea and south of Carmel ("Naphoth Dor," or "heights of Dor," a region presumably near the city Dor, 12:23; 17:11; 1 Kings 4:11).

11:3 *Canaanites . . . Amorites, Hittites, Perizzites and Jebusites . . . Hivites.* After the naming of the kings and the geography, the inhabitants are named, numbering six prominent nations (9:1; 12:8) whose defeat God has promised (3:10). That such diverse groups unite for war indicates their desperation. The Jebusites are better known from their kin in Jerusalem (15:63; 2 Sam. 5:7).

region of Mizpah. From Gilgal it is far northeast below Mount Hermon. The alternate spelling "Mizpeh" occurs in 11:8 (see ESV).

11:4 *all their troops and a large number of horses and chariots.* The coalition is at full force, as shown from the word *kol* ("all") and the term *rab/rob* ("large/huge/numerous") repeated three times. This is the first time the Hebrews face chariots. Their

The Canaanite army of combined forces from the northern Canaanite cities includes horses and chariots. This relief from one of the bronze bands commissioned by Shalmaneser III for his palace gate at Balawat depicts chariots engaged in battle (858–824 BC).

mobility and platform make them adept for battle in the plains, although flooding of the Kishon will make Hazor's chariots immobile in Barak's battle (Judg. 5:21). Only the most powerful armies are equipped with chariotry (17:16–18; Exod. 14:7). Hazor's international connections make it a likely partner in a lucrative trade of horses and chariots (cf. 1 Kings 10:28–29).

as numerous as the sand. Reference to the innumerable "sand on the seashore" is reminiscent of the promise made to Abraham (Gen. 22:17).

11:5 *Waters of Merom.* The location is unknown but likely west of Hazor, perhaps ancient Meiron. Perhaps the waters flood as at Kishon (Judg. 5:21).

11:6 *by this time tomorrow.* Reference to a specific time underscores the certainty of the promise's fulfillment (cf. 2 Kings 7:1).

I will hand . . . over. The participle indicates impending action, "I [Yahweh] am about to give/hand over."

hamstring . . . and burn. Hamstringing meant cutting the connecting tendon in the hind leg, disabling a horse's running capacity. Instead of strengthening their military capacity, Israel fulfills this command, showing their confidence in the Lord rather than in military might (David, 2 Sam. 8:4). The Lord prohibits Israel's kings from multiplying horses (Deut. 17:16). Hamstringing the horses because of their military function was an exception to the general policy of Israel toward creatures. The compassionate and just treatment of wild and domestic animals was characteristic of Israel's life, based on the theology of creation and covenant with all creatures (Gen. 9:12; Deut. 5:14; 25:4). A mark of a righteous person was humane treatment of God's creatures (Prov. 12:10).

11:7 *suddenly.* As at Gibeon (10:9) Joshua's smaller army gains advantage. By attacking first, he shows no fear.

11:8 *Greater Sidon, to Misrephoth Maim . . . Mizpeh.* The pursuers split, chasing the enemy northwest to Sidon and Misrephoth Maim on the coast (13:6) and northeast to Mizpeh (cf. comments on 11:3, above).

11:10 *turned back.* Joshua reassembles his divided troops and assaults Hazor.

11:11 *totally destroyed . . . burned Hazor.* As with Jericho and Ai (6:24; 8:19), all is devoted to God (*herem*) and the city burned (11:13).

11:14 *not sparing anyone.* The narrative repeats (11:8, 11, 14) that Joshua fulfills the command to kill all the living (Deut. 20:17).

11:15 *the Lord commanded Moses.* This phrase begins and ends the verse, stressing that the command comes from the Lord, not Moses. "Commanded" (*tsiwwah*) appears three times for emphasis (also 11:12, 20).

Theological Insights

God promises to give the Israelites the victory over their enemies, if they show courage. This is the same exhortation to Joshua from the start (1:6–7, 9; 10:25). Fear is the natural response for an army confronting Canaanite warriors who are trained, equipped, and seasoned champions. The Israelites have gained experience, but they are no match for the northern kings, whose armies are numerous, coordinated, and especially equipped with chariotry (11:1–5). But Israel's faith is mightier than the most valiant Canaanite warriors, because they place their trust in the word of the Lord, not in strategy or their own power. Israel has no chariotry, and it is woefully outnumbered. By disabling the horses and burning the chariotry the Israelites show that they trust in the Lord, not in armaments. The coalition comes together, motivated by a common fear, and they have refused to accept that the Lord is the Almighty God (cf. 9:1–5; 10:1–2).

Israel's faith is not for faith's sake—an empty faith. Their faith is not merely hopeful wishing—a "Gotta believe!" mentality. Faith itself is not what achieves the victory. Theirs is a faith based in the reality of the revealed Divine Warrior. They have a reasoned faith and are motivated by assurance in the Lord's truthfulness and goodness, as shown in the past. It is a faith placed in the right object, namely, the God of Abraham, Isaac, and Jacob (1:6; 24:3–4), who has more than proven himself fully trustworthy. Faith in the Lord means accepting his word despite appearances. He has called the Israelites to an impossible task. The formidable Canaanite system of city-states is too entrenched to be removed by a rabble of desert wanderers. Yet Israel will burn the trappings of Canaanite hegemony (11:6). God uses the Israelites to judge the Canaanites for their rebellious sin and in doing so to announce to the world of nations that he is mightier than their false gods. Israel too learns that it must not yield to the lure of the Canaanites, whose urban life otherwise is attractive.

God gives the Israelites a chain of command that reflects God's ultimate authority (11:12, 15). The Lord has commanded Moses to destroy the indigenous Canaanite inhabitants, and in turn Moses gives the directive to Joshua. In both cases, Moses and Joshua vigilantly carry out the Lord's instructions, knowing that God demands absolute submission. Compromise is as foolhardy as the reckless response of the northern kings, who believe that they can overwhelm the Israelites with force. The repeated attention to Joshua's obedience, "he left nothing undone" (11:15), speaks to his exceptional character from his youth to his final years. "Moses was the great 'law-giver' in Israel. Joshua appears here as the great 'law-keeper.'"[3]

Teaching the Text

The common idea of promise-fulfillment in the battle narratives (6:1–11:15) continues in this account. Similarly, the demands of God and the careful obedience of his people reappear. These messages are indispensable in teaching the book of Joshua. The repetition of a message should not dissuade the teacher from teaching the core truth of a lesson. It is tempting to teach a peripheral message because an audience often wants to hear something new. Teaching core truths requires setting before each generation the faith to be realized once again in the community (4:6, 21; Deut. 4:9; Jude 3). Concentrating on the author's message, which climaxes with the remarkable achievement at

Hazor, places the proper emphasis on God. God is the chief actor, giving the reader opportunity to contemplate his character and actions. The theology of Joshua tells the reader about the Lord as Deliverer and Sovereign over his people. Translating what Joshua says about Israel's God into the theological framework of the Triune God helps Christians better understand the divine purpose expressed uniquely through Jesus Christ (e.g., John 1:1–18). Jesus is the person through whom we know God as Deliverer and Victor over sin and evil (Col. 1:15–20).

The battle narratives conclude with Hazor, showing that despite how towering the difficulty appears, the Lord is to be believed. Israel's valor encourages readers to face fearful opposition (11:6; Matt. 10:16–33). The Lord honors the leadership that exhibits determined confidence in him. Joshua and the people of Israel grow in their faith as a consequence of their trials and challenges. Christians grow in faith through confronting challenges again and again (James 1:2–4; 1 Pet. 1:6–7; 1 John 5:3–5). We have confidence in the Lord, who helps us overcome the world's temptations.

The Israelites destroy the population of Hazor, "not sparing anyone that breathed" (11:14). Hazor, like Jericho and Ai, is totally burned (11:10–11, 13). Here, it is useful to point out that the passage gives an insight into the necessity of war with the Canaanites. Deuteronomy 20:10–15 says that an offer of peace is incumbent upon Israel for nations that live afar, but cities of those groups that dwell nearby must be destroyed (Deut. 20:16–18). What differentiates the two policies is not ethnicity but the threat of idolatry. It is assumed in this command that the peoples whose religion is threatening are ones who will not accept peace terms. When the Deuteronomy passage and the Hazor narrative are read together, the comment in Joshua 11:19 makes good sense. The verse presupposes that nations refuse to engage in peace negotiations, unlike the Gibeonites, who seek it. God gave the Israelites the specific command to defend themselves in war, but our marching orders are to resist evil. Christians face opposition, and in some cases, imprisonment and violence. Our response is to resist evil by expressing love and praying for those who harm us (Rom. 12:21).

Illustrating the Text

Be strong in your convictions and unwilling to compromise.

True Story: Author Palmer Chinchen shares a story about a time when he and his brothers went white-water rafting down the fast and dangerous Zambezi River in Zimbabwe. Their guide gave them the following instructions: "When the raft flips, stay in the rough water. You will be tempted to swim toward the stagnant water at the edge of the banks. Don't do it. Because it is in the stagnant water that the crocs wait for you. They are large and hungry."[4] It is our natural human tendency to seek the easy road, but the easy road often leads to destruction. It might have seemed easier to the Israelites to simply live among the Canaanites, but that was where temptation to compromise God's standards would be the greatest. Be strong in your convictions even if it means a more difficult life. Beware of the danger of compromise.

Faith is living out what we claim to believe.

Poetry: Author Wilbur Rees wrote a poem called "$3.00 Worth of God." This poem is an indictment of Christians who want enough of God to make them feel good but not enough of God to change their lives. His poem is a challenge to those who are not willing to really believe God and step out in faith and obey him.[5] As we see in the book of Joshua, the Lord's blessings and the power of God are seen when his people live out what they claim to believe. Wanting just three dollars' worth of God robs us of taking risks that allow us to see God do what only he can do. Ask your listeners, "What would it look like for you to live out this week what you claim to believe about God?"

Courageous faith begins with a right perspective on God.

Humor: Children's perspectives on God can be quite humorous. The following is a sample of quotes from letters written by children to God:

> "Thank you for the baby brother but what I prayed for was a puppy." (Joyce)
> "Maybe Cain and Abel would not kill each [other] so much if they had their own rooms. It works with my brother." (Larry)
> "I bet it is very hard for you to love all of everybody in the whole world. There are only four people in our family and I can never do it." (Nan)[6]

Our perspective on God impacts the choices we make. If our God is small, aloof, or powerless, then our life choices will be impacted by that perspective. Courageous faith begins with a right understanding of the nature of God. What are you doing to grow in your knowledge of God?

Summing Up the Conquest

Big Idea *God proves truthful and faithful by enabling his people to defeat their enemies and possess his blessing.*

Understanding the Text

The Text in Context

The purpose of 11:16–12:24 is to describe the success of Israel's entrance into the land. The passage concludes the previous narratives at two levels: first, it closes the first half of the book (1:1–11:15), and, second, it closes the battle narratives (6:1–11:15). It bridges the acquisition of the land (1:1–11:15) and its distribution (chaps. 13–19). Chapters 10 and 11–12 exhibit an approximate parallel arrangement: a battle report (10:1–15//11:1–15) is followed by a description of the conquered kings and lands (10:16–43//11:16–12:24). The geographical summaries in 10:40 and 11:16 are similar in description. Joshua 11:16–12:24 divides into two parts: (1) conquered lands (11:16–23) and (2) conquered kings (12:1–24).[1]

(1) The inventory of the land (11:16–23) includes geographical boundaries (11:16–20), defeat of the Anakites (11:21–22), and a summary (11:23; cf. 10:40). The language "Joshua took this / the entire land" in verses 16 and 23 marks the boundaries of the paragraph. Focus on the defeat of the Anakites in verses 21–22 contrasts with the wilderness Israelites' failure to trust God for fear of the Anakites (Deut. 1:28). The summary's "inheritance" and "divisions" (11:23) prepares for the distribution of the land to follow (chaps. 13–19).

(2) The catalog of kings in 12:1–24 consists of the kings of Transjordan defeated by Moses (12:1–6) and those west of the Jordan defeated by Joshua (12:7–24). Verses 7–8 present a summary. The pattern of naming the city and counting "one" suggests that a catalog in whole or part is used. "Jericho" and "Ai" head the list (12:9). Verses 10–16a mostly name sites known from the southern campaign (chap. 10). Verses 16b–24 begin with Bethel, after

Joshua 12 includes a list of the kings conquered by Joshua and the armies of Israel. Other examples of conquest accounts can also be found throughout the ancient Near East. This wall relief at Karnak, Egypt, records a list of Canaanite cities captured by Thutmose III (1479–1425 BC).

which are fourteen locations, including five cities mentioned in the northern campaign (11:1–15). Verses 16b–18 name cities in the central region, and verses 19–24 generally pertain to those in the north.

Since the list of chapter 12 includes cities not mentioned in the conquest narratives, the author of Joshua does not report all the battles, indicating a broader conflict than told in the battle stories. Also, the battles he does include are the more significant and representative ones.

Historical and Cultural Background

Conquest accounts were common in the ancient Near East, and the biblical account shares many of the same features.[2] (1) One aspect of agreement is the rhetoric used in conquest narratives. The accounts describe an all-out war between the subsequent victors and a virulent enemy, whom they justly destroy. Hyperbole describes the overwhelming victory, annihilating the population and taking full control of the defeated territories. Biblical accounts of Israel's wars against the southern and northern coalitions (10:1–43; 11:1–23) use the same rhetoric of total devastation and complete control of towns and territories (10:28–43; 11:16–20). The biblical author uses the expected historical and rhetorical description, meant to be interpreted accordingly by the audience. (2) Listing conquered cities after narrative reports, as in Joshua 12, parallels Assyrian practice. Assyrian lists of conquered cities were selective, including cities whose capture was not told in the narratives. Joshua 12's partial listing therefore conforms to this ancient practice and should not be considered a mistake.

Key Themes of Joshua 11:16–12:24

- The Lord has "hardened the hearts" of Israel's enemies so that they might be decisively defeated.
- The people honor God's instructions by courageously engaging the enemy.
- Capture of Canaan's cities prepares for Israel's inheritance.
- The listing of sites both east and west of the Jordan reflects the unity and continuity of the community with the promises of the past.

Interpretive Insights

11:16 *region of Goshen.* Goshen is the name of a district in the hills of Judah (10:41); additionally, it is the name of a city in Judah (15:51) and of the location of the Hebrews in Egypt (Gen. 45:10).

11:17 *Mount Halak . . . to Baal Gad . . . below Mount Hermon.* Halak, southwest of the Dead Sea (12:7), and Baal Gad (uncertain), below Hermon in the north (12:1, 5) mark the north–south limits.

11:18 *a long time.* The conquest took five or seven years (14:7, 10).

11:19 *not one city made a treaty of peace.* Except for Gibeon, there is no lull in the struggle.

11:20 *hardened their hearts.* This recalls the destruction of Egypt's army (Exod. 14:17; cf. Rom. 9:17). That God has "hardened [*hazaq*] their hearts" does not imply that the kings otherwise would have been submissive. Canaanite kings, excepting the Gibeonites, consistently show hostile intentions toward the Israelites (9:1–2; 10:1–4; 11:5). The correspondence from Canaan to Pharaoh in this period shows violent chaos in the city-states. The same and similar expressions describe the Lord hardening the heart of Pharaoh, resulting in the liberation of Israel. But Pharaoh already had a determined animosity (*hazaq*, Exod. 7:13, 22); he had oppressed the Hebrews and many others in perpetual slavery as well as inflicted genocide. Moreover, Pharaoh "hardened" (*kabed*) his own heart, breaking his promise to release the Hebrews (Exod. 8:15[11]). Pharaoh becoming more obstinate means that the Lord progressively revealed what were already Pharaoh's evil intentions. The Lord displayed before the nations the glory and judgment of God against Egypt and its gods (Exod. 12:12; 18:11).

11:21 *Anakites.* These warriors exhibit the pinnacle of power (Deut. 9:2). Caleb, who does not fear them (Num. 14:24, 30), subjugates Hebron's Anakites (Judg. 1:20).

11:22 *No Anakites . . . only in Gaza, Gath and Ashdod.* Some opposition survives the conquest, centered in Philistine cities (13:3).

11:23 *rest from war.* "Rest" (*shaqat*) means "to be quiet, have peace," showing that the wilderness wandering is over and the people are free from the sounds of battle (14:15; Judg. 3:11). Disengagement from their enemies enables them to have a stable and prosperous everyday life. "Resting place" (*nuah*) is common in Joshua (e.g., 1:13; NIV: "rest"). And the promise of security is being fulfilled (1:13, 15; Deut. 12:9–10).

12:1 *east of the Jordan.* The Transjordan plateau is bounded on the south by the River Arnon (Num. 21:13) and on the north by Mount Hermon.

12:2 *Sihon . . . Heshbon.* Sihon possessed Ammonite and Moabite lands, from the Jabbok River (north) to the Arnon (south) (Num. 21:21–30). Heshbon, his capital, if it is Tell Hesban, is fourteen miles southwest of Amman.

12:4 *Og king of Bashan.* Og controlled the fertile region Bashan (Num. 32:33; Deut. 32:14), east of the Jordan Valley, from Gilead (south) to Hermon (north) (Num. 21:33–35).

Rephaites. These members of a giant-sized people were dispossessed, leaving Og the last one (Deut. 2:10–11, 20–21). His gargantuan iron bed (13.5 by 6 feet) remained in Rabbah (Deut. 3:11).

12:6 *Moses, the servant of the* LORD. This description occurs fourteen times in Joshua, twice here. The iconic hero, however, is still only second to the Lord.

possession. "Possession" (*yᵉrushah*) refers to the tribal "inheritance" from the Lord. The Transjordan tribes have fulfilled their obligation to their fellow Israelites (1:15; Deut. 3:20). Defeat of the Amorites is the first stage of fulfilling the promise (Num. 32:33; Deut. 2:31–3:3), and it alarms the Cisjordan Canaanites (2:10; 9:10).

12:7 *list of the kings.* Verses 9–24 name thirty-one kings.

conquered on the west side of the Jordan . . . gave. "Defeated" (*nakah*; NIV: "conquered") and "gave" (*natan*) parallel Moses (12:6), elevating Joshua's achievements. The geographical breadth is from Lebanon (northwest) to Halak (southeast), east of Edom's Seir (11:17).

inheritance . . . tribal divisions. The singular "possession/inheritance" indicates the whole, and the plural "allotments" (NIV: "divisions") indicates the distributed parcels (11:23).

12:8 *The lands included . . . the lands of.* The six geographical sectors (10:40; 11:16) are inhabited by six nations (3:10; 9:1; 11:3; 24:11).

12:9 *Jericho . . . Ai.* The first two cities to fall (chaps. 6–8) illustrate Israel's obedience and disobedience.

12:10 *Jerusalem . . . Hebron.* Jerusalem's Adoni-Zedek has led the southern coalition (10:1–3). The city is not permanently captured until the reign of David (15:63; 2 Sam. 5:6–9). On the Anakites of Hebron, see 11:21.

12:13 *Geder.* This unknown site, appearing only here in the Old Testament, may be Khirbet Jedur, near Bethlehem and Hebron.

12:14 *Hormah . . . Arad.* These cities, located in the Negev (15:30; 19:4; Judg. 1:16–17), are not in the battle narratives and come from the wilderness narratives (Num. 14:45; 21:1–3). "Hormah" (*hormah*) is related to *herem* ("destruction"; on the term, see "Christian Interpretation" in the introduction) and is associated with Israel's aborted first attempt to enter the land (Num. 14:45). Its inclusion in the victory list reverses that painful memory.

12:15 *Adullam.* This city (in Judah, 15:35) is known for its cave where David takes refuge from Saul (1 Sam. 22).

12:16 *Bethel.* Bethel is with Ai (12:9), whose king probably rules over Bethel (cf. Judg. 1:22–26). Historically, Bethel is important to Israel's religious life (Gen. 35; Amos 3:14).

12:17–18 *Tappuah . . . Hepher . . . Aphek . . . Lasharon.* These four cities are in the central region (as Bethel) and absent in the narratives.

12:21–22 *Taanach . . . Megiddo . . . Kedesh . . . Carmel.* These four (north), including the significant cities Taanach and Megiddo, are also absent in the narratives, showing that the narratives do not base inclusion on strategic importance alone.

12:23 *Gilgal.* The Greek text reads "Galilee" (cf. ESV, NRSV), which suits the context of the northern region. If "Gilgal" is correct, it is not Gilgal near Jericho in the central area (4:19).[3]

12:24 *Tirzah.* The last city named is in the central highlands and appears out of place geographically in the arrangement of the list, but it puts the Israelite conquests geographically nearer to their strongholds in central Canaan. Later, Tirzah is the first capital of the northern tribes (1 Kings 14–16).

Theological Insights

Theologically, this passage contributes appreciably to the chief message: God, the Divine Warrior, fulfills his promise. Although Moses and Joshua are named the conquerors, the passage attributes victory ultimately to the Lord (11:20). They are but "servants of the LORD" (cf. 12:6), for it is God who orchestrates the conquest. By "hardening" the resolve of the Canaanites, the Lord sets Israel on an arduous but victorious course (11:18). This hardening exposes the hostilities of the Canaanites (10:1–2; 11:1–5; cf. Exod. 4:21) and leads to the destruction of the religious system and immorality that threaten to seduce Israel (Deut. 7:4).[4] The opposition is evidently fiercer than the few battle stories indicate ("long time," 11:18). The Transjordan kings, for example, aggressively oppose Israel using divination despite their pleas for peaceful relations (Num. 21:21–23, 33–34; 22:4–6). The real enemy is the Israelites' fear, not the Canaanites per se. Repeatedly, it is necessary for the Lord to dissuade them from their fears (Deut. 20:3; Josh. 8:1; 10:8), for the Canaanites have the military advantage in their eyes (cf. Num. 13:28–33). The ultimate purpose is to show that the Lord is the only true God (cf. Exod.

Mount Hermon, shown here, is the northern boundary of the territory now controlled by the Israelites. Formerly under the control of Og, king of Bashan, this region is one of the first areas conquered just prior to the Israelite entrance into the promised land.

9:16; Rom. 9:17). The people's faith is tried repeatedly, yet they demonstrate their faithfulness (11:20, 23). Unlike the generation in the wilderness, Joshua's generation believes God's word, undeterred by Canaan's powerful city-states.

That the passage's scope is broad geographically and numerically shows that Canaan suffers an irreversible blow. The land becomes known as "Eretz Israel," the land of Israel (e.g., 1 Sam. 13:19). Future generations can look back to this celebrated time when their forefathers proved themselves loyal subjects. Joshua's victories can function as an exhortation to eradicate sin in their midst and restore their broken relationship with God. Although there is much more to be done in securing their inheritance, the people can take solace that if God secures such astounding victories by such extraordinary means, they can persevere confidently in their future challenges.

Teaching the Text

This passage revisits the theological message of the first half of the book, since it sums up chapters 1–12. The promissory expectation of 1:2–6 has its fulfillment stated in the passage (11:16–17, 23). "Then the land had rest from war" (11:23b) sums up the consequence of the battles listed in chapter 12. "Rest" means that there was a cessation of prolonged war, liberating the people to work and live in peace and prosperity. The writer to the Hebrews shows that the Israelites entered into God's "rest" (e.g., Josh. 21:44), but the promise of "rest" ultimately pointed ahead to the eternal rest that has been secured forever through Jesus (Heb. 4:1–11).

This passage also shows the outcome of those who are hostile toward the Israelites. The king/city list is included to show that God's promises are fulfilled but also to warn any who might consider rebellion against the Lord, including the Israelites themselves (6:18). The detailed list gives a historical picture of what God has accomplished. The stories are not entertaining fiction. Also Israelite readers of this passage for generations to come are residents of the cities named. This gives them a historical linkage with the past when their ancestors out of faith defeated the mighty fortresses that once dominated the land. They too must consider how they will respond to similar challenges in their own day. In Israel's history, generations face the questions of obedience and faith when neighboring armies and great empires threaten to dispossess them. Christians too learn from these heroes of the faith who carry out tasks they are not humanly capable of completing apart from the Divine Warrior (e.g., Heb. 11). One outcome of recalling God's salvation of Israel is to serve as instruction for us today (1 Cor. 10:6, 11).

The widespread opposition to the Israelites is motivated by fear. Ancient Near Eastern kings feared "outsiders" because they considered them enemies of their rule and civilization. This included their authoritarian power and the intellectual environment of polytheism that sustained their government and social structure in Canaan. What the kings feared was Yahweh and the people's devotion to him alone, which they saw as undermining their treaties and relationships with other cities (e.g., Gibeonites, chap. 9). Similarly, Christians can expect opposition to the gospel they proclaim and live out. The hostility in character and intensity will vary in different circumstances, but every Christian holds in common the potential of participating in the suffering of Christ (Matt. 10:16–25; 1 Pet. 4:12–19).

Illustrating the Text

Fear is one of the great enemies of faith.

History: President Franklin D. Roosevelt famously declared, "Let me assert my firm belief that the only thing we have to fear is fear itself—nameless, unreasoning, unjustified terror which paralyzes needed efforts to convert retreat into advance." These words were spoken during the height of the first Great Depression and were a reminder that it was fear that was helping stoke the fire of economic turmoil.[5] Roosevelt knew personally the physical disability of paralysis in his legs due to contracting polio when thirty-nine years old. Yet he overcame his fears and resumed his political career, achieving the highest office in the nation. Fear is also one of the great enemies of faith, as it paralyzes us from taking important steps of obedience. For example, if we fear our future economic security, we might be paralyzed when it comes to investing financially in the kingdom of God. If we are afraid of rejection, we might be paralyzed from sharing the gospel. The antidote to fear is faith expressed in acts of obedience. It is when we take steps of faith that we realize the Lord is powerful and faithful.

Trust is a response learned through steps of faith.

Comics: *Peanuts*, by Charles M. Schulz. In this popular comic strip, an ongoing challenge for Charlie Brown is to kick the football that his friend Lucy offers to hold for him. Each time Charlie runs up to kick the ball, Lucy pulls it away at the last moment, so Charlie falls on his backside. After this happens to poor Charlie Brown numerous times, he wavers despite Lucy's assurance that she will really, really hold the ball this time. Unfortunately, he does not learn. We all have experiences like Charlie Brown, times when people make empty promises and we end up falling on our backside. The impact is that we can learn to harbor a distrust of people. Sadly, we can take this deep distrust to our relationship with God. What is the solution? To realize that because of the nature of God (he is truthful, faithful, and sovereign), he can always be trusted.

The Lord invites you into his rest.

Testimony: In Matthew 11:28–30, Jesus extends an invitation to his disciples to come to him for rest. Share a story from your own life that describes a time of weariness, discouragement, or fear and how, by responding to the invitation to turn your heart to the Lord, you experienced rest for your soul.

The Transjordan Land

Big Idea *Faithful obedience by God's people results in them receiving their inheritance.*

Understanding the Text

The Text in Context

After the battles are recalled in chapters 1–12, the author turns to the goal of the hard-fought victories—the distribution of the land. Chapter 13 introduces the second half of the book (chaps. 13–24), which focuses on the tribal allotments (chaps. 13–19). The location remains Gilgal (14:6) until the camp moves to Shiloh for the final distribution (chap. 18). However, the relationship of setting the boundaries for the Transjordan tribes in chapter 13 and Joshua's farewell address at Shiloh to the two and a half tribes may mean that the distribution for these tribes is also at Shiloh (22:1–9).

Chapter 13 has two parts: (1) introduction to the distribution of the whole land (13:1–14) and (2) distribution of the land for the Transjordan tribes (13:15–33). Each part ends with the same observation in similar wording: "But to the tribe Levi, [Moses] gave / had given no inheritance" (13:14, 33). Reference to the Levites' inheritance prepares the reader for chapter 21's naming of their forty-eight cities.

(1) Verses 1–14 name peoples and regions west of the Jordan River that remain to be taken by the nine and a half tribes (13:1–7), recount Moses's victory over the Transjordan region and describe the lands delegated to the two and a half tribes (13:8–13), and comment on the Levites' special inheritance (13:14).

(2) Verses 15–33 describe the inheritance that Moses has given to Reuben (13:15–23), Gad (13:24–28), and the half tribe of Manasseh (13:29–32). Each section begins (13:15, 24, 29) and concludes (13:23, 28, 31) with parallel formulaic

The Israelites have not yet conquered the region of the Philistines, which would include the cities of Gaza, Ashdod, Ashkelon, Gath, and Ekron and the territory they controlled along the southwest coastal plain. In this relief from Medinet Habu, Egypt, which depicts the capture of the invading Sea Peoples by Ramesses III (twelfth century BC), Philistines can be identified by their distinctive feathered headdresses.

descriptions. Verse 32 provides a summary, and verse 33 ends the chapter, commenting again on the Levites' inheritance.

Historical and Cultural Background

The Philistines were not ethnic Canaanites but immigrants from the Aegean region. They were related to the Peleset, who were members of the non-Semitic "Sea Peoples," as they are called in an Egyptian text. They were a loose confederation of peoples whose sweeping and gradual migrations by sea and land resulted in political and cultural chaos across Asia Minor, Syria, and Canaan, and also challenged Egypt (ca. 1300–1150 BC). The name Palestine derives from the name Philistines. The Philistines eventually occupied Gaza, Ashdod, Ashkelon, Gath, and Ekron along the southwest coastal plain. The five Philistine rulers bore the title *seren* ("leaders/tyrants"), not *melek* ("king"), suggesting that the five made up a council of leadership. The Philistines remained formidable opponents until David's reign (Judg. 14:1; 1 Sam. 31; 2 Sam. 5:17–25). They developed iron before the Israelites, which gave them a cultural and military advantage (1 Sam. 13:19–22).

Interpretive Insights

13:2–3 *Philistines . . . Geshurites . . . Avvites.* The geographical locations are in the southwest region, with the land of the Philistines most prominent (see "Historical and Cultural Background," above). These "Geshurites" are in the south (cf. 1 Sam. 27:8), not the same as those across the Jordan (13:13; 2 Sam. 3:3). The "Avvites" are obscure; they are displaced by the

- The Lord encourages Israel by promising to acquire for it the yet-unconquered cities and territories.
- The Lord reminds Israel of his faithfulness by giving to the Transjordan tribes the land promised by Moses.
- The twelve tribes of Israel remain unified around the promises.
- Joshua brings to completion Moses's promise to the Transjordan tribes.

Caphtorim, a member of the Sea Peoples (Deut. 2:23).

13:4 *Sidonians.* The strip of northern coastal land is occupied by the Phoenicians, whose chief cities are Sidon and Tyre ("Greater Sidon," 11:8; 19:28).[1]

13:5 *Byblos . . . Lebanon.* Byblos (ancient Gebal) is a Phoenician city on the coast north of modern Beirut. Lebanon is the western mountain range just east of the coast.

13:6–7 *I myself will drive out.* God will complete the victory, as he first promised (3:10; Exod. 34:24). Israel fails to "drive out" some enemies (13:13), indicating that Joshua and his generation must rely on the Lord to finish the task (23:5, 13).

allocate . . . divide. Joshua oversees the final allotments to the tribes—a fitting reward for his faithful obedience.

13:8 *Moses had given . . . had assigned.* Joshua will send home the eastern tribes to their possessions (22:1–6) in fulfillment of Moses's provision (Num. 21:23–26; 32:33), showing continuity in Israel's leadership.

13:10 *all the towns of Sihon.* Sihon's territory reaches from the Arnon River to the area of the city Heshbon.

13:12 *whole kingdom of Og.* Og's territory continues north from Heshbon to Mount Hermon.

13:13 *Geshur and Maakah.* These regions are northeast of the Sea of Galilee in the Golan, with the Yarmuk River their southern border and Mount Hermon the northern border, located at the western border of Bashan (12:5; see 2 Sam. 3:3; 10:6–8).

13:14 *tribe of Levi . . . food offerings.* The Levites enjoy a special relationship to God; they receive a portion of the offerings from the altar offered by the people (13:33; Num. 18:20–24).

13:15 *Reuben.* The first official allotment goes to Reuben (13:15–23), Jacob's firstborn by Leah (Gen. 29:32); Reuben receives Sihon's territory.

13:18 *Jahaz.* Jahaz is where Israel has defeated Sihon (Num. 21:23).

13:22 *Balaam.* Balak king of Moab hired this diviner to curse Israel, but the Lord turned Balaam's imprecations into blessings (24:9–10; Num. 22–24). Balaam, along with the princes of Midian, who led Israel into idolatry, was killed by Moses's army (Num. 31:8). Balaam became a symbol of opposition to the gospel (2 Pet. 2:15; Rev. 2:14).

13:24 *Gad.* Gad was born to Jacob's wife Leah by her surrogate, her servant Zilpah (Gen. 30:11). The inheritances of Gad's tribe and the half tribe of Manasseh generally correspond to Og's territory. Gad's possession ranges roughly from Heshbon in the south to Mahanaim in the north.

13:29 *Manasseh.* He is the elder son of Joseph (Gen. 41:51). This inheritance covers the Bashan territory, ranging in the south from Mahanaim to Mount Hermon in the north (13:29–31).

13:31 *Makir.* He is the grandson of Joseph, born to his son Manasseh (Gen.

50:23). His descendants are especially influential, for their name equates to the tribe of Manasseh.

Theological Insights

Chapter 13 describes the outcome of Israel's wars—possession of the promised land. This passage encourages Israel, showing that the Lord is fulfilling his promises. It describes the territories east of the Jordan River that God has already secured for the two and a half tribes. Although the remaining tribes have yet to receive their inheritance, they can take solace that the promises will be fulfilled to them as well. Although the land is divided by the Jordan, the twelve tribes have a historical and theological unity that transcends geography. The whole nation fights together in Transjordan against the Amorite kings and the tribes are united in the battles fought west of the Jordan. The tribes share the common history of the Sinai revelation and the continuity in leadership between Moses and Joshua.

The chapter is also an encouragement because the Lord guarantees Israel that the remaining territories will someday fall into the nation's hands (13:6). This happens during the kingships of David and Solomon. As a consequence later readers of the tribal distribution can be encouraged that although their land is under siege at various times and they are even at times dispossessed, the Lord can yet again recover the land for a repentant Israel. This occurs when the people return from the Assyrian and Babylonian exiles (sixth century). History confirms what the Lord assures. The conquest is only the beginning of the divine purpose for Israel in the land.

This passage also illustrates that there are rewards for obedience. However, rewards are grounded in acts of divine grace, not based merely on commercial exchange. The reward for Israel's obedience is its peaceful and prosperous occupation of the land, but it is also "promised" land that the Lord graciously bequeathed to Israel's fathers. The recurring theme in the book of Joshua is the Lord's call for obedience, which results in victory, but the call for obedience presupposes a covenant bond resting on God's election of Israel, not on Israel's national reputation (Deut. 7:6–8). Moreover, Israel's election is not based on its righteousness. The defeat of the Canaanites is because of the Canaanites' wickedness (Deut. 9:4–6). The Lord does not disregard the nations; rather, the deliverance of the nations is his ultimate goal (Exod. 19:5–6; Deut. 4:4–8; 32:8). Reward for obedience in the Bible is not a simple payment for services rendered. Rather, obedience comes from faith and a thankful heart for what God has already done in a person's life—in this case, the life of the nation.

Teaching the Text

The passage shows that the promissory inheritance is a gift grounded in God's prior covenantal relationship with Israel. "Inheritance" is the key term that repeatedly occurs in the chapter. The primary object of God's gift of the land is Israel's life with him. The land is his, and it is where he

dwells among his people. The *relationship* with God is the true value of the inheritance they enjoy. The passage also speaks theologically to Christian readers, whose reward is their identity in and life with Christ in the consummated kingdom. "Reward" is the realization of the promise that is the

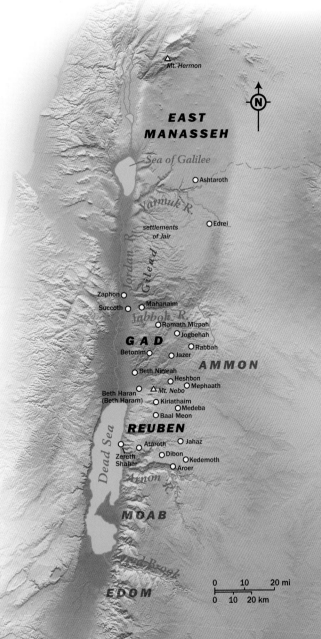

The Gadites, the Reubenites, and the half tribe of Manasseh receive allotments in the Transjordanian territory that Israel has taken from Sihon, king of the Amorites, and Og, king of Bashan.

All the tribes of Israel receive an inheritance in the promised land. For all the tribes except Levi, that inheritance is an allotment of land. For the Levites, who will serve at the sanctuary, their inheritance will be cities throughout the promised land and the food offerings presented to the Lord. This Egyptian tomb painting shows an offering table piled high with food for the god Anubis (Temple of Hatshepsut, Karnak, Egypt, sixteenth century BC).

eschatological worship of God (e.g., Matt. 5:12; Heb. 10:35–36; 11:6).

The naming of the Transjordan tribes' inheritance at the start of the land distribution (chaps. 13–19) reflects the theme of "all Israel" in the book. Also, although the Levites receive no land, their inheritance is not omitted in the reporting of the distribution of the land (13:14, 33; 18:7; 21:1–45). The twelve tribes achieve purposeful unity by their common commitment to the Lord. The two and a half tribes forgo peace to maintain the unity of the nation. They agree to join their brother tribes for the long battles ahead and win with them an inheritance for all. The Transjordan tribes leave their privileged lands and families for the common good of the covenant community in the land. The memorial altar they erect, although misunderstood at first by their brother tribes, indicates their covenant devotion to the Lord and zeal for their kin (22:10). God calls Christians to set aside personal preferences, seeking unity in the body of Christ, so that the church might be effective as a witness to the world (John 17:21–23; Rom. 15:1–7; Eph. 4:1–6).

Another teaching point is that there remains a task for the Israelites to achieve. The Israelites secure the land, enjoying a newfound peace and prosperity. Yet there are enclaves of enemies that remain (13:2–7). What the Israelites have witnessed in their battles is that the Lord fights for them (10:42; 23:3, 10). He promises anew that he will defeat the remaining Canaanites: "I myself will drive them out" (13:6). The church collective has the responsibility to spread the gospel, to maintain a Christian witness, and where possible to impact culture as salt and light (Matt. 5:13–16; John 17:18; Rom. 10:13–17). Christians must undertake Jesus's prayer: "Your kingdom come, your will be done, on earth as it is in heaven" (Matt. 6:10).

Illustrating the Text

The unity of God's people is to be a priority for all.

Music: For an orchestra to be effective there must be one designated leader, with all the members of the orchestra agreeing to yield to that person's leadership. Imagine if the strings section decided they did not like the chosen music and so began playing their own music. The result would be disastrous.

This illustration would be particularly effective if you have people with instruments on the stage and each began playing his or her own, individual music. Now, imagine that all the sections (string, brass, woodwind, and percussion) yield to the authority of the leader and play their music together. The music would be beautiful. If you have the sections represented on stage, have them now play together. The leader, or head, of the church is Jesus Christ. When every believer yields to his authority, the church can accomplish great things for the kingdom of God. What might it look like if, rather than every person seeking his or her own agenda, we worked together in unity, under the authority of Jesus Christ?

Faith is strengthened as we remember the faithfulness of God.

Testimony: God's victory through Joshua and the Israelites, against all odds, became a great reminder to the people of the faithfulness and sovereignty of the Lord. But the power of these events to strengthen the faith of Israel would last only as long as they continued to remember what God had done. The same is true for us. Prior to the service or class, select two or three people to share short testimonies of how they have seen the Lord fulfill his promises in their lives.

The promise of spiritual inheritance for all Christians is a blessing.

News Story: There are many aspects of our spiritual inheritance (i.e., the promises of God) that we have already experienced. Examples include the presence of the Holy Spirit, the peace of Jesus, and the Bible. But there are still promises to come, such as the promise of eternal life. And we are to live in light of these future promises. When Princess Diana died in 1997, her will stipulated that her multimillion-dollar estate would be evenly divided between her two sons, Prince William and Prince Harry. But the money was held in trust until they reached the age of thirty (Diana's will originally stipulated twenty-five, but it was changed by the executors of the will). Prince William and Prince Harry could live, in the time of waiting, in the security of knowing that this money would be theirs.[2] In the same way, every Christian will inherit the future promises of God and can live, in the meantime, in the security of knowing that these promises will be theirs.

Caleb's Inheritance

Big Idea *God fulfills his assurances to his servants by granting them promised blessings.*

Understanding the Text

The Text in Context

After the description of the Transjordan allotments (chap. 13), chapter 14 introduces the parcels for the nine and a half tribes. Chapters 14–19 are a unit, framed by the same reference to Joshua, Eleazar, and the tribal leaders who oversee the distribution at Gilgal and then Shiloh (14:1; 19:51). Chapters 14–17 are a subsection, describing the allocations of the major southern tribe (Judah, chaps. 14–15) and northern tribes (Ephraim and Manasseh, chaps. 16–17). Chapter 14 has two parts: (1) Verses 1–5 introduce chapters 14–19, which give the inheritance for the remaining nine and a half tribes. (2) Verses 6–15 begin the land distribution for Judah by focusing on Caleb, Judah's favorite son. Acknowledgment of Levi's inheritance in 13:14, 33 occurs again in 14:3b, 4b.

Since Caleb's story represents the main idea of the book—faith in God's word—his request appears first (14:6–15). His trust in the Lord's promise to give the land to Israel has resulted in his successful entrance into the land. Whereas his generation perished in the wilderness, Caleb acquires his inheritance (Num. 14:24). A second report on Caleb's inheritance occurs in 15:13–19, giving more details about his family's possession. There are five accounts of special requests for land grants: Caleb (14:6–15), Aksah (15:18–19), Zelophehad's daughters (17:3–6), Joseph's tribes (17:14–18), and Levi's descendants (21:1–3). Chapter 14's introduction provides new information about the process of allocating the land. First, Joshua is joined by Eleazar and representative heads of the tribes to supervise the distribution (14:1). Second, the allotments are determined by casting lots (14:2). Third, the double inheritance of Joseph's tribe (Manasseh and Ephraim) retains the traditional twelve-tribe configuration, since Levi does not receive a parcel (14:3–4).

Tribal inheritances are assigned by lot. Cultures of the ancient Near East, including Israel, believed that when lots were cast, their god controlled the outcome. Dice were sometimes used. This pair is from Jerusalem (Herodian period).

Historical and Cultural Background

Casting lots was a widely practiced form of divination in the ancient Near East. However, it was not oracular divination but served to discern the will of the gods in making a choice, such as choosing the order of temple personnel (1 Chron. 25:8), a sacrificial animal (Lev. 16:8), or division of land (Josh. 14:2; 18:6; 21:4). The word *goral* (14:2) appears twenty-six times in Joshua, translated "lot" or "allotment" (i.e., the assigned portion), used primarily of land division. In the ancient Near East the lots were possibly pebbles, stones, or clay pieces. In one method the lots were placed in a container that was then shaken, forcing the lot out. Another possibly involved tossing the lot in the container or on the ground (cf. Prov. 16:33). Many times the procedure was in the presence of the gods, since it was deemed a divine decision (e.g., "presence of the Lord," 18:6, 8, 10; cf. 19:51). The method employed by the Israelites is uncertain. It was possibly related to the Urim and Thummim that were placed (in a pouch?) in the breastplate of the high priest (Lev. 8:8) and used for divine decision making (Num. 27:21).

Interpretive Insights

14:1 *Eleazar the priest.* Eleazar is involved because of the casting of lots, probably the Urim and Thummim (Num. 27:15–23). He, unlike his father, Aaron, survives the wilderness since he is a member of the new generation. His burial in Canaan is a sign of God's faithfulness to his promises (24:33).

14:2 *assigned by lot.* "By lot" (*beʿgoral*) is at the head of the Hebrew sentence,

emphasizing its role in revealing the divine will (see "Historical and Cultural Background").

the Lord had commanded through Moses. The dimensions of each allotment must correspond to the population base of the tribe (Num. 26:52–56; cf. Joseph's allotments, 17:14–18).

14:4 *The Levites received no share.* The absence of a grant to Levi provides one of the two tracts granted to Joseph (Ephraim and Manasseh) because of its numerous population, preserving the twelve-tribe number.

14:6 *the people of Judah approached.* Judah as the first tribe to approach Joshua reflects its zeal for its promised possessions (cf. 21:1). This contrasts with Joshua's perplexity over the seven tribes that are reluctant to come forward (18:2–3).

Caleb . . . said to him. Caleb and his family (cf. 15:13–19) represent the ideal faith by claiming and achieving what God has promised. Caleb has the same courageous spirit that he has shown at Kadesh Barnea (Num. 14:24). Caleb is a Kenizzite (Kenaz/Kenez), whose people have been absorbed into the tribe of Judah (cf. Num. 13:6). He is the older brother to Kenaz (15:17; Judg. 3:9). The name Kenaz may reflect a genealogical linkage with the Edomites

Why These Detailed Lists?

To the casual reader the extensive lists of boundaries, cities, and territories in Joshua have no modern relevance. But that the lists are detailed and carefully follow literary schemes shows their importance to the author. The lists in chapters 13–19 follow different patterns: boundary and city lists, land grants for individuals, and various regularly appearing features, such as the phrase "according to its clans / by their clans," which occurs twenty-eight times in chapters 13–19 (e.g., 13:15; 15:1; 16:5; 18:11; 19:1). The scope of the detail for each tribe reflects the importance attributed to the tribe—for instance, Judah receives the most extensive description (14:6–15:63). Theologically, (1) these lists demonstrate that the covenant promises are fulfilled; (2) the details remind future descendants of the costly wars; (3) the stories of individuals receiving land grants (e.g., Caleb) and the repetitious reference to "clans" show God's interest in individuals and families; (4) the descriptions seal the legality of claims on the land by clans; and (5) the possession of the land was evidence of covenant membership; thus the specifics of topography and the naming of towns give concrete expression to participation in the inheritance.[a]

[a] Howard, *Joshua*, 315–23.

(Gen. 36:11, 15, 42). Othniel as "son of Kenaz" is nephew to Caleb. The land of the Kenizzites is promised to Abraham's descendants (Gen. 15:19).

You know. In the Hebrew the inclusion of the pronoun "you" (*'attah*), preceding the verb, highlights "you"; Joshua is a witness to the bequest by the Lord (through Moses) (Num. 14:24, 30).

Moses the man of God. The honorific title "the man of God" reinforces the authority by which Caleb makes his appeal (Deut. 33:1).

14:7 *forty years.* By the reference to "eighty-five years old" (14:10), the conquest can be calculated to have lasted five or seven years.

Moses the servant of the LORD. Caleb presents his case with another reference to Moses's stature.

according to my convictions. Literally, "as with my heart," the phrase means "exactly what I thought."[1] Caleb reports his fervent belief, not what others necessarily want to hear.

14:8 *my fellow Israelites.* Caleb refers to the ten Israelite spies who gave the negative report.

made the hearts . . . melt. Literally, "melted the heart," this is an ironic twist on the fear of Israel's enemies at the conquest (2:9, 24). "The hearts of the people" contrasts with Caleb's courageous "heart" ("convictions," 14:7).

wholeheartedly. The word "wholeheartedly" translates the idiom "to fill/fulfill after" (*mille' 'ahare*), meaning "to be loyal to" (Deut. 1:36). Its three appearances show progression: Caleb's loyalty to God (14:8), to Moses's God (14:9), and to Israel's God (14:14).[2] It characterizes Caleb's faithfulness (Num. 14:24; 32:12), in contrast with the disloyal majority report (Num. 32:11; cf. 1 Kings 11:6).

14:9 *your feet have walked.* The language recalls the promise (1:3; cf. Deut. 1:36; 11:24); as a figure of speech, it indicates possession (Deut. 2:5).

14:10 *has kept me alive.* The term "preserved" (*heheyah*) also describes Rahab's survival ("spare," 2:13; 6:25). Caleb recognizes that his continued existence results from God's benevolent promise (Num. 14:30, 38).

forty-five years. The number is approximate: about forty years for the wilderness and five years for the conquest.

Today. Caleb's claim is forcefully stated, clear-cut, and irrefutable.

14:11 *as strong today.* "Strong" (*hazaq*) may be an irony since the ten spies report that Canaan's inhabitants are "stronger" than Israel (Num. 13:31).

to go out. The idiom "for going and coming" expresses "daily tasks" (HCSB) or competence in leadership (Num. 27:17; 1 Kings 3:7).

14:12 *that day.* The expression occurs twice in the verse (NIV: "that day . . . then"), capturing the definiteness of the events.

Anakites. They are remembered for their imposing size (Num. 13:28, 33), creating fear among the people. However, Caleb relishes the challenge they present (15:14).

but, the LORD helping me. His courage and victory assume that the source of his strength is the Lord, not himself.

14:13 *Joshua blessed Caleb.* Joshua invokes God's favor; "bless" (*barak*) indicates peace and prosperity.

Hebron. Hebron is significant in Israel's history—the burial site of Sarah (Gen. 23:19), a Levitical possession (Josh. 21:13), and David's first capital (2 Sam. 2:11).

14:15 *Kiriath Arba.* Literally, "the city of Arba," it is named for the leader Arba; that Hebron eventually lost its connection with the Anakites shows Caleb's report is right (Num. 13:22–33; 14:24).

Theological Insights

Chapter 14 is another testimony to the major theme of the book—God's gift of the land. That Caleb's story is the narrative's focal interest amplifies the chapter's role, for his faith and his reward are examples of the author's message. If Caleb's generation had agreed to his exhortation to press ahead into the land (Num. 13:30–31), the people would have obtained their inheritance. His zeal for the inheritance is a relevant message for future generations, especially those that struggle with faith and

Caleb is given Hebron as his inheritance. Shown here is the southern hill country of Judah near the modern city of Hebron.

courage. Caleb is a prime example of the Lord's instructions to Joshua, "Be strong and courageous" (1:6; Deut. 31:23).

Another important aspect of the promise-fulfillment theme in this chapter is the extent of the promised inheritance. When Caleb remarks, "Just as the LORD promised, he has kept me alive" (14:10), he shows that the promises are intended for individual families, not only for collective tribal groups. God sees individuals and their individual journeys of faith. The promises are also perpetual: "your inheritance . . . your children forever" (14:9). God will not withdraw his promise. Only Israel's sinful behavior results in the dispossession of the land. Although this occurs at the exile of Judah in the sixth century, the exiles return and reinhabit the land. It is a time of chastening, not a permanent rejection.

The casting of lots is one means whereby the people discover the will of God. No aspect of the promise and its fulfillment is left to chance. Chapters 18–19 specify that the lots are thrown in the "presence of the LORD" (18:6, 8, 10) and at the entrance of the sacred tent (19:51). The casting of lots is assumed by the Israelites to be under the direction of the Lord (Prov. 16:33). Lots are used for settling disputes (Prov. 18:18), identifying the guilty (Jon. 1:7; cf. 1 Sam. 14:41), and selecting for service (e.g., Lev. 16:8; Acts 1:26).

Teaching the Text

The chief teaching goal is to show that Caleb has a full life of persevering faith despite obstacles from within and from outside the community of faith. The threats to his faith are the negative report of his ten fellow spies, his old age, and the formidable opposition of the Canaanites. Yet his trust in the Lord's word of promise sustains him during the long forty-five-year wait. The apostle Paul expresses similarly the exhortation to carry on: "Let us not become weary in doing good, for at the proper time we will reap a harvest if we do not give up" (Gal. 6:9; see also 2 Thess. 3:13).

The story of Caleb's life as a whole presents another opportunity to show how the book of Joshua indicates the grace of God liberally extended to all those who place faith in him. Caleb is a "Kenizzite" (14:6, 14) who receives the promised inheritance because "he followed the LORD" (14:14). The primary definition of a covenant member is loyalty to God, not one's ethnicity. The recurring theme of the insider-outsider appears again in the distribution of the land.[3] Rahab and the Gibeonites are outside the covenant initially, but they become "insiders" because they submit to the Lord and his people (chaps. 6; 9). We cannot permit ethnic divisions in the church, lest our mission to announce the salvation of the Lord is impeded (Acts 11:17–18; Rom. 10:11–13; Eph. 2:14).

Last, the casting of lots deserves attention since it was the means by which the people discovered the will of God (14:2; 19:51). The relevant point is *not* the method of discovering God's will but one's careful dedication to *following* God's will (Num. 33:54–55; 34:13; Ps. 78:55). Since the New Testament reports only one casting of lots by the church (Acts 1:26; cf. Matt 27:35; Luke 1:9), it is foreign to the church's practice of learning God's will. The means by which Christians learn God's will today is primarily through prayer and the study of

Holy Scripture (Deut. 29:29; Rom. 1:10; 8:27; 12:2).

Illustrating the Text

Refuse to allow racism or ethnic distinctions to divide God's community of faith.

Christian Life: In her blog titled *Dear Pastor: From a Black Female Congregant*, Trillia Newbell talks about her perspective as a young black woman worshiping in a predominately white southern church in America. In the essay, Newbell talks specifically about culture and writes, "Overall the music, activities and general environment should consider the entire congregation. Did you catch that? I'm not just saying music, but really the activities as well. My church has had wonderful events, but they are often geared towards one audience. . . . If your church is truly seeking diversity (in any way) your activities must be diverse as well."[4] Newbell reminds us that racism can become integrated into the life of a church if it caters to one particular ethnicity. It is not enough to simply invite members of different ethnic groups to join us if we are asking them to adapt to us. It is important for churches to seek to reflect their community in worship style and activities. Ask your audience, "Are we willing to make changes in order to reach our community?"

Serve the Lord faithfully to the very end of your life.

Quote: *Nearing Home*, **by Billy Graham.** A common refrain heard from the elderly in many churches is, "I've done my time serving the church; it's time for a new generation to serve and lead." This sentiment is certainly not seen in the life and attitude of Caleb. In his book *Nearing Home*, evangelist Billy Graham provides advice and perspective to the elderly. He emphasizes the truth that the elderly should be leading the way. Graham writes, "Are we producing fruit that replenishes others? . . . Many elderly people, without realizing it, taint the purpose God has for them: to impact the younger generations by exemplifying reliance on Him and hope in His unchanging promises."[5] It would be particularly helpful to use a specific example from your congregation or the community of an elderly person whom others would know. Connect that example to the example of Caleb.

Remain faithful regardless of the obstacles you face in life.

Biography: Joni Eareckson Tada. In 1967, a diving accident left Joni Eareckson Tada a quadriplegic in a wheelchair, unable to use her hands. After two years of rehabilitation, she learned how to paint with a brush between her teeth. She has also told her story and expressed her faith in the Lord by writing numerous books. Joni could have given up. She could have become bitter toward God. Rather, she chose to remain faithful to the call of the Lord. Consider this quote from Eareckson that describes her fighting spirit and faithful life: "My weakness, that is, my quadriplegia, is my greatest asset because it forces me into the arms of Christ every single morning when I get up."[6]

Judah's Inheritance and Caleb's Family

Big Idea *The Lord's people receive promised blessings, because he honors their zeal for his word.*

Understanding the Text

The Text in Context

After the description of Caleb's inheritance (14:6–15), chapter 15 continues the account of Judah's inheritance. It is the longest and most detailed account of the tribes' allotments, due to Judah's importance in Israel's history. The chapter is highly organized. Verses 1 and 20 read the same, introducing each of two parts. (1) Verses 1–19 describe the borders (15:1–12) and tell the story of Caleb's family (15:13–19). (2) Verses 20–63 list the cities. The borders in 15:1–12 are bracketed by the two accounts of Caleb (14:6–15; 15:13–19), emphasizing his family's fervent faith in the Lord.

The borders are described according to their southern (15:1–4), eastern (15:5a),

northern (15:5b–11), and western (15:12a) boundaries. Verse 12b gives a summary statement. Although Judah is the southernmost tribal allotment, more detail traces the northern border than the southern in order

Precise descriptions of land boundaries similar to what is observed in Joshua have been found in Hittite treaties. For example, this thirteenth-century BC treaty inscribed on a bronze tablet confirms the detailed land boundaries between the territories ruled by the Hittite king Tudhaliya IV and those governed by King Karunta of Tarhuntassa that were agreed upon by the previous rulers of those lands.

to clarify the boundaries between Judah and its neighbors Dan and especially Benjamin, which shares its border with Judah (cf. 15:5–11 and 18:15–19). Unlike Benjamin, Dan's relationship to Judah was minimal because the Danites soon migrated north (Josh. 19:47; Judg. 1:34; 18:1–31). The author was uninterested in Dan's boundaries and only named its cities (19:40–48). A unique feature of Judah's allotment is its relationship to Simeon's, whose allocation of cities (no borders) falls within Judah's portion (19:1, 9). The two join forces to obtain their allotments (Judg. 1:3, 17), and eventually, Simeon is absorbed into Judah.

More cities are named in Judah's allotment than any other tribe, indicating its prestige. The cities are grouped according to region: the Negev (= south, 15:21–32), the western foothills (= lowland, i.e., Shephelah, 15:33–44), the Philistine coastal plain (15:45–47), the hill country (15:48–60), and the wilderness (15:61–62). The final verse describes Judah's failure to take possession of Jerusalem (15:63)—the chief city in Israel's history.

Historical and Cultural Background

The extensive descriptions of the tribal allotments in chapters 13–19 share many features known from documents in the ancient Near East, as early as the third millennium. Boundary descriptions and town lists in Joshua have parallels to treaties, land grants, and administrative texts from Sumer, Alalakh, Hatti, and Ugarit. Joshua's boundary descriptions in 8:30–35 and chapter 24, presented in the context of covenant, closely parallel Hittite treaties that detail the borders between lands. Catalogs of towns and persons from Alalakh and

Key Themes of Joshua 15:1–63

- The Lord gives Judah the largest tract of land.
- The Lord designates many cities, including those yet unconquered.
- Caleb's nephew Othniel and daughter Aksah show faith and courage, relying on the Lord's promises.
- Judah fails to drive out the Jebusites from Jerusalem.

Ugarit, similar to those in Joshua, function for administrative purposes (e.g., 15:21–62; 18:21–28). The typical pattern (but not always) is a preface, border description and/or town list, and a conclusion, a pattern also found in Joshua. That similar descriptions are attested in cuneiform texts of the second millennium suggests that the boundary/town list reports in Joshua are an authentic memory of the settlement period.[1]

Interpretive Insights

15:1 *extreme south.* Judah's border is the southernmost boundary of the land (Num. 34:3).

15:2–4 *Dead Sea . . . Mediterranean Sea.* The southern border runs roughly from the southernmost end of the Dead Sea (Salt Sea) westward to the Mediterranean Sea.

15:5 *eastern boundary . . . northern boundary.* The eastern boundary is the Dead Sea, beginning where the Jordan feeds into the sea. The northern boundary runs westward from the Dead Sea to the Mediterranean.

15:8 *Valley of Ben Hinnom.* This valley is on the southern slope of Jerusalem (18:16). It is notorious as the place for child sacrifice (2 Chron. 28:3; 33:6; Jer. 7:31). The Greek Old Testament at 18:16 translates it "Gehenna" (*gaienna*), which in New Testament times is the place for burning refuse. It became a picture of fiery judgment and is typically rendered "hell" (*geenna*, Matt. 5:29).

15:12 *Mediterranean Sea*. Literally, "Great Sea" (1:4; 15:47).

15:14 *Caleb drove out*. This second account of Caleb's capture of Hebron (1) supplies important details (14:6–15; cf. Judg. 1:10–15) and (2) shows the passing of the torch from the desert to the settlement generation.

Sheshai, Ahiman and Talmai. The ten rebellious spies feared these three Anakites (Num. 13:22; cf. Judg. 1:10–15), but Caleb's defeat of the Anakites vindicates his trust in God.

15:15 *he marched against . . . Debir*. Although the location is uncertain, Debir is commonly identified with Khirbet Rabud, southwest of Hebron. The inclusion of the former name Kiriath Sepher ("City of Scroll/Book") distinguishes it from other cities named Debir (13:26; 15:7). It also reminds readers that the city initially was populated by different ethnic groups.[2]

15:16 *my daughter Aksah in marriage*. Marriage to the daughter of a prospering landowner perhaps means receiving a handsome dowry (cf. 1 Sam. 18:17–28).

15:17 *Othniel son of Kenaz, Caleb's brother*. Othniel is Caleb's nephew and cousin to Aksah (cf. Judg. 1:13). He is especially remembered for his deliverance of Israel (Judg. 3:9–11). The diverse accounts of Debir's capture credit different parties: Joshua (10:38–39), Caleb (15:14–15), Othniel (15:16–17; Judg. 1:12–13), and Judah (Judg. 1:10–11). The best explanation for these variants is that the various narratives describe the capture from different levels as incremental to its completion.

15:18 *she urged him*. That Othniel captures Debir shows his faith and aggressive personality, but Aksah is as aggressive as, or even more so than, her husband. The passage does not say why it is necessary to press Othniel or why Caleb has not already offered a field. The story may have compressed two separate requests into the same scene, perhaps to underscore Aksah's admirable zeal. Othniel requests a "field," which the text assumes Caleb grants, and then the narrative focuses on Aksah's additional request for water in the arid Debir. Her persuasive appeal reflects her insistence on an inheritance (cf. Zelophehad's daughters, 17:3–5).

she got off her donkey. Aksah expresses respect for her father. The event is reminiscent of Rebekah's response at seeing Isaac for the first time (Gen. 24:64; cf. 1 Sam. 25:23).

15:19 *Do me a special favor*. (Cf. Judg. 1:15.) The literal rendering is "Give me a blessing." "Blessing" indicates favorable treatment. "Give" (*natan*) occurs three times in her request, showing that her request requires special benevolence.

land in the Negev . . . upper and lower springs. The "Negev," meaning also "south" and "southland," names the arid region south of Hebron. This area depends largely on rainfall for water. Two springs located near Khirbet Rabud, if this is ancient Debir, may correspond to the biblical description of the upper and lower springs.

15:32 *twenty-nine towns and their villages*. A fixed expression characterizes the town list: "X [number] cities with their villages." "Villages" (*hatserim*) refers to a town's suburbs. The parallel term, "towns" (*banot*; lit., "daughters"), occurs in verses 45 and 47 (NIV: "settlements"). The absence of the stock phrase for the Philistine cities may indicate that Judah has lost control (15:45–47; Judg. 1:18). These cities are given prominence among the areas remaining unconquered (11:22; 13:3).

15:63 *the Jebusites.* The Jebusites are members of the "seven nations" in Canaan (Deut. 7:1). Joshua defeats those in the hill country (9:1; 11:3; 12:8; 24:11) as God has promised (3:10). The Jebusites in Jerusalem, however, are only temporarily displaced (Judg. 1:8, 21; 19:12). Jerusalem finally falls when David reigns, and it becomes known as the "City of David" (2 Sam. 5:5–10). Bethlehem too holds that distinguished name in New Testament times, since it is the birthplace of David and of David's greater son, Jesus (Luke 2:4, 11).

to this day Jebusites live there with the people of Judah. The comment refers to a time before David, since the city is still occupied by the Jebusites. Recounting Judah's most glaring setback suggests that the account is historically authentic, not merely a politically motivated story. Both Judahites and Benjamites (Judg. 1:21) live with the Jebusites in Jerusalem. The Jebusites are among the remaining nations that lead to Israel's intermarriage and idolatry (Judg. 3:1–7). The precise relationship of Judah and Benjamin to Jerusalem is uncertain since it falls within the scope of both inheritances (15:8; 18:16, 28). Although the city is formally Benjamin's, the surrounding villages and fields may have been Judah's. Or perhaps the two tribes collaborated to displace the Jebusites, as in the case of Simeon and Judah (Judg. 1:3, 17), but failed to drive them out permanently.

Theological Insights

The fulfillment of promise is central to the theology of Joshua. Literary elements in the passage evoke memories of the patriarchs, such as the capture of Hebron, the donkey scene, and the idea of "blessing" (the key word in Genesis). The extensive boundaries and numerous cities given to Judah recall Jacob's blessing, which elevates the tribe over its brother tribes (Gen. 49:8–12). The passage shows that the fulfillment of the blessing for Judah is under way. The possession of so many cities recollects the promise to give Israel "cities you did not build" (Deut. 6:10), a promise that is fulfilled by Moses and Joshua (24:11–13). Moreover, the passage anticipates the future defeat of the Philistine cities and the possession of Jerusalem—the most sacred city in Israel's history. These cities elude capture, but they remain part of the inheritance that will yet fall into Judah's hands. The favorite son of Judah, King David, leads Judah and all Israel to claim what has been promised for the people (2 Sam. 5:5–10, 17–25; 8:1).

Another theological aspect of the chapter is the message of inclusion in the promised inheritance. Caleb is a Kenizzite (cf. 14:6) whose father is Jephunneh, who is said to be from the tribe of Judah, probably by adoption (Num. 13:6). The gift of land is for all those who profess allegiance to the Lord, regardless of ancestry (e.g., Rahab). The inclusion of a woman in the account is appropriate since women are important to the possession of the promises and have rights to ownership (cf. Zelophehad, Num. 27:1–11). What is required of them is the same trust in the Lord's promises as exhibited by the men. Aksah demonstrates the same measure of zeal and courage as her father, Caleb, and husband, Othniel.

The passage also shows that the Lord provides for his people. The Lord meets the needs of Israel as the tribes face the challenge of dispossessing hostile nations. Judah's territory includes choice land that enables the families to thrive (5:6; Exod. 3:8; Deut. 8:7–10). The parcel of land given to Othniel and Aksah also requires a natural water source for the land to reach its potential of rich harvest and growing herds. Aksah receives from her father the Lord's provision whereby her descendants will receive a profitable inheritance.

Teaching the Text

The description of Judah's inheritance shows that God accomplishes his promises on behalf of his people. The echoes of the ancestry of the tribe of Judah bring to mind the successes and failures of the man Judah and later of the tribe. Members of the tribe such as Caleb's family represent the best of God's people. Yet the tribe is not perfect in carrying out the assignment to drive out the nations. The defeat of the Jebusites of Jerusalem by Joshua is temporary (12:10; Judg. 1:8), and the permanent possession of the city is not achieved (15:63; Judg. 1:21). Nonetheless, God's plan via Judah's tribe for his people was not frustrated. Christians too experience success and failure in Christian faith,

but we should not be discouraged. God accomplishes his purposes for our lives, and we can press ahead in faith, knowing that the Lord works patiently with and through us (Gal. 6:9; Phil. 1:6). The account of the settlement shows that "outsiders" are included as recipients of the promises. Non-Israelites are initially outsiders to the promises, but provision is made for them through the witness of the Israelites. The inclusion of Caleb, a Kenizzite (cf. 14:6), and the inclusion of women such as Aksah and Rahab are examples of the promises' ultimate purpose of including all who profess allegiance to the Lord (15:13–17; 6:15–25; cf. Gal. 3:7–9, 28). Teaching this passage includes showing that God is not partial, for he welcomes all regardless of ethnic origin, gender, or age. We, in accord with the Lord's character and mandate, must show the same love and openness toward all people (Deut. 10:17; Col. 3:11; James 2:1–9).

Also, the account of Othniel and Aksah's request for larger springs points to the couple's forward-looking instincts (15:18–19). They are acting on their faith, believing that they will subdue the land and that they and future generations will prosper (Deut. 8:7, 10). Although this passage does not teach that believers necessarily receive material rewards for their faith in every circumstance, it illustrates confidence in the Lord's provision for our lives (Matt. 6:31–33; Phil. 4:12–13).

Illustrating the Text

Faithfully complete all the work the Lord gives you.

History: General MacArthur, commander of the American forces in the Philippines, experienced his own "Pearl Harbor" on December 8, 1941, at 12:35 p.m., ten hours after the attack on Hawaii. Japanese fighter planes caught MacArthur's air fortress still parked on the ground. Although MacArthur was aware of the Pearl Harbor disaster and received a direct cable from Washington commanding him to implement planned countermeasures, his inaction resulted in the Japanese occupation of the Philippines. A widely held view by scholars is that MacArthur's delay was a compromise to appease the political leadership of the Philippines, who had hoped to maintain neutrality.[3] There are times in our lives when we compromise or make poor choices because we are caught ill-prepared for the faith challenges that life brings. We need to always be vigilant.

God accomplishes his purposes despite our failures and limitations.

News Story: In the 1980s, Pastor Gordon MacDonald was a shining light in the Christian community. He was the author of many books, the senior pastor of a large church, the president of World Vision, and then the president of InterVarsity Christian Fellowship. But his world came crashing down around him when he publicly admitted to an adulterous affair.

MacDonald lost his job and his reputation. But he did not run and hide. Rather, after taking time away to process his decision and failure, he wrote a book titled *Rebuilding Your Broken World*, to help others who have suffered similar brokenness. When he returned to preaching at Grace Chapel in 1993, R. Judson Carlberg, a longtime friend of MacDonald, said, "His [MacDonald's] preaching now is even more deep and sensitive and compassionate than it was before this. He certainly has an authority to address hurting people." He also met numerous times as a counselor for President Bill Clinton following his public scandal with Monica Lewinsky.[4] Despite Pastor MacDonald's moral failure, the Lord continues to accomplish his purposes through MacDonald. If we confess our sin, grow from our mistakes, and depend again on the Lord, he will use us.

Avoid partiality by welcoming all people to the church.

Culture: We want to believe that everyone, regardless of age, race, gender, appearance, and so on, has equal opportunities at success in life. However, in 2010 *Newsweek* conducted an online survey of 202 corporate hiring managers as well as a telephone survey of 964 members of the public, which found that looks and age matter in all elements of the workplace. The beautiful people are simply more successful and more quickly promoted. *Newsweek* summarized the results: "Our surveys suggest managers are looking beyond wardrobe and evaluating how 'physically attractive' applicants are."[5] The church should never be guilty of such shallow favoritism but needs to express the same grace to all people.

Joseph's Inheritance

Big Idea *The Lord graciously grants his people their inheritance, although they do not always show obedience.*

Understanding the Text

The Text in Context

After extensive reporting on Judah's inheritance in chapter 15, the author turns to the most influential tribe in the north, the tribe of Joseph (chaps. 16–17). Chapters 16–17 consist of one unit, respectively describing the territories assigned to Ephraim and (western) Manasseh, Joseph's sons. They are treated together because they represent one tribe (Joseph), and they speak as one united people (16:4; 17:4).

(1) Joshua 16:1–4 introduces the whole unit, presenting a general description of the southern border of the Joseph inheritance.

(2) Joshua 16:5–10 consists of three parts: (a) the boundaries of Ephraim (16:5–8), (b) an exception (16:9), and (c) acknowledgment of Ephraim's failure to expel the inhabitants of Gezer (16:10).

(3) Chapter 17 begins and ends similarly with the requests of Joseph's tribe: first, the daughters of Zelophehad for an inheritance (17:4), and second, the tribe's petition for an enlarged inheritance (17:14–18). These are the third and fourth special requests reported in chapters 14–19 (cf. Aksah, 15:18–19). Chapter 17 has three parts similar to

chapter 16: (a) verses 1–10 give the boundaries of Manasseh's territory and include the brief narrative of Zelophehad's daughters, who receive their father's inheritance (17:3–4); (b) verse 11 gives an exception to the boundaries; and (c) verses 12–13 describe the failure of Manasseh to remove the Canaanites. Verses 14–18, however, have no parallel in chapter 16. Here, Joseph's tribes make a special request for an expanded land grant due to their numerous populations.

Interpretive Insights

16:1 *The allotment for Joseph began at the Jordan.* Generally, the allotment was in the central hill country bordering Dan and Benjamin in the south and terminating in the north just south of the Jezreel Valley. Verses 1–4 describe the southern border, which is most important in differentiating it from the larger tribe of Judah. The southern border stretches east to west from the Jordan River to the Mediterranean. The southern border abuts Benjamin and Dan and equates to their northern borders. The emphasis on "Jericho" (3x; see ESV) reveals its strategic importance and recalls the first and great victory of Israel (chap. 6).

16:2 *Arkites.* This people is known only by "Hushai the Arkite," a counselor to David (2 Sam. 15:32). This group, "Arkites" (*'arki*), is not to be confused with the similar name "Arkites" (*'arqi*) in Genesis 10:17.

16:3 *Japhletites.* This group is unknown, occurring only here. Both of these peoples are on the southern border of Ephraim. That the Arkites and Japhletites do not occur in the battle stories shows that the conquest stories are selective accounts.

16:5 *the territory of Ephraim.* Verses 5–10 describe the southern border of Ephraim, which corresponds in verse 5 with the description of Joseph's southern border in verses 1–3.

16:6 *Mikmethath.* Mikmethath's location at the northernmost point of Ephraim is uncertain. That it has the definite article in Hebrew, "*the* Mikmethath," may indicate it refers to a geographic feature, not a city. There are towns assigned to Ephraim that fall within the borders of Manasseh to the north (16:9; e.g., see also 17:11).

16:10 *to this day . . . forced labor.* "To this day" refers to the monarchy or earlier,

Key Themes of Joshua 16:1–17:18

- The Lord blesses Joseph with numerous descendants and fulfills his promise to Zelophehad's daughters.
- Tribal unity is illustrated by the unity of the Joseph tribes.
- Ephraim and Manasseh initially fail to drive out the Canaanites, but there is hope for their descendants.
- Joshua chooses what is best for the people, not what is best for himself.

since the occupants of Gezer are not expelled until Solomon (1 Kings 9:15–17). Forced labor was common in the ancient Near East. Although this is permitted if foreigners offer peace to the Israelites (Deut. 20:11; cf. Gibeonites, Josh. 9), the Israelites choose to conscript the Canaanites for financial gain (see also 17:13; Judg. 1:28, 30, 33, 35). The practice reaches its peak with the building projects of Solomon (2 Chron. 8:7–8). In the settlement period, the Israelites embrace the Canaanites through intermarriage and adopt their idolatry (Judg. 3:5–8).

17:1 *Joseph's firstborn.* "Firstborn" (*bᵉkor*, 2x) recalls the blessing of Jacob, who chooses the younger son Ephraim over Manasseh (Gen. 48:13–22).

Makir . . . great soldiers. Manasseh's possession in the Transjordan is stated first, referring to the Makirites, whose warriors are especially fearsome (13:31).

Mentioning the Makirites, who have dispossessed the Amorites (Num. 32:39), may be a slight against their brothers in the west.

17:4 *among our relatives.* Literally, "our brothers"; it is a common expression. Moses's command occurs in Numbers 27:1–11. The incident merits a new law that provides a father's inheritance for daughters if their father has no sons. Daughters, however, must marry within their father's clan, to retain the father's legacy in his tribe (Num. 36:1–12).

17:5 *ten tracts.* Five tracts are for five clans (17:2; Num. 26:30–32), and the sixth clan, Hepher's, receives five by Zelophehad's five daughters (17:3).

17:8 *Tappuah itself.* That tribal inheritances overlap is not rare (17:8–9, 11).

17:12 *Yet the Manassites.* "Yet" expresses a contrast between the fact that the land is their inheritance and the fact that, by failing to expel the enemy, the Canaanites remain entrenched there.

17:13 *the Israelites grew stronger.* Subjecting the Canaanites to forced labor is true of other tribes (e.g., 16:10; Judg. 1:28, 30, 33, 35) and may be a general statement describing the custom. The NET brings out this nuance: "*Whenever* the Israelites were strong militarily . . ." (italics mine).

17:14 *Why have you given us only one allotment and one portion . . . ?* The request has the tone of complaint, different from the zeal of Caleb and the daughters of Zelophehad. The first-person singular pronouns "me" (NIV: "us") and "I" (NIV: "we") reflect the united voice of the people.

Many cities in the Jezreel and Harod Valleys have not been conquered by the Israelites because the Canaanites possess iron chariots, giving them a fighting advantage on flat ground. This Assyrian relief depicts a horse-drawn chariot heading into battle (from the palace at Nineveh, 645–635 BC).

Some English versions read "one allotment and one portion" as a hendiadys, meaning two nouns expressing a single idea, which emphasizes that the tribal allotment is one united heritage (cf. "one tribal allotment" [HCSB, NET] or "one portion of land" [NLT]).

the LORD has blessed us abundantly. The population and prestige of the tribes fulfill the blessing of Moses (Deut. 33:17). Compare Joshua 17:17. Their argument may be that they deserve another allotment, since the Lord has blessed them.

17:15 *If you are so numerous.* Joshua's retort is in effect, "If it is true as you say, then you should have no problem increasing your inheritance."

hill country of Ephraim. Joshua specifies the area he has in mind, whereas the tribes may have desired a broader area by using the general description "hill country" (17:16).[1]

Perizzites and Rephaites. The Perizzites have joined coalitions warring against

Joshua (9:1; 11:3). They are members of the "seven nations," whom the Lord assures Israel that they will destroy (3:10). These Perizzites must have remained a small pocket in the hill country. The Rephaites are reputed to be giants (Deut. 2:10; 3:11; see also Josh. 12:4; 13:12).

17:16 *chariots fitted with iron.* Chariots require a relatively flat landscape, as opposed to the hilly terrain that the Israelites occupy. That they fear the chariots is in direct disobedience to God's promise (Deut. 20:1). They have already witnessed God's faithfulness in Israel's defeat of the chariotry of Jabin (11:6–9; cf. Judg. 4:1–16). The iron component of ancient chariots was an overlay that strengthened the frame. Iron retrieved from disassembled chariots was kept as a spoil of war (22:8).

17:18 *forested hill country.* The allotment is not ideal, because it possesses two obstacles—the forest and Canaanite chariots. For agricultural purposes the forest must be cleared and the land terraced. In order for them to progress, however, they must first rid the area of Canaanites. But their success against the enemy is only partial (Judg. 1:27–29, 35).

Theological Insights

This passage reinforces the fundamental theology of the book: conquest and possession of the land require obedience to the instruction of the Lord. "Obedience must accompany miracle."[2] The tribes, however, do not exhibit perfect obedience. They fail to dislocate some Canaanites, and Joseph's descendants want more land instead of first fully claiming what is initially given. They choose economic gain by enslaving the Canaanites (16:10; 17:13; cf. Judah, 15:63).

This concession leads to assimilating Canaanite religion (Judg. 2:1–3). The consequence is their own undoing because they choose ease over obedience.

God's true and faithful word is fulfilled, shown by allotting land to Ephraim as the favored tribe in accord with the blessing of Jacob (Gen. 48:20). Also, the Zelophehad family receives their promised possession, providing a legacy for generations to come (17:3–4). What is more, Joshua's prediction that the tribes will expel the Canaanites and take possession of their inheritance reflects confidence in God's promises to the nation as a whole (17:15–18). Although it will take time before the Canaanites are completely dislodged, the people can have hope, knowing that the Lord will fulfill his promises of total possession.

The passage also shows what the proper focus of godly leadership is. Although Joshua is an Ephraimite (Num. 13:8; Josh. 19:49–50; 24:30), he does not favor his own tribe over others. Joshua pointedly challenges his own tribal people. He puts God's kingdom (14:2) above his own interests (cf. Lev. 19:15; James 2:9). Joshua's achievements on behalf of the nation garner trust by the people.

A successful distribution of the land requires a cooperative spirit among the tribes. From this passage there are two examples of the community's unity. First, although the inheritance of the Zelophehad daughters means that they receive five of the ten tracts assigned to Manasseh (17:5), there is no envy or infighting among the clansmen, because they accept the command of the Lord. The second example, although not a totally flattering episode, is the unity of the two Joseph tribes in bringing their case to Joshua (17:14).

Teaching the Text

In contrast to Joseph's descendants who must be spurred on to obedience, the passage honors the faith and passion of Zelophehad's daughters. They illustrate the commitment that is incumbent on the people. The challenge is for the Israelites to show their faith in God's promises by acting on them. Christians experience the similar challenge of acting on our faith in the face of obstacles and doubts. Our assurance that the Lord will enable us to overcome obstacles to our obedience arises from our daily perseverance in faith (Heb. 3:14, 18).

The tribes chose prosperity over obedience by enslaving the Canaanites instead of dispossessing them. Temptations to ease and distraction will ultimately prove to dissuade them from receiving the full portion of their inheritance. We too must follow God's will despite difficulty in our lives, for the Lord tests our hearts through troubles to strengthen our devotion to him (Deut. 8:2, 16; 1 Pet. 4:12; 2 Pet. 2:9).

Joshua does not favor his tribe of Ephraim over others. He is not swayed by the special appeal of Manasseh and Ephraim, nor is he intimidated. Christian readers, however, must not draw a direct line of application in all respects between Joshua as leader and the leadership in the church today by pastors and elders. Joshua held a special position in the life of the nation at a special time. To oppose Joshua's directives was tantamount to rejecting God's word. Christian leaders do not have the same kind of direct authority. They are accountable to the teaching of Scripture and to the people they serve, showing pastoral care and gentle correction (2 Tim. 2:14–16; 1 Pet. 5:1–4).

The tribes retained their own distinctive heritage, but they cooperated with one another, giving unity priority over their diversity. Unity by itself is not the goal, however, for they can be unified in resisting the word of God. The purpose of unity for the tribes is to achieve collectively the purposes God has for Israel. They cannot succeed in realizing the divine promises independently of one another. Christian unity based on our mutual love for the Lord and for one another is our witness to the unbelieving world (see the comments on 1:18; see also 22:21–34; cf. John 17:21–23; Rom. 15:1–7).

Illustrating the Text

Beware of choosing comfort and prosperity over obedience to the Lord.

History: The story of the Donner party is a reminder that shortcuts are not always the best choice. In 1846 nine covered wagons left Springfield, Illinois, on the 2,500-mile journey to California. The journey would end as one of the greatest tragedies in the history of the migration to the west. The problem was that the Donner party put their trust in a book, *The Emigrants' Guide to Oregon and California*, which advertised a new shortcut that would save 350–400 miles in the journey. Unfortunately, what the Donner party did not know was that the trail had never been tested. Even though warned while on the journey by a fellow traveler that the "shortcut" would not work, the party continued on its course. Of the ninety-one people associated with the Donner party, forty-four died because of the shortcut.[3] We need to heed this lesson from history that shortcuts are not always the best path. There are times in life when

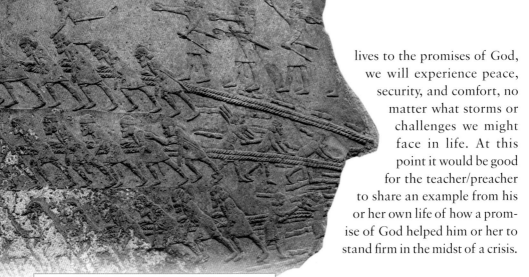

lives to the promises of God, we will experience peace, security, and comfort, no matter what storms or challenges we might face in life. At this point it would be good for the teacher/preacher to share an example from his or her own life of how a promise of God helped him or her to stand firm in the midst of a crisis.

As the Israelites settle in the land and become stronger and more prosperous, they choose to subject the indigenous Canaanite populations to forced labor rather than driving them away. Conquered peoples were often used as laborers as shown in this Assyrian relief from the palace of Sennacherib at Nineveh (700–692 BC). Here prisoners of war are pulling ropes to move a colossal stone bull (not seen in this panel) as part of a construction project.

we are tempted to make choices for short-term happiness, comfort, and security, but these choices can bring about tragic results.

The promises of God can bring great comfort and security to our lives.

Props: Bring an anchor to the service, to be used as an image of the impact of God's promises for our lives. When sailors properly anchor a boat, they can have confidence that the boat will be secure. Despite strong currents or intense storms, the anchor keeps the boat stable by holding it in place. In the same way, when we properly anchor our

Love is expressed when we sacrifice to give to others what God wants for them.

News Story: In choosing not to favor his own tribe, Ephraim, Joshua exhibited a principle to be followed by all believers: love is best expressed when we are willing to give up what we want for ourselves to give others what God wants for them. On September 30, 2013, Dwayne Johnson covered his thirteen-year-old daughter as a rock slide crashed down on them. Although Dwayne died, the sacrificial action of this father is credited with saving the life of his daughter. A friend said of Dwayne, "Probably his only regret is that he didn't jump in front of his whole family [other family members were killed]; he's just that type of guy."[4] Joshua reminds us that we are to live not for our own agenda but in obedience to God. Are you willing to give up what you want for yourself in order to give to others what God wants for them?

Inheritance for the Remaining Tribes

Big Idea *The Lord ensures that all his people receive his promised blessing, even when they show fear.*

Understanding the Text

The Text in Context

Chapters 18–19 complete the distribution of the land. There are three phases: (1) Moses's earlier allotment for the Transjordan territories (chap. 13), (2) at Gilgal the territories for Judah and Joseph (chaps. 14–17), and (3) at Shiloh the territories for the remaining seven tribes (chaps. 18–19). The seven tribes are tersely treated compared to the large tribes of Judah (chaps. 14–15) and Joseph's sons (chaps. 16–17). Chapters 18–19 evidence a carefully planned report. References to the tent of meeting at 18:1 and 19:51 mark the boundaries of the unit. Sandwiched in between are two parts.

(1) Joshua 18:2–10 describes the preparation for the seven allocations, including a delegation of surveyors. They are reminiscent of the spies sent by Moses from Kadesh Barnea (Num. 13) and by Joshua from Gilgal (Josh. 2).

(2) Joshua 18:11–19:50 describes each tribal allotment in a similar pattern of introduction and conclusion statements: "the [second, third, etc.] lot came up/out

The tent of meeting has moved from Gilgal to Shiloh. Shown here is the tell at ancient Shiloh (modern Khirbet Seilun) with its visible Middle Bronze walls.

for [name of tribe], for the descendants of [tribe] according to their clans" (AT) (18:11; 19:1, 10, 17, 24, 32, 40); and "This was the inheritance of [tribe] according to their clans" (AT) (18:20; 19:8, 16, 23, 31, 39, 48). These descriptions name boundary perimeters and/or city lists. Some peculiar features can be mentioned here: (a) Benjamin, one of the smallest tribes, has the longest description, since it lies strategically between Judah and Joseph's sons, serving as a buffer between these influential tribes (18:11–28). (b) Simeon's inheritance contains only a city list; these cities lie within the borders of Judah, since Judah receives a lot larger than needed (19:1–9). (c) Levi also receives no land, only cities throughout the land (18:7). Simeon and Levi receive no land because of their ancestors' violent sins (Gen. 34:25–30; 49:5–7). (d) Dan is named last, perhaps because it becomes a center of idolatry (Gen. 49:17; Judg. 18:30–31). Also, Dan does not permanently possess its original allotment, choosing instead to migrate to the north (19:47; Judg. 1:1–31).

Historical and Cultural Background

Boundary descriptions were critically important during the settlement period of Israel. Such boundary descriptions were part of treaties in the ancient Near East and defined the borders of neighboring nations. There could be topographical boundaries formed by rivers or mountains, but lacking that, the borders could well be described in terms of cities and the cultivated fields or grazing areas around them. In that sense, there were often no definitive boundaries circumscribing a territory, as we would have today. This helps explain, for example, how Simeon's possession can be fully within

Key Themes of Joshua 18:1–19:51

- Joshua exhorts the seven reluctant tribes to possess what God has promised.
- Joshua sends representatives from each tribe to survey the land.
- Each allotment's size corresponds to the size of the tribe so as to provide equitable distribution.
- Joshua receives his inheritance, but only after he has completed the distribution to all the tribes.

territory given to Judah (19:1, 9), as some towns within Ephraim and Manasseh belonged to one tribe or the other (16:9; 17:9). Towns in border descriptions listed within the borders of another nation are attested in Hittite treaties.[1]

Interpretive Insights

18:1 *Shiloh . . . tent of meeting.* Shiloh is in the hill country of Ephraim, identified with the modern Khirbet Seilun, which is about twenty miles north-northeast of Jerusalem. The tent is mentioned only twice in the book (18:1; 19:51; see the sidebar). Presumably the ark is present, implying that the casting of lots is "before the LORD" (AT; 19:51; cf. Judg. 20:27).

brought under their control. The land is essentially constrained so that there is no excuse for the timidity of the seven tribes. "Brought under control" (*kabash,* "subdue") recalls the creation charge to subdue the earth (Gen. 1:28); the term can convey the nuance of rule (2 Sam. 8:11).

18:3 *God of your ancestors.* The promise made to the patriarchs (Gen. 15:18) is the basis for taking the land in faith (1:6; 21:43).

18:4 *Appoint three men.* The vast land requires three men per tribe to cover the territories.

18:5–7 *You are to divide.* Joshua summarizes the land already apportioned (chaps. 13–17). Levi is specifically mentioned since it receives only cities, which accounts for the reference to seven tribes instead of eight (18:1–2).

18:9 *wrote . . . on a scroll.* The recording of the survey as a document (*seper*) indicates that the boundaries are written contemporaneously with Joshua. The document, however, is not to be equated with the boundary lists presented in the book of Joshua but probably served in some modified way as a resource for the book.

18:11–28 *Benjamin.* The description includes boundaries (18:11–20) and twenty-six cities (18:21–28). Benjamin lies between Judah and Ephraim. Naming Jericho and Gibeon is reminiscent of Israel's previous battles (chaps. 4; 9–10). Gibeah becomes a future threat (Judg. 19–20), and Jerusalem's location overlaps with Judah (15:63).

19:1–9 *Simeon.* The smallest tribe, Simeon, receives only seventeen cities, which lie within the territory of Judah (Gen. 49:7). This enables the original boundaries of Judah to remain intact while accommodating one of the seven tribes, leaving sufficient areas for the remaining tribes (cf. 1 Chron. 4:38–43).

19:10–16 *Zebulun.* Zebulun is located in Galilee, with Asher as its west boundary, Naphtali as its east boundary, and Issachar on its south side. Although there are "twelve towns," only five are named (19:15), which are probably only representative. "Bethlehem" is not the Bethlehem of Judah (19:15). Isaiah describes Zebulun as shrouded in darkness because of Assyrian oppression (eighth century), but it will see the dawning of a great light (Isa. 9:1–2).

Matthew says this is fulfilled by Jesus's ministry in Galilee, which brings spiritual light (Matt. 4:13–15).

19:17–23 *Issachar.* Issachar's eastern boundary is the Jordan, its southwest and southern border is Manasseh, its western boundary is Asher, and its northwest and northern boundaries border Zebulun and Naphtali. Mount Tabor is at its border (Deut. 33:18–19).

19:24–31 *Asher.* Asher lies along the Mediterranean coast in Phoenicia, from Mount Carmel north to Sidon (19:28), and is bordered on the east by Zebulun and Naphtali (19:27). Asher fails to drive out the Phoenicians at Akko and Sidon (Judg. 1:31).

19:32–39 *Naphtali.* Naphtali is located in Galilee. Its western boundary is Asher, its southern border is Zebulun, and its eastern border is the Jordan.

19:40–48 *Dan.* The borders are not given, only cities; the location is south of Ephraim, north of Judah, and west of Benjamin, with its western border at the coast.

19:47 *Leshem and named it Dan.* Judges 18 details the migration of Dan, who failed to occupy its original allotment (Judg. 1:34). Leshem (also "Laish," Judg. 18:7) is located at Tell el-Qadi (Tel Dan), about eleven miles north of Lake Huleh at the foot of Mount Hermon. Apparently, Samson's judgeship occurs before the Danites move, since he faces the Philistines whose cities are in the southwest portion of Judah adjacent to Dan (Judg. 15:20).

19:49–50 *Timnath Serah.* The location (Khirbet Tibnah) is in the heart of Ephraim, where Joshua lives and is buried (24:30; also named Timnath Heres, Judg. 2:9). There is no specific passage that recounts the command of the Lord to provide Timnath Serah. The author probably has in mind the general promise made to Joshua and Caleb (Num. 14:30). Joshua requests a city that requires him to rebuild and perhaps dispossess it, as is the case with the courageous Caleb (14:6–15).

Theological Insights

Although there is no dialogue between Joshua and the Lord, the presence of the Lord is evident by the phrase "before the LORD" (AT; 18:6, 8, 10; 19:51) and "by the command of the LORD" (AT; 19:50). What transpires at Shiloh is under the same divine superintendence as in earlier distributions. That the allocation occurs at the tent of meeting shows that the Lord is the landlord (Lev. 25:23).[2] Another indication of God's presence is the reappearance of the key term "give" (*natan*), referring to the Lord (e.g., 1:2; 12:6) or Moses (e.g., 1:14–15) or Joshua (e.g., 17:4), who "gives/gave" the land. As is common in the book, the passage affirms that the land is the Lord's gift (18:3, 7). But Israel "gave" to Joshua his

Tent of Meeting

The tent of meeting symbolizes that God lives among his people (Exod. 29:43–45). It is his "home," where he is worshiped; it houses the sacred ark of the covenant. Exodus 25–40 describes its construction at Sinai. This "tent" should not be confused with the temporary tent outside the camp used by Moses (Exod. 33:7–11) or the tent David prepares to house the ark in Jerusalem (2 Sam. 6:17). As a portable structure it is disassembled and moved wherever the nation journeys in the desert until the people's entrance into the land, where the tent of meeting is established at Shiloh (Jer. 7:12). It remains at Shiloh until subsequent moves to Nob (1 Sam. 21) and Gibeon (1 Chron. 16:39; 2 Chron. 1:3) and its final location in Jerusalem (2 Chron. 5:5).

inheritance in accord with God's instruction (19:49–50).

Another theological idea is worship. The "whole assembly" gathers at Shiloh (18:1), and Joshua ensures that all the tribes either have received or will receive their inheritance (18:3–10). Reference to Shiloh's tent of meeting makes it the first reported case that the fulfillment of the demand for exclusive worship occurs (Deut. 12:5; Jer. 7:12). "Dwelling for his Name" (Deut. 12:11; 14:23; 16:2, 6, 11; 26:2) refers to any legitimate place for Yahweh worship, which includes the location of the tent. Ultimately, the only legitimate place becomes the sanctuary at Jerusalem (Jer. 7:10). What provides unity is Israel's exclusive commitment to the Lord as its God.

Joshua exhibits a leadership that puts the Lord's people above himself, instead of demanding the first share in the land

The tent of meeting has been a transportable structure, the place of God's presence as the Israelites travel from Mount Sinai to the promised land. It appears that the ark of the covenant finds a more permanent home at Shiloh, where sacrifices are brought and the ark is housed until it is taken into battle and captured by the Philistines in 1 Samuel 4. This replica of the tent of meeting has been erected at Timna, Israel.

as Israel's leader. His possession is said to be from the Lord, and he can argue for a right of precedence for this reason. Joshua also does not cling to the exclusive right of parceling out the land; he is joined by Eleazar the priest and the tribal elders. Only after he has completed the task of dispersing land to all Israel's tribes does he make his personal request.

Finally, this passage provides another example of faithfulness in contrast to the hesitancy of the remaining seven tribes and the Danites' failure to capture their land. Joshua, who has been commissioned to carry out the distribution of the inheritance, acts decisively. He puts a plan in motion to move this second generation of Israelites forward. The sending forth of the surveyors reflects his good judgment but also is reminiscent of the twelve spies dispatched by Moses from Kadesh Barnea (Num. 13–14). Symbolically the surveyors' reports in effect reverse what the unfaithful spies contended.

Teaching the Text

Since the distribution of the land is in the shadow of the "tent of meeting" (18:1; 19:51), the passage indicates that the inheritance is not a secular transaction but an act of worship. The tent is the meeting place between God and the people of Israel. The tent is the place where he "dwells" among his people (Exod. 25:8; 29:42–46; Num. 35:34; Deut. 12:4–7). Any attempt to worship apart from the legitimate place of God's presence is understood as apostasy (Josh. 8:35; 22:27). Christians too make worship central to their experience with the Lord, given out of love and obedience

(John 4:23–24; Eph. 5:18–20; Col. 3:16; Heb. 10:24–25; 12:28–29). For Christian readers the promise of an eternal inheritance is for all believers (Eph. 1:11–18; Heb. 9:15; 1 Pet. 1:3–5). Our proper response to the Lord's good gift of new life must be in a spirit of thanksgiving and worship (Col. 3:15–17; James 1:17).

At the conclusion of the distribution, the narrative describes the inheritance that Joshua receives, "as the Lord had commanded" (19:49–50; 24:28–30). The two chapters end on this special notice, showing that God is fulfilling his promises to individuals, such as Joshua and Caleb (14:6–15; 15:13), and to the tribes collectively. Joshua receives his inheritance because of God's faithfulness to his promises and Joshua's response in faith (Num. 14:30, 38; Deut. 1:38; 3:28; 31:6–8). We can have confidence in the Lord's ability and desire to fulfill his promises to each of us through Christ (1 Cor. 1:18–22; Eph. 1:11–14). That the Lord is fulfilling his promises in our lives should motivate us to offer thanksgiving, obey his word, and practice spiritual holiness (2 Cor. 1:20; 1 John 3:1–3).

Illustrating the Text

The people of God are to worship the Lord as a priority of their lives.

Christian Life: In a study conducted by Kirk Hardaway, an Episcopal Church researcher, and Penny Marler of Samford University, 20.4 percent of the American population actually attends church on a weekly basis.[3] This low percentage reflects the declining value many Christians place on the need to gather for corporate worship. The following represent perspectives your listeners might hear from people who claim the Christian faith. Read each statement, and give your listeners time to consider how they might respond: "I don't go to church because I worship God entirely on my own. You don't need formal religion or to go to church in order to worship God." "I don't go to church because it's filled with hypocrites. I don't need church to connect with God." After giving your listeners time to think about each statement, share your own perspective on each. It is important to emphasize the priority of God's people gathering for worship.

Selfless living is to be a mark of committed followers of the Lord.

Everyday Life: When a family or group gathers for a meal, the cook will often be the last to serve himself or herself. It is the cook who has done the work, thereby earning the right to the best and choicest portions. But by waiting until last, the cook extends the service of preparing the meal to the selfless sharing of its enjoyment as well. As Joshua was willing to sacrifice for the sake of the community by waiting until the end to select his inheritance, so we are to live with selfless service in our relationships with one another.

Choose to live with an attitude of gratitude toward the Lord.

News Story: For thirty years Peggielene Bartels served as the secretary to the Ghanian embassy in Washington. When the king of Otuam, Ghana, died, the elders prayed and poured schnapps on the ground while they read the names of the king's twenty-five relatives to determine their new king. The process selected Peggielene, who was appointed king. This woman who had very few possessions now has a driver, a chef, an eight-bedroom palace, and more than a thousand acres of land.[4] When we come to put our faith in the Lord, we become heirs to the kingdom of God. And our selection is even more gracious than Peggielene's. This reality should inspire us to lead a life filled with gratitude toward the Lord.

Cities of Refuge

Big Idea *The Lord is just and requires justice among his people.*

Understanding the Text

The Text in Context

Chapters 13–19 detail the boundaries of the tribes' inheritance in the land, excepting the Levites. The Lord allots to the Levites forty-eight cities and their pasturelands. Chapters 20 and 21 delineate the cities.

Since the distribution of the land has been accomplished (chaps. 13–19), the next allotment is naming the cities of refuge.

If a person kills someone accidentally, he or she can flee to a city of refuge, stand in the entrance of the gate, and state his or her case before the elders of the city. Civic and judicial affairs were conducted at the city gate, where gate chambers may have been part of the gate construction to facilitate that process. Shown here is the north gate complex entrance to the city of Shechem, one of the cities of refuge.

That the Lord directs Moses to distinguish six cities in the land presupposes that the people will accomplish the dispossession of the Canaanites (Num. 35:9–15; Deut. 4:41–43). Previously, during the wilderness period, an offender received sanctuary by grasping the horns of the altar of burnt offering in the tent of meeting (Exod. 21:14; cf. 1 Kings 1:50–53; 2:28–34).

Four passages in the Pentateuch describe the procedure regarding the cities of refuge (Exod. 21:12–14; Num. 35:6–34; Deut. 4:41–43; 19:1–13). The steps in the process can be reconstructed as follows. (1) When a homicide occurs, the offender flees to one of six designated cities of refuge (Josh.

20:7–8) and receives *provisional* safety from the pursuing "avenger of blood" (Num. 35:6, 12). The underlying assumption is that a convicted murderer must be put to death (Exod. 21:12; Lev. 24:17), and a ransom for a murderer's crime cannot be paid (Num. 35:31–32).

(2) Elders of the city return the offender to the town where the killing has occurred, and the offender is judged before the "assembly" (Num. 35:24–25). Although not specifically stated, the jury may have been constituted of elders from the city of refuge and elders from the offender's town.

(3) If it is determined that the homicide is accidental, "without malice aforethought" (Deut. 4:42; Josh. 20:5), the slayer receives sanctuary in the city of refuge (Num. 35:25). If the homicide is deemed murder, the slayer is handed over to the avenger to be executed (Num. 35:21; Deut. 19:11–12).

(4) If the homicide is accidental, the slayer must remain in the city of refuge or be subject to the avenger (Num. 35:26–27). Only at the death of the high priest may the slayer return home, free from the retribution of the avenger (Num. 35:25, 28; Josh. 20:6).

Chapter 20 has three parts: (1) verses 1–6 give instructions for the procedure, (2) verses 7–8 name the six cities, and (3) verse 9 summarizes the legislation.

Interpretive Insights

20:2 *cities of refuge . . . through Moses.* "Refuge" (*miqlat*) is a technical term, used twenty times in the Old Testament and only in association with the cities of asylum. Numbers 35:9–15 gives the Lord's instructions to Moses.

Key Themes of Joshua 20:1–9

- The Lord is merciful toward those who kill by accident—without premeditated malice—by requiring equitable retribution for the offense (*lex talionis*).
- Provisional protection for resident aliens indicates that the Lord's justice and mercy are inclusive, not ethnically conditioned.

Why Cities of Refuge?

"Cities" of asylum appear only in Israel and not elsewhere in the ancient Near East. The six cities are also members of the Levitical forty-eight cities (Josh. 21). They are distributed equally, three cities on each side of the Jordan. These six are distinctive, having dual purposes: first, as Levitical cities they provide security and prosperity, and, second, for all Israelites they function as havens of protection. The Lord grants the six cities as sanctuary for a person who kills someone, so that the community must guarantee a fair hearing. The institution of cities of refuge permits family feuds to be controlled, curbing potential bloodbaths. Also, the offenders do not need to escape to a foreign country, thereby preserving the community solidarity of the tribe and family. Additionally, the concept of the cities addresses the need to account for the threat of cultic impurity in the land due to the spilling of blood. The threshold for determining premeditated murder is high, requiring more than one witness (Num. 35:30; Deut. 17:6; 19:15) and establishing the motive of the killer (Num. 35:20; Deut. 19:4, 6, 11). An alternative to the role of the blood avenger is the action taken by the whole community. The death sentence is typically carried out by stoning, and the witnesses are the first to cast stones, followed by the whole congregation (cf. Deut. 17:7). For the case of murder, neither commutation nor atonement is possible (Num. 35:33). Although the offense is a private matter, it impacts the whole community's culpability.

20:3 *anyone who kills.* The same word occurs for "manslayer" and "murderer" (*rotseah*). Premeditation defines whether a person is guilty of murder or manslaughter. Numbers 35:16–24 and Deuteronomy 19:4–6, 10–11 provide representative cases that constitute manslaughter or murder. Modern jurisprudence also metes out a

Avenger of Blood

The role of the "avenger of blood" (*go'el haddam*) is described in Numbers 35; Deuteronomy 19; and Joshua 20 (cf. 2 Sam. 14:11). The word *go'el* refers to a family member who restores (*ga'al*, "to redeem") a relative from financial loss or slavery, or a childless widowed sister-in-law, or who accounts for loss of life (Lev. 25:25, 47–49; Num. 35:12–29; Ruth 2:20). The description "blood" specifies the *go'el*'s role of retaliation on behalf of a fallen relative in the case of manslaughter or murder. The NLT reflects the family connection by translating "relatives seeking revenge" (Josh. 20:3). The role of the *go'el* achieves social equilibrium and confines justice to a local and family matter.

penalty based on malice and the extent of premeditation.

find protection. The cities are not asylums for every crime but specifically delegated for protection from the victim's avenger, who acts "in a rage" (lit., "his heart/passion is hot," Deut. 19:6).

20:4 *city gate.* The gate is the place where a city's commercial and legal transactions occur (e.g., Deut. 17:8; Ruth 4:11).

20:6 *until the death of the high priest.* The penalty for manslaughter is restriction to the city of refuge until the death of the high priest. The high priest's death is a symbolic sign, indicating that atonement for the killing is needed to reconcile the killer to God and return the individual to home. The idea is that the atonement provides the means for restoring the killer to the life that person had before the incident (Deut. 19:10). Cultic atonement typically requires a time of isolation from the community for purging and includes a sacrifice before re-entry into the community can occur. In this case, the time factor is the duration of the priest's life, and his death is equivalent to the ritual. If the killer leaves the city before the priest's death, no atoning reconciliation to God has occurred, and the avenger who

brings divine sanction against the culprit is obligated to carry out the deed. If the avenger kills the person who has returned home after the death of the high priest, the avenger is probably deemed guilty of murder and is the object of the community's retaliation (Deut. 19:10).

their own home. The passage assumes the killer wants to return to the city of origin, but there is no clear admonition to return. Possession of ancestral property is that person's strongest motivation to return.

20:7–8 *they set apart.* No two cities of sanctuary are in the same tribal allotment, making the six cities widely accessible.

20:9 *any foreigner residing among them.* The term "foreigner" may be misunderstood by readers today. The term "resident alien" (*ger*) refers to a permanent immigrant who identifies with the Lord and Israel by observing the covenant. A *ger* has the same opportunity as the native citizen for an impartial trial.

Theological Insights

This passage reflects two qualities of God. First, the Lord is just in his dealings with his people (e.g., Deut. 10:18; Ps. 7:11). The spilling of innocent blood requires redress (e.g., Gen. 9:5–6; Num. 35:30). Second, the Lord is merciful when dealing with his people, because he acts in accord with the degree of seriousness of their crimes. Although the Lord demands recompense for killing a person, he takes mitigating circumstances into consideration. Additionally, the Lord does not discriminate against any people group (Lev. 24:22; Deut. 10:17–18). Each person, regardless of social standing, is held responsible for his or her own behavior (Jer. 31:29–30; Ezek. 18).

Also, the passage indicates the high value of human life. The presumption is that human life is uniquely created in the image of God (Gen. 1:26–27) and therefore must be guaranteed special protections (Gen. 9:2–6). The extensive attention given to the question of manslaughter and premeditated homicide shows the importance of human life and death in God's eyes. The community as a whole must address the issue if there is to be order. Miscarriage of justice incurs God's wrath because it causes ritual impurity in the land, and the people are therefore subject to God's condemnation (Num. 35:33). The highest penalty for taking human life is execution (Exod. 21:12), but only after sufficient evidence warrants it and proper criminal procedure has occurred. The system of asylum effects the just treatment of human life, and it also keeps a family's avenger from committing the crime of murder against one who does not deserve death (Deut. 19:6).

Teaching the Text

The passage shows that special provisions are established for maintaining the sacredness of the land. The land, as God's possession and dwelling place, requires justice and accountability for human life. Animal sacrifice is required to purge the land of its uncleanness even when there is an unexplained death (Deut. 21:1–9). The sacredness of human life, created in the image of God (Gen. 1:26–27; 9:5–7), means redress is necessary for shedding blood, whether by intention or by accident. Christians too must pursue justice and protections

Cities of refuge are part of the Israelite justice system and guarantee a trial to determine whether a killing was intentional or accidental. In cases ruled murder, the laws of Israel demand the punishment be death by the hands of the family "avenger of blood." In cases ruled manslaughter, the punishment is banishment to the city of refuge, a practice that provides protection for the killer and prevents blood feuds. No ransom can be paid in either case. This system differs from those of some other ancient cultures that allowed the "avenger of blood" to choose retaliation or payment. In Tablet A of the Middle Assyrian Laws (ca. 1400–1000 BC), shown here, it says, "If either a man or a woman has entered a man's house and killed either man or woman they shall turn over the murderer to the next of kin; He may have them executed, or he may choose to accept compensation in property" (translation from Alan Humm, "Middle Assyrian Law Code Tablet A," http://jewishchristianlit.com/Texts/ANElaws/midAssyrLaws.html).

for human life. Every life, regardless of circumstance, has a purpose in the heart of God that Christians must recognize and honor (Jer. 29:11; Eph. 2:8–10). Also,

Kedesh ●

Abdon ○
ASHER
Rehob ○ **NAPHTALI**
Mishal ○
Kartan ○
Nahalal ○
Helkath ○ **ZEBULUN**
○ Daberath
Kishion ○
Jokneam ○ **ISSACHAR**
Jarmuth ○

EAST MANASSEH

Sea of Galilee

Golan ●

Hammoth Dor ○
En Gannim ○

Taanach ○

Ramoth Gilead ●

MANASSEH

Shechem ●

Mahanaim ○

Jabbok R.

○ Gath Rimmon
○ Shiloh

GAD

EPHRAIM

DAN
Eltekeh ○
Gezer ○ Beth Horan ○
Gibbethon ○ Aijalon ○
Gibeon ○
Beth Shemesh ○
Libnah ○ ○ Holon

Bethel ○
BENJAMIN
○ Geba
Almon ○
Anathoth ○

Jazer ○ **AMMON**
○ Mephaath

Heshbon ○

Bezer ●

Dead Sea

JUDAH
Hebron ●
Debir ○ ○ Juttah
○ Eshtemoa
○ Jattir

Jahaz ○
REUBEN
○ Kedemoth

Arnon

MOAB

SIMEON

Zered Brook

EDOM

0 10 20 mi
0 10 20 km

> Each Israelite tribe is to designate towns for the Levites within its inheritance in the promised land. Six of those towns are to be places of safety for those who have caused the death of someone unintentionally. The towns of Hebron, Shechem, Kedesh Bezer, Ramoth-Gilead, and Golan, shown on this map, would become the cities of refuge.

by the gift of his Spirit (1 Cor. 12:13; Eph. 2:15–19). For Israel, foreigners who were members of the covenant community received the same protections and also had the responsibility of covenant duty. Christians too acknowledge that all—regardless of race, economic standing, or national origin—who join the community of faith have equal standing in God's eyes (Rom. 3:28–30).

Another important feature of the passage is that the manslayer is released from confinement to the city of refuge at the death of the high priest rather than by animal sacrifice. Sacrificial atonement is required for unintentional sins (Lev. 4; 5:1–6:7). The principle is that atonement requires a living sacrifice, whose blood purges ritual pollution. If this sacrifice is not carried out, the result is sacrilege of the land. Perhaps the high priest's role as representative of the nation and of the sacrificial system explains how his death can account ritually for the shedding of innocent blood. For Christian readers, it is a reminder that reconciliation to God and to life in his community has been fulfilled by the death of Jesus (Heb. 9:11–10:18). The New Testament, however, does not specifically refer to Jesus in terms of the

we are charged to treat another person in the household of faith with loving respect (Rom. 12:10; James 3:9).

The tradition of the "avenger of blood" (20:3) reflects the cultural ideology of community coherence. Nevertheless, the passage indicates that the establishment of justice and protections for the sanctity of the land apply as well to "any foreigner" (20:9). As was the case with Israel, Christian community is grounded in God's relationship with those who acknowledge his lordship, cities of refuge, with the possible exception of Hebrews 6:18.[1]

Illustrating the Text

God's justice and the sanctity of life should impact our social views.

Personal Reflection: The reality that all of us are made in the image of God has profound implications in terms of our social views. This teaching of Joshua 20 provides an opportunity for the preacher/teacher to challenge the listeners to consider how they should think about the following societal challenges: How should the Bible shape our perspective regarding capital punishment? How should the Bible shape our perspective regarding abortion? How should the Bible shape our perspective regarding the taking of human life in war?

The community of faith is to live out God's love for all people.

Biography: Elijah P. Lovejoy. After graduating from Princeton Seminary, Lovejoy began his preaching ministry. He was deeply moved by the plight of slaves in the United States, and he focused his attention and influence on abolitionist issues, particularly through the publication of an antislavery newspaper, the *Saint Louis Observer*. Some people believe that his strong abolitionist views were the result of being forced to watch a slave burned at the stake. Even though he was continually threatened and had his printing presses destroyed by mobs, Lovejoy refused to stop working on behalf of the freedom of slaves. In 1837, incited by the arrival of a new press, a mob in Alton, Illinois, tried to set his home on fire, and as he ran out of his house he was shot and killed.[2] As a Christian, Lovejoy refused to accept the enslavement of any human being. In the same way, we should be unwilling to accept any kind of bigotry, racism, or sexism in our hearts, in the church, or in our world. This would be a good time to provide specific opportunities for your congregants to engage in the battle against bigotry.

God provides boundaries of justice in the world.

Literature: *Lord of the Flies*, by William Golding. Golding's classic novel provides a poignant picture of life without the boundaries of justice. In the novel a group of boys survive a plane crash near an isolated island in a remote region of the Pacific Ocean. The society that these well-educated children produce soon regresses into savagery and cruel acts of injustice. As we see in Joshua 20, as well as in many other Bible passages, the Lord graciously provides clear boundaries for community, helping to ensure that individual rights are protected. Ask your congregants to imagine what the world would be like if the Lord did not provide just boundaries. It would be good to pause and give thanks to the Lord for his justice and his teachings, which help to create a better world.

The Levites' Towns

Big Idea *The Lord's appointed leaders instruct his people in God's commandments.*

Understanding the Text

The Text in Context

Joshua 21:1–42 details the naming of forty-eight towns provided for the Levites from the tribal allotments (also 1 Chron. 6:54–81). Chapter 20 names the six cities of refuge, five of which (excepting Bezer) are named in chapter 21 as Levite possessions (21:13, 21, 27, 32, 38). The final paragraph of chapter 21 (vv. 43–45) is the concluding summary statement of the distribution of the land narrated in chapters 13–21.

The listing of towns is highly structured, following this scheme:

1. Introduction (21:1–8)
   a. Preface (21:1–3)
   b. Kohathites: twenty-three cities (21:4–5)
   c. Gershonites: thirteen cities (21:6)
   d. Merarites: twelve cities (21:7)
   e. Synopsis (21:8)
2. Kohathites' cities (21:9–26)
   a. Aaron's priestly descendants: thirteen cities (21:9–19)
   b. Rest of the Kohathites: ten cities (21:20–26)
3. Gershonites' cities: thirteen cities (21:27–33)
4. Merarites' cities; twelve cities (21:34–40)
5. Total: forty-eight cities (21:41–42)

Generally, the cities are named geographically in a counterclockwise arrangement, beginning with Judah and ending with the Transjordan tribes of Reuben and Gad. Because Aaron founded the lineage of the priests, his cities are distinguished (21:9–19; 1 Chron. 6:2–15).

Historical and Cultural Background

After the distribution of the land occurs at Gilgal (chaps. 14–17), the tent of meeting moves to Shiloh, from which seven tribes receive their inheritance (18:1–19:48). Shiloh is identified as Khirbet Seilun, which is located about midway between Shechem and Bethel in the hill country of Ephraim, north of Jerusalem. Apart from a return to Shechem for the covenant renewal (24:1, 25–26), the tent of meeting remains at Shiloh, but the ark is captured by the Philistines in the battle at nearby Ebenezer (1 Sam. 4:1–11). Shechem was an important setting for covenant renewal since it was historically connected with the patriarchs. Shiloh too was an appropriate background for the distribution of the land because of its long association with an ancient cultic site. Archaeologists have concluded that Shiloh most likely was a worship center, during the Middle Bronze IIB/C (1700–1500 BC) to Early Iron (1200–1000) periods. Cultic items were recovered, such as cultic stands and votive bowls, and the site did not reveal residential settlement. Settlement surveys show, however, that many local towns can be explained perhaps as a result of Shiloh's shrine. The burned remains of buildings in the eleventh century agree with the biblical suggestion that Shiloh was destroyed by the Philistines (Jer. 7:12–14).[1]

Ancient boundary lists distinguished the borders of city-states by physical features, such as mountains and rivers, and by towns. Economic transactions between individuals included descriptions of the properties and distinguished the borders by houses and fields of those properties. Boundary descriptions and town lists often appeared in treaties between city-states; for instance, descriptions of the borders between vassal states under the Hittite king occur under his supervision and with the effect of diminishing potential rivalries. The Levite towns are determined by God (by lot), and the Israelites are bound to acknowledge

Shiloh's history as a sacred site may have influenced the decision to locate the tent of meeting there. The discovery of objects such as this incense stand from the seventeenth to sixteenth century BC provide evidence that Shiloh was the location of an ancient worship center.

Key Themes of Joshua 21:1–42

- The Levites' inheritance is the Lord and the tent of meeting's ministry.
- By the Lord's command the Levites receive towns and their pasturelands as gifts from the tribes.
- The Levites instruct the people and influence them by godly behavior.
- That the Levites receive a possession shows that they are recipients of the divine promises.

the Levites' property rights. (See "Historical and Cultural Background" in the units on 15:1–63 and 18:1–19:51.)

Interpretive Insights

21:1 *approached Eleazar the priest.* The same word "approached" (*nagash*) describes the initiation of the distribution at Gilgal (14:6). Eleazar, the son of Aaron, is named before Joshua since the chapter pertains to the priestly and Levitical clans.

21:2 *The LORD commanded through Moses.* A similar phrase occurs in 14:2 (cf. 20:2; 21:8; 22:9; Num. 35:1–5). The inclusion of "the LORD" and "through Moses" underscores the legitimacy of the claims made by the Levites.

pasturelands for our livestock. The suburbs of the towns provide open land for herds and flocks. These include animals presented to the Levites by the people as the tithe of their possessions (Num. 18:21).

21:3 *out of their own inheritance.* The Levitical cities are the gifts of the tribes who relinquish

Why Levitical Towns?

The book of Joshua repeatedly acknowledges that the Levites did not receive a territory as did the other tribes (13:14, 33; 14:3–4; 18:7). Rather, their inheritance was the Lord and the offerings presented at the tent of meeting by the Israelites (13:14; cf. Num. 18:20–24; 35:1–3; Deut. 10:8–10; 14:27). The towns were given by each tribe from its territory in proportion to the size of the territory (Num. 35:8). The Levites had the unique position of serving as priests and as custodians of the ark and tent of meeting. The Levites were teachers and interpreters of the commandments, ruling on cultic boundaries and thus preserving the sacredness of the community (e.g., Lev. 10:10–11). They were spokesmen for the people before God, offering blessings and oracles (Num. 6:22–27; Deut. 33:8; 1 Sam. 1:9–20; 14:41). They were diviners regarding war and supervised the ark in times of battle (Josh. 6; 1 Sam. 4; 2 Sam. 11:11). They probably functioned as local tax collectors (Exod. 30:11–16). The location and wide distribution of the towns suggest that the Levites were the cultural vanguards against encroaching military threats and religious idolatry of the Canaanites.

them in obedience to the Lord's command. The inheritance of the Levites, however, is the Lord himself, not the cities.

21:4 *first lot came out for the Kohathites.* Joshua casts lots for the Levitical cities, using the same means as before to discern God's will for the tribal allotments (e.g., 14:2; 18:10). The Kohathite towns are named in two groups—those belonging to Aaron's family (21:9–19) and to the remaining Kohathite families (21:20–26). Judah, Simeon, and Benjamin contribute the thirteen cities that belong to Aaron's priestly lineage. Simeon's allotment lies within the borders of Judah (19:1, 9) and therefore can be counted under the auspices of Judah's territory. Judah is especially large, yielding nine cities, whereas Benjamin gives four cities.

21:5 *rest of Kohath's descendants.* Dan, Ephraim, and the half tribe of Manasseh contribute ten towns. The Danite cities named in chapter 21 are in the original tribal location in southwest Canaan (21:23), possibly indicating that this list of names reflects a time before the tribe has migrated north (19:47; Judg. 18:29). Alternatively, the list may be an idealized account of what should be the Danite contribution from their original allotment.

21:6 *Gershon . . . thirteen towns.* These towns are in the northern regions, including the Transjordan half of Manasseh.

21:7 *Merari . . . received.* Eight cities are in the Transjordan (from Reuben and Gad), and four are widely distributed west of the Jordan in Zebulun.

21:11–12 *Arba . . . Anak . . . Caleb.* The recurring reference to the imposing and infamous Anakites in the book underscores the faith of Caleb, who obtains his inheritance (14:6–25; 15:13–19; Num. 13:28–33).

21:42 *Each . . . had pasturelands.* The word "pasturelands" (*migrash*) occurs fifty-five times in this chapter. Numbers 35:1–5 gives a detailed description of the pasturelands' dimensions, indicating the importance attached to the pasturelands.

Theological Insights

Chapter 21 shows the inclusiveness of God's grace. No tribe is left out of the blessing. One important difference from the other tribal allotments is that the Levites receive their portion from the tribes. The tribes share out of their abundance with the Levites, who are especially set aside by the Lord for the work of the ministry. This practice is also reflected by the custom of tithing. The Levites receive a tenth of all the offerings presented at the tent of meeting (Num. 18:21–24; 31:30). The Levites too must practice tithing by presenting a

tenth of what they receive to the work of the Lord (Num. 18:26–28). Initially, the Levites receive cities instead of a land tract because of their ancestor's sins (cf. Gen. 34; 49:5–7). But the heroic response of the Levites against the idolaters of the golden calf transforms the judgment into a blessing (Exod. 32:25–29; cf. the Levite priest, Phinehas, Num. 25:6–8).[2]

The blessing for the Levites results in benefits for all the tribes through the teaching of God's word. Because the Levites are distributed among the tribes, the Lord's ministers are better positioned to teach and model the ordinances of the Lord. That the Levites exhibit influence in Israel's history can also be seen by the negative influence they exert (Judg. 17–18; Mic. 3:11; Mal. 2:8).

The theology of promise and fulfillment appears in this chapter, reflecting the primary theology of the book of Joshua. The Lord's instructions to Moses in Moab to set aside towns for the Levites imply that the Lord will fulfill his promise of giving Canaan to the Israelites (Num. 35:1–5). That the Lord specifies the exact number of "forty-eight towns" indicates that the Israelites will eventually have numerous

possessions (Num. 35:7). Since the theme of Israel's obedience to the Lord's commands in the book is foundational to the theology of Joshua, it appears again in this chapter, detailing that the Israelites carry out the command precisely. Although the cities named have not yet all been won, the naming of them anticipates the success of Israel's future possession of Canaan.

Teaching the Text

The tribes give their cities to the Levites as an essential part of their dedication to the Lord's service. The Bible is replete with exhortations and examples of God's people contributing from their possessions to sustain the worship of the Lord (e.g., Deut. 26:1–15; Neh. 10:37–39; 2 Cor. 8:1–15; Phil. 4:18). Jesus sends his disciples to preach the gospel and instructs them to rely financially on those who receive their message (Mark 6:6–13; Luke 9:1–6). Offering gifts for the Lord's work is a privilege enjoyed by Christian believers (2 Cor. 8:3–5).

The wide distribution of the Levitical cities provides all the tribes the opportunity to learn the statutes of the Lord for doctrine, worship, and godly living. Joshua reinforces the significance of obeying the statutes so that the people might continue life in the land (8:30–35; 24:1–28; Lev. 10:10–11). The same principle is at work in the Christian community. The church is furnished with appointed leaders who are gifted teachers (Rom. 12:6–8; Eph. 4:11–14). The elders of the church who work effectively receive their due reward from the members of the church who are the beneficiaries of the elders' labor (1 Tim. 5:17–18; cf. 1 Cor. 9:9, 14; Deut. 25:4).

The passage provides another opportunity to show that God's blessings for his people are inclusive. In receiving God's blessing, laity and priests are interdependent. The laity provide the financial support of the Levites through gifts and offerings to the Lord. In turn the laypeople rely on the Aaronic priests and on the Levites to function as cultic mediators between the Lord and the people. Furthermore, they depend on the appointed leaders to teach them the word of God. Similarly, the church shows interdependence between appointed leaders and the laity. Church leaders are the recipients of the laity's service to the Lord, and they are servants and spiritual protectors of the laity (e.g., Acts 20:28; 1 Pet. 5:1–3). But there is an important difference between the priestly orders in Israel and the clergy in the church. The church's leaders are not priests in the same sense. For Christians the high-priestly function is carried out by Jesus. Individual Christians and collectively the church are the temple, the sacred space, in which the Spirit dwells, that must be maintained by godly living (1 Cor. 3:16–17; 6:19; Eph. 2:21–22).

The tent of meeting has been moved to Shiloh, so this is where the Levite family leaders come to ask for their inheritance. This small plateau on the ancient site of Shiloh is one possible area where the tent of meeting may have stood. The mention of doorposts and doors in 1 Samuel seems to indicate that the tent structure would be replaced by something more permanent.

Illustrating the Text

How much is the gospel worth?

Anecdote: W. A. Criswell, pastor of First Baptist Church, Dallas, used an illustration of how giving to the Lord's work by parents teaches their children what value to place on the gospel. A parent took his son on Saturday to the fair, where he splurged on tickets, rides, and sweet treats. But on the following day, Sunday, when the offering plate passed down the pew the father tossed in a dollar—a pittance. What did the parent teach his child? The Lord's work is unimportant!

You can affect eternity.

Quote: Henry Brooks Adams. The American literary giant Henry Brooks Adams (1838–1918) in his autobiography, *The Education of Henry Adams*, warned in 1918 that teachers in the new century had a powerful influence on the direction of society. The oft-quoted line attributed to Adams, "Teachers affect eternity; no one can tell where their influence stops," can have a positive or negative side.[3] Nevertheless, the observation is sobering for teachers and students. The apostle Paul insists that his successors who teach the church must adhere to the authentic gospel and to the teaching of the apostles if the church is to survive the onslaughts of its opponents (2 Tim. 1:13; Titus 1:9; cf. Jude 17–20).

God gives perfect gifts.

Everyday Life: Kit Yarrow, a researcher in consumer behavior, names the six gifts you should *not* give to a person. First, "the all about me gift," which is not wanted or needed, tells more about you than about the recipient. Second, "the obvious regift" says you do not care enough to give a present that is especially for the recipient. Third, "the statement gift" is a gift that makes an evident declaration, not of appreciation, but of disapproval. Fourth, "the well-meant misfire" gives a present that is well intended but hurtful, such as an acne solution kit for a person with skin problems. Fifth, "the passive-aggressive gift" is a kind of statement gift that is an expression of hostility wrapped up in a decorative package. Sixth, "the non-gift" is often a gift that would need to be bought anyway, such as socks; but worst is the one given between members of the same financial household that is an expensive purchase that the recipient had no input in getting, such as a new car.[4] The Lord furnished the Levites good gifts, gifts of towns and pastures, so that they might prosper like the other tribes. James 1:17–18 reminds us that "every good and perfect gift" comes from the "Father of the heavenly lights," who bestows salvation's new birth.

Rest in the Land

Big Idea *The divine promises are fulfilled by establishing God's people in his ways.*

Understanding the Text

The Text in Context

Joshua 21:43–45 is a summary statement that completes the former section describing the distribution of the land in 13:1–21:42. It is reminiscent of an earlier summary in 11:23 that completes the former section narrating Joshua's conquest of the land in chapters 6–11 (see also 10:40–42). Chapter 12 is transitional, bridging the conquest stories and the disposition of the land. The present passage functions similarly as a bridge between the former part of the book of Joshua in chapters 1–21 and the latter part in chapters 22–24. Chapters 22–24 describe what life is like in the early days of Israel's settlement. Joshua 21:43–45 provides the platform for understanding this following section narrating the settlement era during the lifetime of Joshua and the elders of the nation (chaps. 22–24). Some scholars observe that verse 43—"gave to Israel all the land" (AT)—summarizes chapters 13–21; and verse 44—"not one withstood them from their enemies" (AT)—recalls the battles in chapters 1–12. And verse 45—"every good promise was fulfilled" (AT)—is a reflex of all the foregoing in chapters 1–21.

The passage has two parallel constructions. (1) The expression "had sworn (to give) to their ancestors" (AT) occurs in 21:43 and 21:44a. This repetition reveals the focus of the passage—the oath of God to Israel's forefathers. (2) Another parallel structure appears in 21:44b and 21:45 by "not one . . ." and "not one . . ." The logic of this parallelism is the following: since not one enemy withstands the Israelites, then not one of God's promises fails. The promises made to the fathers have been realized because of the defeat of Israel's enemies. Thus, sandwiched between the divine oath (21:44a) and the divine promise (21:45) is the reason for the fulfillment of the promissory oath—that is, the Lord enables the Israelites to rout the Canaanites (21:44b).

Interpretive Insights

21:43 *So the LORD gave.* The word "gave/give" (*natan*) occurs three times in the Hebrew text (four times in the NIV) of these three verses, reiterating a common term in the book of Joshua (e.g., 1:2). This summary statement underlines the favor of God. The divine landlord grants his people their own land, where they might prosper in peace (Lev. 25:23).

all the land. The word "all/every" (kol) appears six times in this short span of three verses. The largesse of the Lord is again in view, indicating that the Lord provides fully what he has promised (e.g., 24:3; Gen. 13:15; Deut. 19:8).

he had sworn. That God takes an oath is not customary, and it emphasizes the assurance of the divine promise. The word "swear" (shaba') occurs for both human and divine oaths. On the human plane in the ancient Near East, people invoked the gods as witnesses to an oath (cf. 23:7; Heb. 6:16). The Israelites made oaths, but only in the name of the Lord or by those things that were deemed sacred because of their association with God (e.g., 2:12; 1 Sam. 20:42; Matt. 23:16–22). On the divine plane, the Lord alone was the true God and could swear an oath only on the basis of his own integrity (e.g., Gen. 22:16; Heb. 6:13). In biblical orthodoxy witnesses to

Key Themes of Joshua 21:43–45

- The Lord's gift of the land is accomplished.
- The Lord's blessing for Israel is peace from its enemies and prosperity in the land.
- The Israelites carry out the possession of the promised inheritance.
- The ancestors and their descendants are unified throughout the generations by the divine promise of blessing.

divine oaths must be inanimate, such as Moses's song (Deut. 31:21) or the heavens and earth (e.g., Deut. 30:19; Isa. 1:2)— never the gods.

their ancestors. "Ancestors" translates the word "fathers/forefathers" ('ab), referring most likely to the patriarchs, Abraham, Isaac, and Jacob (1:6; 24:3–4; see, e.g., Exod. 6:8; Deut. 10:15). Moses has explained that God chose Israel because of his love for the fathers (Deut. 4:37–39), not because of Israel's strength in numbers (Deut. 7:7–8) or because of Israel's righteousness (Deut. 9:5–6). The possession of Canaan is due to God's faithfulness to his promises.

they took possession. The word "possess" (*yarash*) is very common in Deuteronomy, Joshua, and Judges. The term means "to seize, dispossess, and drive out." The land is called, literally, "the land of your possession" in 1:15, indicating from the outset that the Israelites are promised a possession but must also play a role in acquiring their inheritance (e.g., 13:13; 15:63; 18:3). Yet it is God who will "certainly drive out" the Canaanites (3:10; cf. 23:9).

settled there. "Settled there" describes the Danites' migration to Leshem, where they take up a new residence and adopt a new name (19:47; Judg. 18:28). The idea in the present verse is that the Israelites are immigrants who take up permanent residence. This is the promise God makes to the fathers (Gen. 15:7–8). The Israelites are wilderness refugees who against all odds become entrenched in Canaan as newly settled immigrants.

21:44 *gave them rest.* The word "rest" (*nuah*) also appears in 23:1 in the sense of a respite from Israel's enemies. It also occurs in conjunction with possessing the land as the place of rest (1:13, 15; 22:4). "Rest" is the security that the Lord affords the covenant people through the gift of the land, a land that is their possession and gives them prosperity.[1] A more specific term is "rest from war" (*shaqat*), indicating the pacification of the land (11:23; 14:15). It is the common term appearing in Judges to describe the cessation of hostilities by the nations against the Israelites (e.g., Judg. 3:11).

Not one . . . withstood them. The comment is not absolute, since there remain pockets of Canaanite resistance (e.g., 15:63; 17:12; Judg. 1:19; 2:21). This summary statement is the reversal of the Israelites' defeat at Ai, where they do not "stand against their enemies" (7:12–13). The language reflects Moses's sermon that predicts Israel's victory over its enemies (Deut. 12:10; 25:19). But Israel experiences defeat if it disobeys the covenant: "You will not be able to stand before your enemies" (Lev. 26:37 AT). The literal rendering is "not one from all their enemies stood against them," indicating that their wars recounted in chapters 6–11 result in overwhelming victories.

21:45 *Not one . . . promises . . . failed.* The verse states emphatically that the divine promise of dispossessing the inhabitants of Canaan has occurred (cf. 23:15; Jer. 33:14). "Israel" is literally "house of Israel," which occurs in Joshua only here. The expression is inclusive, meaning all the tribes benefit from the victories God has promised, "every one [promise] was fulfilled" (lit., "came to pass"). For a discussion of hyperbole as a legitimate rhetorical device in battle reports, see "Inheritance of the Land" in the introduction.

Theological Insights

This passage shows that God is faithful to keep his promissory word. The weight of the responsibility rests ultimately on God's shoulders, not the Israelites'. Although the settlement era under Joshua is characterized by faithfulness on Israel's part, more often the Israelites are disobedient. This is the case once Joshua and the elders pass away (24:31; Judg. 2:7–13). Nevertheless, the Lord preserves the Israelites because of his commitment to their ancestors (Exod. 34:6). Joshua acknowledges that the land is not fully pacified, and future generations must do their part to claim their possession

(23:4–5). What is more important is the implication of Israel's failures for God's integrity and reputation. If the Lord does not fulfill his word, then the nations will conclude that the God of the Israelites is unreliable and impotent (Exod. 32:12–14). The book shows that the conquest is progressive and that the Lord gradually ensures the reality of the promises. The result is that the conquest creates awe for Israel's God among the nations (Deut. 4:6–8).

The description of the Israelites' victorious conquest of the promised land contains rhetoric similar to that found in battle accounts across the ancient Near East. For example, the Taylor Prism (691 BC), shown here, which recounts the military success of Sennacherib, recognizes the role of the Assyrian god when the inscription says that the god Assur "has made powerful my weapons," "encouraged me," "gave me courage," "supported me," and "gave ear to my prayers and came to my aid." The Israelites, too, acknowledge that the Lord, YHWH, gives the land, gives them rest, and gives their enemies into their hands.

The covenant that God made with the fathers and their descendants has bound the people together across generations (21:43). Unity is derived from their common relationship with the Lord, not the consequence of common ethnicity or cultural heritage. Also, the assurance of God's promises and the constancy of his elective love supersede time (4:6, 21; 22:24–28). Communal life is based on the promises of old that continue with future generations who love the Lord (Deut. 7:9).

The passage reflects the goodness of God (Exod. 33:19). God alone is inherently good (Mark 10:18), whereas all others act with benevolence toward others by virtue of a preexisting relationship. Joshua declares that the promises are "good," indicating God's generosity (21:45; 23:14–15), and that their inheritance is the good land (23:13, 15, 16). By this he means that they will prosper as a nation. The ultimate purpose of the Lord's benevolence toward Israel, however, is to convey his saving grace toward all nations (Exod. 19:6; Deut. 7:6; Isa. 43:21).

The synergy of the Sovereign Lord and human enablement occurs in this brief summary. The Lord has "sworn," taking on himself the fulfillment of the promise, yet Israel has "possessed" Canaan, indicating the role of the people themselves. The coexistence of these two facets creates an uneasy tension in the minds of many modern readers. The idea of God's "all-causality" asserts that the Lord is *ultimately* the causal factor for all that happens. Whereas today people say, "*It* rained," the Bible says that "God sent the rain" (Gen. 2:5; Jer. 5:24; Matt. 5:45). But biblical narratives acknowledge that nature and people are intermediate causes. For example, the Lord uses the Assyrian army to accomplish his greater purpose of purging Israel of its wickedness (Isa. 10:5).

Teaching the Text

This brief passage gives teachers the opportunity to summarize all that has gone before in the book of Joshua. The author back-references all the previous major sections and paves the way for the final section of the book, chapters 22–24. The passage by itself gives the reader a theological summary of the main message of the book by drawing in key terms that have recurred—"gave," "ancestors," "possession," "rest," "enemies," and "promises." Several of the words recall chapter 1's terms and theological emphases. Coupling the chapters together, the teacher can show the theology of promise in chapter 1 and the theology of fulfillment in 21:43–45. The emphasis of the passage is the trustworthy character and promises of God (cf. Exod. 33:14). This message shows us that we can place full confidence in God's eternal promises for us (Heb. 3:6).

The theological idea of "rest" throughout the Bible concerns the achievement of stability and order in a way that can be accomplished only by God, whether it is in the political kingdom of Israel or the spiritual kingdom of God (in both "already" and "not yet" terms; Matt. 11:28–30; Heb. 3–4). Regardless of the perspective a person has regarding the relationship of a future redeemed Israel and of the church, all views have in common the lordship of Christ, who fully achieves the promises and completes ultimately the Christian's spiritual inheritance of eternal life (Rom. 6:22–23; Eph. 1:9–18; Heb. 11:8–10; 1 Pet. 2:3–4). By building on the idea of possession of Canaan, the writer to the Hebrews sees the generation of Joshua as a type of the Christian's own journey of faith, experienced now by those who have believed the gospel (4:1–5; 12:22); yet still to come for those who persist in faith is possession of the ultimate heavenly inheritance of Christ (e.g., 11:16; 12:22, 28). Whether in Israel's possession of Canaan or in the Christian's present pilgrimage, the theology of "rest" means not inactivity but freedom to strive in faith and godly living—expressing faith through obedience to God's word. The message of Hebrews serves as an exhortation to continue in faith and as a warning to those who have not entered that rest.

The passage invites reflection on the goodness of God, for his "good promises" (lit., "good things," 21:45) consist of his grace extended to his people. Not Israel's might or goodness but God alone provides a secure land (Lev. 26:5). The "good land," rich in beauty and resources, sustains Israel (Deut. 8:7–10). God provides a sacred land, for the land is the habitat of the Lord where Israel and God commune (Exod. 29:46). The goodness of God ought to elicit praise and thanksgiving from believers (Ps. 54:6) and obedience to God's word (Josh. 23:15). Christian readers have experienced in communion with Christ a mere taste of the goodness of God, which incites them to persevere in godly living (1 Pet. 2:3). Our faith is in a God who showers his people with spiritual blessings (Matt. 7:11; James 1:17).

Illustrating the Text

Faith is choosing to act in light of the commands and promises of God.

Human Experience: Teaching a toddler to swim can be a frustrating experience for the parents and a terrifying experience for the child. The process often involves allowing the child to flounder in the water, and possibly even begin to sink, with the parent's loving arms there to catch or rescue the toddler. The child's willingness to engage in the learning process will be a reflection of his or her confidence in the promise of the parent, "I will be with you and won't let anything happen to you!" The more faith the toddler has in the parent's promise, the more willing he or she will be to practice the swimming technique until there is confidence and competence. A child who does not trust the promise of the parent will not be willing to take the step of faith. And as the parent proves faithful to his or her promise to the child, the toddler gains confidence and deepened trust and faith. In the book of Joshua we see that Israel's willingness to take the land against astronomical odds of victory is a reflection of its trust and faith in the promise of God. And as the Israelites find the Lord faithful in battle after battle, their trust and faith in the Lord deepen. But this lesson is learned only when they are willing to take the step of faith. Ask your congregants, "What step of faith is the Lord asking you to take?"

Obedience to the Lord leads to spiritual rest.

Object Lesson: In general, it is not a good idea to use power tools in the kitchen. Bring to the service a power drill, cake mix, and related items to make a cake. Place the ingredients for the cake in a mixing bowl, and then use the power drill to attempt to mix the ingredients. Obviously the drill will be an ineffective tool to accomplish the purpose. After attempting to mix the ingredients with the power drill, use a kitchen mixer. Explain that it is a good idea to use tools in ways that are consistent with their purpose. For example, it would be better to use a knife than a saw to slice a roast. Read Matthew 11:28–30 to your listeners. Explain that the point Jesus is making is that spiritual rest is found as we live the life we were created to live (in obedience to God). Just as tools function best when used according to their purpose, we will find rest when we live according to life's design and purpose.

Choose to respond to the goodness of God.

Applying the Text: Explain to your listeners the power of the goodness of God. For example, knowing that God is always good means that we never have to worry about the Lord being volatile with us or responding to us in a manner that is not good. Take a few moments to lead the audience in a prayer of thanksgiving, thanking the Lord for his good gifts.

Transjordan Tribes Receive a Blessing

Big Idea *The Lord's appointed leaders invoke God's blessings on those who are faithful to their obligations.*

Understanding the Text

The Text in Context

Chapter 22 begins the last major section in the book, describing the life of the people during the settlement period (chaps. 22–24). The chapter consists of two units. (1) Joshua 22:1–9 introduces the central subject of the whole chapter: the question of loyalty to the Lord by the Transjordan tribes (22:10–34). These tribes have received their inheritance from Moses, but on the condition that they assist the other tribes in winning their lands across the Jordan (Num. 32:1–33). At the permission and with the blessing of Joshua, they leave for their homelands. (2) Joshua 22:10–34 tells

The fighting men from the tribes of Reuben, Gad, and Manasseh, whose inheritance is land on the east side of the Jordan, are told by Joshua to return home with the spoils of war they have received and to divide that among the Israelites who have remained in the Transjordan during the time of the conquest. This relief from the palace at Nineveh (640–620 BC) shows victorious Assyrian soldiers piling up cauldrons, weapons, and furniture while scribes make a record of the plundered items.

how the Transjordan tribes build an altar and the threat that it causes to the solidarity of the twelve tribes.

The present unit has four parts: (1) Joshua first exhorts the Transjordan tribes to remain faithful to the Lord (22:1–5; see 1:12–18). (2) As a consequence of their loyalty, Joshua invokes a blessing for the tribes (22:6–7). (3) In continuing the idea of community solidarity, he commands the tribes to share their wealth with their "fellow Israelites" (22:8). (4) The narrator ends this prelude by recounting that the tribes leave "Shiloh," the place where they have been united by the central sanctuary (22:9).

Interpretive Insights

22:1 *Then Joshua summoned.* The beginning word (*'az*; cf. 8:30; 10:33) shows that only *after* the land has been secured for the western tribes (21:43–45) does Joshua release the Transjordan tribes from their pledge (Deut. 3:18–20). Joshua exerts authority over all the tribes (e.g., 4:4; 6:6; 9:22; 10:24; 23:2; 24:1). His authority is due in part to Moses's investiture but ultimately derives from the Lord alone (Num. 27:12–23).

22:2 *You have done all . . . obeyed me in everything.* The language calls attention to the subject "you" (lit., "you, you have . . ."), focusing on Joshua's commendation. The tribes entirely fulfill their oath to secure the land for their kin. The verbs "done" (*shamar*) and "obeyed" (*shama' b^eqoli*; lit., "heard my voice") highlight complete compliance with Joshua's commands.

22:3 *For a long time now . . . you have not deserted.* The time frame is the seven and a half years of conquest. The verbal

commitment, however, occurred in the last days of Moses, which may be also in mind (Num. 32:25–33). The men of the tribes are separated from their families for a long period, but they do not waver. "Deserted" (*'azab*) means to forsake, but another nuance of the term is the failure to keep one's obligation to God or his people (24:16, 20; Deut. 28:20; Ruth 2:20; cf. ESV).

22:5 *But be very careful to keep.* "But" (*raq*) intensifies the contrast between verses 4 and 5. "Keep" (root word *shamar*) occurs four times in a short span of four verses (22:2, 3, 5 [2x]; the repetition doesn't come clearly through in the NIV; cf. ESV) to emphasize the command for Israel's vigilant obedience.

the commandment and the law. "Commandment" (*mitswah*) and "law" (*torah*) capture the whole of the covenant instructions given to Moses (Exod. 24:12; "Book of the Covenant," Exod. 24:7). The Ten Commandments (Exod. 20) are the heart of the covenant, giving absolute commandments or "policy" by which Israel lives ("you shall / shall not"). The "law" refers to the specific legislative requirements that give practical expression to the covenant policy (Exod. 21–24).

to keep his commands, to hold fast. Moses uses the same exhortation, "to keep his commands," so that they might have life and prosperity in the land (Deut. 30:16). The word "hold fast" (*dabaq*) means "to cling to," as a belt clings to a person's waist (Jer. 13:11; cf. ESV) or as Ruth hugs Naomi as a sign of her devotion (Ruth 1:14). The term also occurs in Genesis 2:24 ("united"), describing the union of wife and husband. Here, its figurative use indicates devotion to God (cf. Deut. 11:22).

to serve him with all your heart and . . . soul. "Serve" (*'abad*) ranges broadly in meaning, from forced labor for human masters (16:10) to the worship of God (22:27). Joshua repeatedly uses "serve," meaning worship, for contrasting Israel's God and the worship of idols (23:7, 16; 24:2, 14, 15). "Heart" (*lebab*) and "soul" (*nepesh*) combine to mean the inner person, indicating here authenticity and passion (Deut. 6:5; 11:13; 13:3). "Soul" (*nepesh*) is not Greek philosophy's eternal, immaterial essence

of a person. Rather, in biblical thought, it refers to the total person (cf. Gen. 2:7, "living being") or to the inner mind and inner desire. "All" (*kol*) commonly occurs in this expression, indicating full allegiance.

22:6 *Joshua blessed them*. Joshua invokes the blessing of God. "Blessed" (*barak*) indicates the favor of God (8:33; 14:13; 17:14). The content of the blessing may have been similar to the priestly blessing of Numbers 6:24–26.

22:8 *great wealth*. The riches of the tribes consist of the booty taken in the preceding years of war (Deut. 20:14; Josh. 8:2, 27; 11:14). These items are the tribes' inheritance, whereas at Jericho they are dedicated to the Lord's service (6:19, 24). The mention of clothing recalls Achan's theft (7:15, 21–26).

large herds of livestock. Large herds motivate the Transjordan tribes to request the eastern lands, especially Bashan (9:10),

Half the tribe of Manasseh returns to the area of Bashan, the modern Golan Heights region shown here, and part of Gilead, both east of the Jordan.

which is known for its timber (Isa. 2:13), lush pasturelands (Num. 32:1–4, 33), and large cattle (Amos 4:1). Bashan, the possession of Manasseh, is east of the Jordan opposite the area of Galilee.

fellow Israelites. These are men who have stayed behind in Transjordan to protect the families and holdings of the warriors.

22:9 *Gilead.* The region is south of Bashan, consisting of two major halves (12:2, 5; 13:31). The northern half is mainly settled by Manasseh and the southern half by Gad. It is prized for spices and medicines (Gen. 37:25; Jer. 46:11).

Theological Insights

Two theological pillars for the book of Joshua are the promises of God and the faithful obedience of his people. The consequence of God's promises and the people's fidelity is the bestowal of land on Israel (chaps. 13–19). The present passage emphasizes the obedience of the people, in particular, the two and a half tribes of Transjordan. The passage assumes that the reader knows that it is God who gives them their lands, not Moses by himself (Deut. 29:7–9). The emphasis in this passage is the obedience of the tribes and the gift of the land for their descendants. Unity based on mutual love for the Lord and shown by cooperation as fellow Israelites is the chief thought here. The idea of blessing is an important feature in the book's theology; it is God's favor expressed toward those who demonstrate covenant faithfulness (8:33–34; Caleb, 14:13; cf. 15:19). Joshua's invocation assures the eastern tribes of peace and prosperity in the land as long as they are faithful (22:6–7).

To Love God

What does it mean to love God? (1) God initiates love between him and human beings. The concept of "love" (*'aheb*) is central to Deuteronomy (cf. Deut. 6:5) and underlies Joshua, although the word occurs only twice (22:5; 23:11).[a] Deuteronomy 10:15 defines "love" in terms of God's covenant election of Israel's ancestors. (2) Second, the nation responds to God's love by covenant loyalty. "Love" means the sole worship of Israel's God (Deut. 13:3). To accept God's love means to keep his commandments (Deut. 7:9), and it means love of those things and persons connected to the Lord, such as his law (Ps. 119:47). Love for God includes thanksgiving for his provision (Ps. 116:1). To love God also means to love one's neighbor (Lev. 19:18).

The New Testament reflects Israel's understanding of God's elective love (*agapaō*; Rom. 11:28). The two great commands combine the ideas of loving God and loving one's neighbor (Mark 12:28–34). Faith and love are related, for by faith in God a person responds in love of God and of believers (Gal. 5:6). The love of the Father for the Son is shared with the believer; love toward one another evidences believers' relationship with God (John 13:34; 14:21–23; 1 John 4:7–13).

[a] See Els, "*'aheb*"; Günther and Link, "Love."

Also important in this passage is the role of the tent of meeting at Shiloh, which houses the ark of the covenant (cf. 18:1). The passage does not specifically refer to the tent, but there is an undercurrent of its importance. The identity of Israel and its intertribal relationships are bound up with the symbolic significance of the tent—the presence of God among his people. It is God's "home," so to speak, and the people are leaving Shiloh (22:9) and the tent for their own homes (22:4, 6, 8). Joshua's concern might be expressed by the proverbial saying: "Out of sight, out of mind." Will the Transjordan tribes remain faithful although they do not have ready access to the tent of meeting at Shiloh? Distance from the central sanctuary and from their fellow Israelites does not allow them to act independently of their covenant commitments. Joshua's call for loyalty prepares the reader for the conflict reported in the remainder of the chapter.

The uniqueness of Israel's God, and the worship of the Lord God only, is a critical feature in the books of Deuteronomy through 2 Kings (Deut. 4:35, 39). God cannot be reduced to an image, as are the gods of the nations. His presence is through his revealed word. Deuteronomy's theology teaches that God alone must be worshiped and only at the place where legitimate worship is conducted (Deut. 12:5). As they intermingle with Canaanites in the land, the people face the temptations of pagan worship. Deuteronomy 12:10–14 commands the people to resist the influence of the nations (cf. Josh. 9:27; 23:7, 12–13). This feature of covenant loyalty is reflected in Joshua 8:30–35 when the people build an altar exclusively in accordance with Deuteronomy's dictates.

Teaching the Text

The reason Israel is the recipient of God's blessing (via Joshua) is not the Israelites' number or character but God's elective love for their ancestors (Exod. 32:9; Deut. 7:7–8; 9:4–6). The word "reward" occurs in the Old Testament and the New Testament, but theologically "reward" in connection to God presupposes a love relationship, one founded on grace, not negotiation. Blessing is anchored in God's love, not in human behavior or industry. Christian obedience does not initiate the relationship with Christ but is an expression of it (1 John 5:2–3; cf. Titus 1:16). "We love because he first loved us" (1 John 4:19).

Related to this is the perseverance of Israel's obedience to God's commandments (22:2, 5). Joshua exhorts the Transjordan tribes to continue the devotion they have shown to God. He does this again for all the tribes in chapters 23 and 24. The Transjordan tribes have demonstrated their love for God, but now they must maintain it. There is no holiday from steadfastness in the Lord. The temptations to compromise their faith by practicing idolatry will be as steadfast. Christians too show faith's authenticity by fervency in the gospel (Col. 1:23; James 1:22–27). Christian works, as imperfect as they may be, nonetheless are bound with faith in Christ (Eph. 2:8–10; 1 Tim. 6:17–19). Faith and works of love come from the same source, Jesus Christ (Gal. 5:6).

Another important feature in this passage is the concept of worship. Obedience to God requires exclusive worship of him— no other god, person, or thing. The Lord does not accept rivals to his rightful place as sovereign ruler (Exod. 20:3; Deut. 8:19). A wedded couple takes marriage vows to love only each other (see the comments on "hold fast" in 22:5, above); divided loyalty breaks the marital oath. The inclusive language with which Joshua implores the Transjordan tribes, "with all your heart and with all your soul" (22:5), indicates fulfillment of their oath (1:12–18). As Jesus teaches his disciples, a person cannot have two masters (Matt. 6:24).

Illustrating the Text

Obedience to God is to be a response of faith and not manipulation for reward.

Television: *Everybody Loves Raymond.* In the Christmas episode from season five of this family sitcom, Ray wants to go with his friends for a golf outing in Myrtle Beach. Ray is afraid his wife, Debra, will not approve, so he wants her to "owe" him. Although Debra only wants a Crock-Pot for Christmas, Ray wants to give her a bigger gift than she is giving him so that she will feel guilty and gladly agree to his golf outing.[1] As you describe the plot, it will be easy for people to "feel" Debra's hurt at the insensitivity of Ray's actions. Ray's "gift" is not really a gift, because it is an act of manipulation. In the same way, when we "do things for the Lord" in order to receive something in return, it is not really an act of love.

Persevere in faith and obedience to the Lord.

Statistics: Every January, millions of Americans make a New Year's resolution to exercise more, often by joining or reconnecting with a gym. Many gyms see a traffic surge of 30 to 50 percent in the first few weeks of January. But the odds that you will keep your New Year's resolution are less than 40 percent.[2] Many people begin their Christian faith with good intentions but then are unable to persevere through trials and temptations (cf. Matt. 13:1–23). This would be a good opportunity to talk about how to persevere in faith.

Love the Lord as the first priority of your life.

Quote: Stephen Covey. Management consultant and author Stephen Covey once said, "Most of us spend too much time on what is urgent and not enough time on what is important . . . the urgent always outweighs the important in terms of the demands it makes on our attention."[3] According to the Bible, what is of ultimate importance is that we love the Lord our God with all of our heart, soul, strength, and mind (e.g., Deut. 6:5; Luke 10:27). But most of us are distracted from that ultimate priority by the life "urgencies" that call for our attention and time. Ask your listeners to reflect on their past week: What would you guess was the percentage you focused on the command to love God as the first priority of your life? Also challenge them to look ahead: What changes can you make this week to keep your heart focused on the Lord as your first priority?

Threat to Unity

Big Idea *The Lord's people resolve conflicts in the covenant community, thereby preserving its unity.*

Understanding the Text

The Text in Context

The introduction to this episode is Joshua's release of the Transjordan tribes to return home (22:1–9). The setting shifts from Shiloh with its tabernacle altar (chaps. 18–21) to the location Geliloth with its replica altar. Also, whereas Joshua is the main character to this point, he is not heard from again in this episode after 22:8. Phinehas the priest and the elders represent the assembly, confronting the Transjordan tribes. The passage consists of four parts: (1) the altar creates a problem (22:10–14); (2) the assembly charges the Transjordan tribes with idolatry (22:15–20); (3) the Transjordan tribes explain that the altar is only a witness, not a place of worship (22:21–29); and (4) Phinehas and the elders are satisfied with the explanation and war is averted (22:30–34).

The passage echoes former trials, including the apostasy of worshiping Baal in the desert (Num. 25) and the incident of Achan's theft at Jericho (Josh. 7). Since the incident centers on the question of loyalty, it prepares readers for Joshua's final exhortations to remain loyal to the

The tribes that occupy the land in Transjordan erect an altar near the Jordan River on the west side. It was not an altar on which to offer sacrifices like this eighth-century BC reconstructed altar found at Tel Beersheba. Rather, the altar at Geliloth was built as a witness to their commitment to worship YHWH at his sanctuary and according to his commands.

covenant. Chapter 23 is his speech calling for the tribes to remain faithful after his death, and chapter 24 describes a covenant renewal ceremony led by Joshua.

Interpretive Insights

22:10 *Geliloth near the Jordan.* "Geliloth" may be a place-name (18:17) or a common noun, meaning "regions" (13:2).

If a place-name, its exact location is unknown, somewhere along the border of Benjamin and Judah.

an imposing altar. The description of the altar, literally, "a large altar in appearance," suggests that the altar is larger than the tent's altar, which measures seven and a half feet long, seven and a half feet wide, and four and a half feet tall (Exod. 27:1–8). An alternative altar for worship is not always illicit (8:30–31; 1 Sam. 7:17), but the worship at an alternative altar must always be directed to the Lord. The erection of the altar by the Transjordan tribes provokes the other tribes to question the purpose of the altar.

22:11 *on the Israelite side.* Compare "the LORD's land" in 22:19.

22:12 *the whole assembly.* The same language occurs in 18:1, where the tent of meeting is at Shiloh. That the tent and its altar are present perhaps creates the visual background for the assembly's meeting. "Assembly" (*'edah*) occurs six times in this passage, emphasizing the community's collective persuasion (22:12, 16, 17, 18, 20, 30). The "whole assembly" (4x) may be another ironical twist, since the two and a half tribes are not present.

to go to war. "War" (*tsaba'*) commonly describes armies at conflict (4:13; NIV: "battle") but also appears as part of a divine title, "LORD of hosts" (*yhwh ts^eba'ot*; e.g., 1 Sam. 1:3; 17:45; NIV: "the LORD Almighty").

22:13 *Phinehas . . . the priest.* Phinehas is the appropriate delegate since he is a grandson of Aaron (Exod. 6:25) and therefore represents the priestly obligation of overseeing tabernacle worship. He is the heroic figure at Peor (22:17) who purges Israel of idolatry (Num. 25:1–18).

Key Themes of Joshua 22:10–34

- The worship of the Lord God constitutes the unity of Israel's nation.
- The Transjordan tribes exhibit zeal for God by establishing a replica of the altar in the tent of meeting.
- The Israelites avert war by investigating the facts before acting.
- The Transjordan tribes secure their future inheritance in Israel's community by naming the altar "Witness."

Gilead. See comments on 22:9.

22:14 *ten of the chief men.* The ten are "leaders of the community" (22:30, 32). That ten are present instead of twelve is a reminder that Israel is fractured.

22:16 *break faith.* The translation renders two words, both from the word group *m'l*, literally, "unfaithful" (*ma'al*) and "to act unfaithfully" (*ma'al*). The terms occur seven times in this passage (22:16 [2x], 20 [2x], 22, 31 [2x]), emphasizing their treachery. At the human level it describes an unfaithful wife (Num. 5:12, 27), but breaches against God concern violations against sacred things (Lev. 5:15). The case of Achan illustrates theft of devoted things (*herem*; see the comments on 7:1). Here, the suspected violation is sacrilege against the holy altar of the tent of meeting (22:19, 29).

turn away . . . rebellion. The word *shub* is very common, meaning "to turn, return" (22:8–9, 32), but metaphorically it means disloyalty (22:16, 18, 23, 29; 23:12), or oppositely, "turning back" to God in repentance (Hosea 6:1). The word group "rebellion, rebel" (*marad*) occurs six times in this passage, three times in conjunction with the verb "turn away" (22:16, 18, 29).

22:17 *sin of Peor.* "Sin" (*'awon*) occurs in verse 20 also. It means "iniquity," the "guilt of iniquity," or even "punishment for guilt" (Gen. 4:13). The "sin of Peor" is Israel's idolatrous worship of Baal, resulting in a devastating plague (Num. 25). God's wrath is appeased by Phinehas, who executes an offender and his pagan wife. Peor is a mountain in the Transjordan region (Moab), which is a significant place to recall in the tribes' charge of apostasy against the Transjordan tribes. The apostasy at Peor is an infamous event in Israel's memory (Ps. 106:28; Hosea 9:10).

cleansed ourselves. The people still suffer in some way from the effects of the plague, although the plague has ceased (Num. 25:7–8). The wicked are executed, but the plague must have fallen upon the innocent too. The infected parties cannot participate normally in the community and cannot appear at the tent of meeting for worship. It is a perpetual reminder of the destructive effects of idolatry on the community and explains in part why the western tribes take swift action.

The Festival of Ingathering, also known as the Festival of Tabernacles, Booths, or Sukkot, was one of the celebrations that required Israelite men to travel to the tent of meeting for worship before the Lord. This festival also required the construction of temporary shelters, perhaps like this one, in which the Israelites lived for seven days. Even though the Israelites were separated geographically, sacred assemblies, celebrations, and rituals like these helped unify them in the promised land.

"Cleansed ourselves" comes from the verb *taher* (here in the reflexive form), meaning that they have not yet purged themselves of the effects of the plague. The term is often used of cleansing ceremonially for the purpose of reentry into the community (e.g., leper, Lev. 14).

22:18 *angry with the whole community.* "Angry" (*qatsap*) may describe human displeasure but more often describes God's wrath. The golden calf incident in Deuteronomy 9:19 includes three synonyms for God's fury: anger (*'ap*), hot displeasure (*hemah*), and wrath (*qatsap*) (see NASB; cf. ESV).[1] The judgments of plague or of foreign invasion impact the whole community, not discriminating between the innocent and the guilty.

22:19 *defiled . . . the LORD's land.* "Defiled" (*tame'*) is another cultic term that describes what is ceremonially unclean; the land is "unclean" if idolatry occurs (Jer. 2:7; NIV: "defiled"). Phinehas's priestly responsibility is to discern between the clean and the unclean (Lev. 10:10). The tabernacle at Shiloh explains why the territory west of the Jordan is named "the LORD's land," specifying that he is its landlord.

22:20 *devoted things.* See comment on 7:1.

22:22 *Mighty One, God, the LORD.* The reverberation of divine names underscores the solemnity of the tribes' oath (cf. Ps. 50:1). "Mighty One" (*'el*) may be translated as "god," "God," the name "El" (which is often compounded with divine names, e.g., El

Shaddai), or the common noun "mighty." One alternative rendering is "the LORD is the God of gods" (cf. HCSB). "God" (*'elohim*) may be translated as the one true God (capitalized) or the plural pagan "gods." The three divine names spoken in a staccato voice reach their crescendo in the name "LORD," the divine name Yahweh.

do not spare us. By taking this oath, the tribes invoke the punishment of death if they abandon the Lord.

22:23 *call us to account*. The Transjordan tribes call on the Lord to administer the curse as their just due if they break faith.

22:24 *No! We did it for fear*. The emphatic negative, "no, indeed," explains that they were motivated only by the anxious concern for their descendants.

22:27 *it is to be a witness*. A "witness" between covenant parties could be an object, such as a heap of stones (Gen. 31:44–45) or an altar (Isa. 19:19–20). Cf. 22:28, 34.

22:28 *replica of the LORD's altar*. "Replica" (*tabnit*), meaning "pattern," is the term used to describe the false altar built by King Ahaz (2 Kings 16:10; see ESV).

22:31 *rescued the Israelites from the LORD's hand*. The oath of the presumed offenders delivers them from the Lord's wrath.

22:34 *Witness Between Us*. The name of the altar is derived from 22:28. The altar becomes a point of mutual reference, testifying to the community's unity under God.

Theological Insights

The central focus of Joshua's speech in 22:1–9 is the covenant loyalty of the Transjordan tribes toward their fellow tribes. Ironically, the building of the altar leads to the question of their loyalty, although the Transjordan tribes mean for the altar to

Holy Days

Three high holy events, the Feasts of Unleavened Bread (Passover), Weeks (Pentecost), and Ingathering (Tabernacles/Booths), require the males of all twelve tribes to appear before the Lord in worship at the tent of meeting (Exod. 34:18–23). Unleavened Bread and Weeks occur in the spring to early summer months, and Ingathering celebrates the fall harvest. This requirement provides occasions for the tribal leaders to renew their commitment to the Lord and to one another. If carried out properly, the holy days stabilize the community despite geography, material culture, and dialects.

demonstrate their allegiance. Two different viewpoints collide. First, the western tribes believe the altar contradicts the instructions in Deuteronomy 12:5, 26 that permit only a legitimate place of worship, one that bears the name of the Lord. In accordance with the covenant, disobedience means the tribes as a "whole assembly/community" (22:12, 16, 18, 20) are subject to God's wrath (cf. Achan, chap. 7). The second view is that of the eastern tribes, who fear their claim to their land as Israelites might be rejected in future generations (cf. the case in Nehemiah's time, Neh. 2:19–20). Once it is understood by all that the altar is a memorial, the potential for war among the brother tribes (fratricide) is averted. The unity of the community is preserved, and the people continue to enjoy the favor of God as they establish themselves in the land.

The unity of the tribes persists despite differences. The Transjordan altar is at a different place (Shiloh and Geliloth) and has a different purpose (the tent's altar and the memorial altar) than the altar at the tent of meeting.[2] The tribes can remain unified, despite the barrier of the Jordan, because of their common commitment to the same God, the God of their ancestors (18:3; 21:43; 24:17). Another binding feature between the tribes is their common salvation.

The Lord has delivered their fathers from Egypt (2:10; 5:2–9; 24:6) and has enabled the tribes to overtake the Canaanites in the land (10:42; 11:23; 21:44; 24:11–13). Further, common worship and the revelation of God given to Moses create a unified people (1:7–8; 5:10–11; 8:30–35; 23:6). And the people have a common purpose, agreeing to secure the land promised them—both east and west (1:12–18). Finally, the people are unified around the common leadership of Joshua (1:16–17; 11:23; 12:7; 22:2).

Teaching the Text

What binds the twelve tribes is not their common land, for there is a "border" that separates them (cf. 22:11). They are bound by their allegiance to the Lord of the covenant and to one another, the "whole assembly/community" (22:12, 16, 18, 20). The Transjordan tribes and the Cisjordan tribes indicate this loyalty in different ways. The Transjordan tribes replicate the altar as a memorial, a statement of their loyalty to the covenant (22:21–29). The Cisjordan tribes insist that the Transjordan tribes abandon their possession if the land is ceremonially "defiled" (22:19), for the land promised as well as the altar is sacred—the "holy land," because the Lord dwells among this people (Lev. 26:11).[3] The Transjordan tribes were meant to live in the promised land (Num. 32:1–33), but they were granted the exception to live outside Canaan. If their possession proves to be marred by the impurities of sin, they must retreat to Canaan. For Christians the holy sanctuary is the spiritual community of the church that is bound by the lordship of Christ. Despite the vast differences in the church's makeup across the

centuries and across the world's geography, Christians hold in common devotion to the one true God, salvation in Christ, and the headship of Jesus Christ (Rom. 12:4–5; Eph. 4:1–16; Col. 3:11–15).

Another lesson related to the first is the accountability of the tribes for the welfare of the whole community. The passage shows that the eastern tribes cannot act independently of the western tribes. Any act on their part impacts the whole nation (22:18, 31). The tribes have previously experienced trials because members disobeyed God (7:1–26; 9:18). The community is deemed guilty too if it ignores criminal acts in its midst (Deut. 19:8–13; 21:1–9; Ezek. 33:7–9), or it can be caught up in God's wrath, which is directed against the guilty (e.g., Num. 16:34; Jer. 26:15). The church too is impacted by the actions of individual members, requiring them to give account for one another (Acts 5:1–11; 1 Cor. 11:17–22; Gal. 6:1–10; James 5:19–20; 1 John 5:16a; Jude 22–23). Christians are commanded to encourage one another in the faith and in spiritual discipline (1 Thess. 5:11; Heb. 10:24–25).

For ancient Israel, syncretism (fusion of different belief systems) was a constant risk. Typically, ancient peoples adopted or adapted the deities of other people groups into their pantheon of gods. The memorial altar might have become a means of merging Yahweh and the popular Baals of the region (e.g., Judg. 17:1–5; 2 Kings 16:1–18). The same threat faced the early church in gentile regions (Acts 14:8–18). American pluralistic culture has produced popular religious systems that are syncretistic in nature, such as New Age, the "Goddess Movement," Unitarianism, and Christian

Science. Christians today must diligently maintain a singular commitment to Jesus Christ and his gospel as they are portrayed by the New Testament (Gal. 1:6–10; 1 Tim. 2:5–6).

Illustrating the Text

There is beauty in the unity of the family of God.

Science: Suzanne Simard, forest ecologist at the University of British Columbia, made a major discovery that trees and plants are able to interact with one another. Simard discovered the existence of an underground fungus that literally connects the trees and plants of an ecosystem, enabling them to share resources. This ability to share resources enables all the trees and plants to draw what they are lacking from other foliage. For example, Simard found that "the big trees were subsidizing the young ones through the fungal networks. Without this helping hand, most of the seedlings wouldn't make it."[4] In the same way, Christians are to visibly express unity as we draw upon the resources of the Lord and one another. For example, we are to share money and possessions with those in need. We are to encourage the discouraged and challenge those who are walking astray. In the church, the Lord has provided what we need to live well and in unity with one another.

Counterfeit religions are best detected by studying the truth.

Finance: Federal agents in Canada are trained to identify counterfeit money by closely studying genuine currency. Once agents master the feel and look of authentic currency, they are better able to identify counterfeit money. The training process to distinguish a genuine bill from the counterfeit is "touch, tilt, look at, and look through." The first step is touch, where agents learn the feel of real money. The next step is to tilt the bill to identify the holographic stripe (which is very difficult to copy). The third step is to "look through," holding the bill to the light to identify several features that are present in authentic money. The final step is to "look at" the currency to identify fine-line printing and particular patterns.[5] By studying the features of authentic currency, the agents are trained to identify the counterfeit. In the same way, by carefully studying and learning the truth as presented in the Bible, we are better able to identify counterfeit religions.

We have responsibility for one another.

News Story: In May 2006, a tornado ripped through the small town of Otwell, Indiana. Kathryn Martin, who lived sixty miles away, had the sense that she just had to help the victims. So Kathryn loaded her car with juice boxes, snacks, and toys and drove to Otwell. She dropped the items off with the Red Cross and then stopped to help a young family sorting through the wreckage that was once their home. Once Kathryn returned home, she organized fund-raisers and used the money to buy a bus that now travels to disaster-torn towns, giving the children there a safe place to play while their parents clean up from the disaster.[6] Too often we turn a blind eye to the pain and struggles of our fellow human beings. Many of us live such individualistic lives that we do not see the responsibility we have for one another. What is one thing you might do differently if you were to open your eyes and see the needs around you the way Kathryn did?

A Call to Faithfulness

Big Idea *The people of God remain faithful when tempted to disloyalty.*

Understanding the Text

The Text in Context

"After a long time" (23:1) signals an undisclosed period of time between chapters 22 and 23. Although there is an abrupt change between chapters 22 and 23, Joshua's farewell address follows logically on the dispute between the tribes regarding the memorial altar built by the Transjordan tribes (22:10–34). The motivation for his final exhortation is Joshua's advanced age (23:1–2), which also explains his distribution of the unconquered land (13:1).

Joshua 23:1–2 is introductory to the chapter. Verses 3 and 10 repeat the same phrase, "the LORD your God who fought/

fights for you," providing the opening and closing refrains of the section. Joshua 23:11 bridges the two parts of Joshua's speech, verses 3–10 and 12–16. The cause for faithfulness to God is verses 3–11, and the consequence of unfaithfulness is verses 12–16. (1) Joshua anticipates that the Israelites ultimately will vanquish the remaining nations as God has promised (23:3–5). (2) Joshua echoes what the Lord initially instructed him (1:7–8), exhorting the people to abide by Moses's teaching (23:6–8). (3) Joshua reminds his audience that God gives them victory despite impossible odds, concluding that they must "love the LORD your God" (23:9–11).

In the final section of his speech, Joshua forewarns them of the consequences if they

When the Lord gives the Israelites rest from their enemies, they are able to occupy the land, build houses, and plant crops. In the hill country, terraced hillsides such as these supported olive groves and vineyards.

worship other gods (23:12–16). This final passage deserves its own commentary unit and is treated separately.

Interpretive Insights

23:1 *a long time . . . rest.* Reference to a time period begins and ends the verse. Sufficient time (lit., "many days") has passed after the Israelites gained their victories for them now to become complacent in their devotion to the Lord. Remnants of the nations remain (13:1–2; 23:4, 7, 12), and Joshua urges the Israelites to complete the task. "To give rest" (*nuah*) means the Lord provides peace and security after years of battle (1:13, 15; 21:44; 22:4).

old man. The leadership of Joshua comes to an end since he is old (lit., "he was old, advanced in days"; cf. 13:1–2; 22:2). He dies at 110 years of age (24:29). Abraham at an advanced age also prepared for his legacy (Gen. 24:1–4), as does Joshua for his ruling successors (Josh. 24:31).

23:2 *elders, leaders, judges and officials.* These are men who hold varied positions of civic authority, representing the wider community (8:33; 24:1). "Elders" (*zᵉqenim*) are men with community authority (e.g., 20:4). "Leaders" (*ra'shim*; lit., "heads") typically are heads of family households (e.g., 14:1). "Judges" (*shopᵉtim*) carry out administrative and adjudicating duties (e.g., Deut. 17:9). "Officers" (*shotᵉrim*) exercise various levels of civil authority (e.g., Deut. 1:15; Josh. 1:10).

23:3 *You yourselves have seen.* The verse echoes Moses's account of the defeat of the Amorite kings in Transjordan (Deut. 3:21–22). The second person plural ("you," "your") occurs multiple times in verse 3, emphasizing the community as a whole. The wording is also reminiscent of the Lord's speech to Israel at Sinai (Exod. 19:4; see also Exod. 20:22; Deut. 29:2).

for your sake. The phrase occurs twice in the passage (23:3, 5; cf. 2:9–11), indicating why the Lord took action.

It was the LORD your God. The construction focuses attention on the subject of the causal clause, literally, "for the LORD your God." The following pronoun, literally, "he (is/was)" (*hu'*), refers back to (restates) "the LORD your God," which is the formal subject in the clause. The significance of the construction is that the Lord alone delivers them. The exact Hebrew sentence occurs in 23:10 and Deuteronomy 3:22. Joshua previously has declared that God "fought for Israel" (10:14, 42), but this time he personalizes it by saying, "for your sake."

23:4 *Remember.* Joshua plays on the word "seen" (*ra'ah*) in the previous verse by using the same term, "See!" (*ra'ah*). The NIV renders it "remember," indicating the idea of a mental image.

the nations I conquered. Joshua specifies the nations located west of the Jordan that he defeated, whereas Moses defeated the Transjordan nations in the east.

23:5 *will push them out . . . drive them out . . . take possession . . . promised.* This verse summarizes in four verbs by rapid succession the vision of what Israel will yet accomplish. Although 23:1 states that "all" of Israel's enemies are defeated, it is a general statement since there still remain city-states to vanquish, such as the Philistine cities (13:1–7).

23:6 *Be very strong.* Verses 6–8 contain repeated exhortations to faithfulness. Verse 6 is a repetition of the sentiment previously spoken by God and by the community (especially 1:7). Joshua now adds his voice. The expression slightly differs, however, from the previous occasions of "be strong and (very) courageous" (1:7; see also Deut. 31:6, 7, 23; Josh. 1:6, 9, 18; 10:25). The emphasis in this verse is shown by the adverb "very" and the additional words "be careful." Other renderings reflect the strong admonition clearly: "therefore overcome diligently" (*katischysate oun sphodra*, LXX); "But be most resolute" (NJPS); and "Therefore strive hard" (NAB).

23:7 *Do not associate.* "Associate" in this context means to intermingle with the nations, probably referring to intermarriage (23:12; cf. Deut. 7:3–4; Judg. 3:6).

do not invoke . . . swear . . . . serve . . . bow down. Each of these four directives has the same syntactical expression—the repetitive negative "not" (*lo'*) precedes the verb. The terse combination of sounds underscores the urgency of Joshua's exhortations. "Invoke" (lit., "remember," *zakar*; cf. Exod. 23:13) and "swear" (*shaba'*) work in tandem, referring to supplication in which an oath occurs (cf. Isa. 48:1).

23:8 *hold fast.* The word *dabaq* has broad meaning, referring at times to physical "clinging" (e.g., Ruth 1:14); here, the figurative use of the word indicates loyalty (22:5; 23:12; for "hold fast" and "swear" together, see Deut. 10:20).

23:9 *great and powerful nations.* The phrase reflects Deuteronomy 4:38; 9:1; 11:23, probably referring to the nations' imposing citadels and large populations (Deut. 7:1; 9:14). The future of Israel is expressed in the same terms (Gen. 18:18; Deut. 26:5), although initially they were a small people. Despite their insignificance, God has chosen them because of his love for their ancestors (Deut. 7:7–8).

23:10 *One . . . routs a thousand.* The metaphor indicates that Israel's unlikely victory resides with the Lord (cf. Lev. 26:8; Deut. 32:30).

23:11 *be very careful to love.* The exhortation repeats the admonition in 22:5 but advances the idea from faithfulness to God's word to faithfulness to God himself. After the command "be very careful," the Hebrew text has a reflexive expression (*l'napshotekem*) that is not translated in the NIV—literally, "for your own well-being" (HCSB) or "to yourselves" (NASB) (cf. Deut. 4:15).

Theological Insights

The chief tension in chapter 22 is the fear that the Transjordan tribes have erected an altar for making offerings to the Lord (cf. Lev. 26:30) rather than appearing at the tent of meeting in accordance with the law of Moses (Exod. 34:18–23). Building such an altar appears to be practicing idolatry since altars are commonplace among Canaan's populace (e.g., Num. 22:41–23:2). Instead, Moses has instructed Israel to tear down pagan altars (Deut. 12:2–6). Now, Joshua's farewell speech reinforces the good judgment of the Israelites, who have rejected the practices of the Canaanites.

"The LORD your God, who fought/fights for you" in 23:3, 10 offers the reason why the Israelites have prevailed and why they ultimately will claim unconquered lands. Moses makes the same assertion at the crossing of the Red Sea when Pharaoh's chariotry drowns. Pharaoh's own army acknowledges that it has fallen prey to Israel's God (Exod. 14:14, 25). This admission reminds us of Rahab's confession (2:8–11). That the Israelites are incapable of such mighty deeds apart from the Lord's intervention shows that the Lord is indeed the Lord God alone (Exod. 7:5; Deut. 4:35; Josh. 3:10; 4:24). God does not employ miracles for entertainment as a magician does. His purposes for his people far outweigh the wondrous deed itself. Moreover, the deeds performed for individuals are not independent of the community at large; the blessing received by leaders is designed to benefit the community too.

Since it is the Lord and no other who delivers the Israelites, it is evident that he is the God who rules over and through historical events. He is not the typical fertility deity worshiped in the ancient world (see the sidebar "Abraham's Ancestral Gods" in the unit on 24:1–18). The book of Joshua, reflecting Deuteronomic theology, shows that history is linear and is not subject to human manipulation through sympathetic magic or incantations. Sympathetic magic is the practice of imitative rites that affect or influence the behavior of pagan deities. This feature of the Israelites' God has serious implications for them if they choose to abandon him for Canaan's nature deities. If God can intervene in history and secure victory for Israel, he can also intervene and secure its defeat. This very thing occurs in the generation following Joshua and the elders. The book of Judges repeatedly reports that the tribes defect from God, suffer defeat at the hands of their enemies, and then are forced by circumstances to turn to the Lord for salvation (e.g., Judg. 2:10–23).

Joshua does not depart from the recurring message, beginning in chapter 1 when the Lord instructs him to pursue obedience to the word of the Lord (1:6–9). Now, at the end of his life, Joshua challenges future generations to continue in the same train of obedience as he and leaders of his time have demonstrated (23:6–11). The book of Joshua carries on the idea of blessing intended for future generations, as emphasized already in Deuteronomy (Deut. 4:9; 32:46). By instructing and modeling for their children, Israel as a nation will enjoy long life in the land (Deut. 6:1–2). Theirs is the choice of either blessing or curse (Deut. 30:19). Blessing is not automatic, nor is curse foreordained.

Joshua warns the Israelites not to serve or bow down to the gods of the nations that remain in the land. This bronze figurine from Tyre (1400–1200 BC) may be a depiction of Baal, one of the gods worshiped by the Canaanites.

Teaching the Text

The primary lesson in this passage is the sufficiency of God to accomplish his promises for Israel. God alone commissions Joshua to lead the people into the land; he alone superintends their wars; and he alone fights for Israel, giving them victory against impossible odds. One commentator observes that verses 3–5 and 9–10 are in "miniature" the claim of the book.[1] By looking back at what the people themselves have seen (23:3) Joshua reinforces what the narrator has forcefully declared—the Lord is the Divine Warrior who has fought and will continue to fight for Israel (10:14, 42; 11:8; 21:43–44). The land is his, and his to grant, but he also fights actively at the forefront of Israel's battles to secure the land as he promised. A similar declaration occurs regarding the sufficiency of Christ, a competence found neither in others nor in Christians themselves (2 Cor. 3:4–6; Col. 1:12). Just as the promissory word of God proves true in Israel, the efficacy of the revealed word in Christ is assured. We can have confidence in the elective love of the Lord that provides believers the eternal security that he has accomplished on our behalf (2 Cor. 1:22; Eph. 1:13).

The authority and faithful promise of the Divine Warrior motivate Joshua and his generation to exhibit confidence in God (23:1–3; 24:31; Judg. 2:7). In contrast to biblical characters who falter in their older years (e.g., Moses, Gideon, Samuel), Joshua remains stalwart in his trust in God throughout his lifetime (Exod. 33:9–11; Num. 27:18–23; Deut. 34:9). Although the great prophet Moses has passed away, the work of God continues in Joshua's time because it is just that—*God's* work—not

whatever Joshua has chosen to undertake. Christians too are but servants in the Lord's household, and the kingdom's work transcends their lives. Believers can be confident that what the Lord has planted in and through Christian service will take root, grow, and blossom under the watchful care of the Lord (1 Cor. 3:6–11; Gal. 6:9).

Yet God's promise to continue to fight for Israel requires that it exercises cautious vigilance in the face of persistent temptation (23:6, 8, 11). The reason for Israel's immediate fall into idolatry after the generation of Joshua and the elders (Judg. 2:7, 10–11) is the rebellious nature of Israel (Deut. 9:7, 24; 31:27). Additionally, the influence of Canaanite culture with its idolatry is an ever-present snare (23:13; Judg. 2:3; Ps. 106:36). By the regeneration ("circumcision of the heart") of the believer by the Holy Spirit, Christians belong totally to God (Rom. 2:29; cf. Deut. 30:6). For Christians, temptation to sin is also an ever-present danger, but the empowerment of the Spirit enables them to persevere (Rom. 6:15–23; 1 Cor. 10:13; 2 Pet. 2:9; 1 John 4:4).

Illustrating the Text

The Lord is powerful to fulfill his promises.

Object Lesson: Because we cannot see God with our eyes, many people have a hard time believing in him and his power to achieve what he has promised. The purpose of the following demonstration is to remind your listeners that there are forces at play in the world that cannot be seen by the naked eye. And just as we trust in these unseen forces each and every day of our lives, we can trust in "the unseen Lord." In his book

77 Science Activities for Illustrating Bible Lessons, Donald B. DeYoung provides an object lesson for illustrating God's invisible power. Bring to the service a magnet and explain that the magnet is completely surrounded by a magnetic field. Place a sheet of paper over the magnet and sprinkle staples or paper clips on it, showing their alignment (if it is a relatively small magnet, you can verbally explain the process).[2] As DeYoung concludes, "We are surrounded by a number of invisible shields, including magnetism and the ozone layer. Even greater is the divine protection that the Lord revealed to . . . his servants long ago."[3]

Persevere!

News Story: In just four months three men ran a grueling four thousand miles across the Sahara Desert. The journey is one of extremes. Temperatures can exceed one hundred degrees Fahrenheit during the day while dropping below freezing at night. Sandstorms can make it difficult to see and even to breathe. Throughout the run, the participants were "stricken with tendinitis, severe diarrhea, cramping and knee injuries all while running through the intense heat and wind—often without a paved road in sight." The three men never gave up and successfully made the journey.[4] Such a journey requires not only endurance but faithfulness to the goal and an unwillingness to quit. During the journey of the Christian faith, we will face many challenges and temptations. There will be times when we will be encouraged to compromise or even give up on our faith. The ability to end well for the Lord requires an unwavering commitment to successfully complete the journey.

Make a plan to take a stand against temptation.

Informational: In a study led by Loran Nordgren, senior lecturer of management and organizations at Northwestern University's Kellogg School of Management, it was discovered that individuals tend to miscalculate the amount of temptation they can truly handle. The miscalculation leads to a greater likelihood of the person yielding to the temptation. Nordgren concludes, "The key is simply to avoid any situations where vices and other weaknesses thrive and, most importantly, for individuals to keep a humble view of their willpower."[5] We must admit and understand our vulnerability to temptation and create a plan to stand firm for righteousness.

Words of Warning

Big Idea *A faithful community of believers must resist sinful enticements or they will forfeit God's blessing.*

Understanding the Text

The Text in Context

This passage concludes the final exhortation of Joshua's speech that began in 23:1–11. Several ideas from the previous passage (23:1–11) reappear in verses 12–16, but here Joshua particularly warns against two failures. (1) The Israelites must not practice intermarriage with the Canaanites, lest they fall into idolatry (23:12–13). (2) The Israelites must not worship other gods, for the Lord's wrath will result in their expulsion (23:14–16). The nearly identical language in 23:13 and 16 distinguishes the literary boundaries of the two parts: "until you perish from this good land, which the LORD your God has given you" // "you will quickly perish from the good land he has given you." Joshua's farewell speech (chap. 23) prepares the reader for the last chapter of the book, which is a covenant renewal ceremony. As in chapter 23, he calls the people to commit themselves to the Lord, rejecting the allure of idolatry (24:14–15).

Just as unsuspecting birds are captured by a hunter's snare, the Israelites will be caught up in the ritual practices and idolatry of the Canaanites if they intermarry or associate with them. This fragment from Nebamun's tomb in Dra Abu el-Naga, Egypt, shows men using a net to catch quail (1350 BC).

Interpretive Insights

23:12 *But if you turn away and ally yourselves.* The adversative ("but," *ki*) indicates a strong contrast with the preceding verses (23:9–11). The alternative translation, "for if" (e.g., ESV, HCSB), explains why judgment falls as described in the subsequent verse 13. "Turn away" (*shob tashubu*) expresses a strong adverbial construction (infinitive absolute + imperfect), more clearly seen in other versions:

"But if you *ever* turn away . . ." (NET, italics mine; also cf. NAB, NASB). The word "ally" (*dabaq*) translates the same word in 22:5 and 23:8, meaning "to hold fast, cling to," indicating allegiance. The word also can describe marital union (Gen. 2:24) and a physical embrace (Ruth 1:14).

intermarry . . . associate. Intermarriage was a common means of forming political or family alliances (Gen. 34:9; 1 Kings 3:1), but it is forbidden as a general practice since it frequently leads to idolatry (Deut. 7:3). "Associate" (NET: "establish friendly relations") renders a word (*bo'*) that is broad in meaning, including sexual relations (Gen. 16:2). Its connotation may mean sexual relations in marriage (e.g., NRSV: "you marry"). The terms "ally," "intermarry," and "associate" together depict acceptance of Canaanite culture by intermarriage (Judg. 3:6).

23:13 *then you may be sure.* The translation "be sure" (*yadoaʿ tedᵉʿu*) is another emphatic construction (infinitive absolute + imperfect), emphasizing the certainty of what the Lord threatens to do.

no longer drive out. "No longer" changes the mood of the exhortation. Whereas in verse 5 Joshua assures the Israelites that the Lord will continue to subjugate the nations, here the reversal is equally sure.

snares and traps. Both words (*pah*, "snare"; *moqesh*, "trap") occur in Amos 3:5 (NIV: "trap," "bait"), describing a bird trap or net that springs up to capture the prey (cf. Ps. 124:7). The metaphorical meaning is the enticement of idolatry that leads to destruction.

good land, which the LORD . . . has given you. (Cf. the comments on 23:16, below.) The "good land" indicates the productivity

and prosperity that Israel will enjoy if it remains faithful (Deut. 6:18; 8:7, 10). The same language appears again in verse 15, and similar language occurs in verse 16. The passage reinforces that the land is a gift that can be rescinded. The focus is on the Divine Warrior, who makes Israel's habitation possible (23:3, 5, 9).

23:14 *Now I am about to go.* The construction emphasizes the solemn character of Joshua's words. The text has the word "today" (*hayyom*), indicating immediacy (cf. NASB, NET). Joshua announces that he is presently dying (HCSB: "I am now going") or that his death is imminent (see also Jacob, Gen. 48:21; 50:5; Joseph, Gen. 50:24; Moses, Deut. 31:16, 27, 29; and David, 1 Kings 2:2).

the way of all the earth. The phrase is a metonymy, associating the earth with the grave (cf. Gen. 15:15). The common expression is "[so and so] slept/rested with his fathers and was buried in . . ." (e.g., 1 Kings 2:10; cf. Gen. 47:30).

all your heart and soul. The same phrase occurs in 22:5 (see also Deut. 11:13; 13:3). "Heart" and "soul" are a synecdoche, referring to the total person. The Deuteronomic phrase "heart" and "soul" usually prefers the verb "to love" or "to serve" (e.g., the Shema, Deut. 6:4–5; cf. Deut. 10:12; 11:13;

30:6), but here it is that the people "know" with their total being that God's promises do not fail.

not one of all the good promises. The emphatic "not one" appears twice in the verse, underscoring the certainty of God's promises. The modifier "*good* promises" (italics mine) is rare (cf. 21:45; 1 Kings 8:56). "Good" appears five times in the passage (23:13, 14, 15 [2x], 16), to focus on God's kindness and also the bounty of his gift.

23:15 *good things . . . evil things.* Joshua now contrasts the "good" and the "evil" that God can bring on Israel. The adjective "evil" (*ra'*) occurs once in Joshua, and the verbal form "bring disaster" (*hera'*, causal Hiphil form) appears once in 24:20 (cf. "disaster [*ra'*] will fall on you because you will do evil [*ra'*]," Deut. 31:29).

23:16 *If you violate the covenant.* Most English translations render the clause as a condition ("if"), but it may indicate an assumption, "When you transgress the covenant" (NASB; cf. KJV). The term "violate" (*'abar*) also means "to cross over," or in its noun form, "crossing over, across." In the book of Joshua, it typically refers to the tribes' crossing of the Jordan (e.g., 1:2; 4:10). The use here is "transgress" (e.g., ESV), as in the case of Achan, who violates the covenant (7:11, 15). The association of the two ideas "cross" and "transgress" suggests a wordplay: although they have "cross[ed]" the Jordan, they must not "transgress," lest God expel them. "Covenant" (*berit*) most often occurs in Joshua in "ark of the covenant," but it also appears as the "treaty" made with the Gibeonites (9:6) and the "covenant" renewed by Joshua (24:25).

bow down. The expression is effectively a synonym for worship (see also 23:7).

anger will burn. This phrase occurs only twice in the book, each referring to God's judgment (7:1).

will quickly perish. The same language occurs in Moses's forewarning (Deut. 11:17; cf. Deut. 9:6).

Theological Insights

The primary emphasis of Joshua's last words is the certainty of God's promises. This certainty, however, has both positive and negative dimensions. Negatively, if the people worship the gods of the Canaanites, they may be just as assured that judgment will happen as they are assured that he will be with them in their faithfulness. The positive is the assurance of divine war against Israel's enemies. The passage shows that the people have responsibility for the outcome (Deut. 11:22–23). Their actions have consequences, and they face the choice of life and death, both as individuals and as a nation (Deut. 30:19). The emphasis on obedience in Deuteronomy and Joshua focuses on the nation corporately, but individuals too are profiled and held responsible (e.g., Rahab's faith and Achan's theft). The message of Deuteronomy indicates that the people must play a vital part in the dispossession of the nations, and the book of Joshua describes what choices the people face upon entering the land. Since God has revealed to the people what their responsibility is, his actions are not fickle but clear and predictable.

Intermarriage with the nations in the land is expressly prohibited (Deut. 7:3). The motivation for this ban is not ethnically determined. Rather, its basis is the immorality that results from such a practice (e.g., Judg. 3:6; Neh. 13:1–2, 23–27). It is virtually axiomatic in the Old Testament that marriage outside the covenant community (exogamy) leads to adopting the polytheism of Israel's neighbors. This prohibition, however, is neither absolute nor permanent (e.g., Ruth the Moabitess; cf. Deut. 23:3–8). Exceptions include women who are taken captives, but they must undergo a cleansing rite before they are integrated into the community as full participants (Deut. 21:10–14). The primary point of the ban is that a spouse whose ethnicity originates outside the assembly must "convert" to the Lord before the marriage is considered legitimate.

The passage depicts God as the ultimate Judge who dispenses his favor or his harm on a righteous basis. Although the word "evil" occurs only once in Joshua (23:15), the idea of divine punishment for disobedience is a major theme. God brings disaster on those who practice evil deeds (24:20; Deut. 28:20). That Joshua's army fails to capture Ai is attributed to the Lord's doing (7:7). This portrayal of God relies on the belief in the ultimate sovereignty of God, whose actions are the cause of what happens to Israel and the nations (Isa. 47:11; Jer. 44:8). Israel acknowledges that its future *ultimately* rests in the hands of God, recognizing that his favor or disfavor

leads to blessing or curse (Num. 14:3; Judg. 6:13). The *immediate* cause for divine favor or disfavor, however, is the moral or immoral deeds of Israel and the nations (e.g., Judg. 6:1; Amos 1:3–5).

Teaching the Text

The principal concern of Joshua's speech is the threat of idolatry, if Israel assimilates with the inhabitants of Canaan (23:7, 12, 16). Idolatry transgresses the two most essential commandments of the covenant: exclusive devotion to the Lord and absolute rejection of idol worship (Exod. 20:3–6; Deut. 5:7–9). The consequence of alliances with the Canaanites is expulsion, for God will no longer fight for Israel (23:13; Deut. 4:25–26). Although this is the general principle toward Canaanites, there are exceptions for those who submit to the Lord and his people, such as Rahab and the Gibeonites (chaps. 6–7; 9). The New Testament also implores believers to take

Intermarriage was forbidden to the Israelites, although exceptions were made in the case of women taken captive after a victory in battle like those shown in this Assyrian relief (700–692 BC). After a time of purification and mourning, they could become wives of the Israelite men.

Joshua 23:12–16

Joshua reminds the Israelites that God's judgment will come if they bow down and serve other gods. The peoples surrounding Israel worship many gods, and the Israelites will be tempted to turn to them as well or return to the gods of their ancestors, rather than worship Yahweh alone. In this Egyptian stele from 1295–1069 BC, a worshiper kneels in prayer before Sobek, the Egyptian crocodile god.

at Ai, for instance, was God's judgment for disobedience (chap. 7). The principle of divine retribution is the same for Israel as for the nations: God destroys sinful nations. A mistake by some Christian interpreters, however, is to equate God's blessing or judgment on the nation Israel with his treatment of individuals today. Also, there is no simple one-to-one correspondence between morality and prosperity or between immorality and suffering. That prosperity or suffering are not always the direct consequence of human behavior is shown by the book of Job and in Jesus's statement in John 9:2–3 that the infirmity of a man born blind is not due to his sin or his parents' sin.

Joshua declares that the Lord is good by providing the "good land" (23:13, 15, 16) for his people. Also, Joshua acknowledges that the people are the recipients of the Lord's "good promises" (23:14). The Bible explains that the Lord is good and the Lord never betrays his own fundamental character of love.[1] His actions are out of love, including his discipline of his people (Ps. 145:9; Heb. 12:5–6; 1 Pet. 2:3). As for judgment against the wicked, if the Lord does not respond to evil by appropriate measures of retribution, then he is not acting justly. Justice is as essential to the character of the Lord as is his love. If there is no justice, then love is empty sentimentality.

special precautions when forming alliances with unbelievers, because Christian faith and values can be compromised (2 Cor. 6:14–18; James 1:27). Intermarriage with unbelievers is proscribed (2 Cor. 6:14–15), but there is no absolute prohibition against relationships with unbelievers, which vary in kind and degree (1 Cor. 5:9–10). Each circumstance requires wise conduct (Col. 4:5–6). The ultimate measure for judging the attitude Christians adopt toward unbelievers is whether it is to "the glory of God" (1 Cor. 10:31; cf. 1 Pet. 4:11).

Joshua forewarns that just as God is faithful in carrying out "good things," his judgment is equally reliable in bringing about the promised "evil things" (23:15). This explicit statement captures what the book throughout has asserted. The defeat

Illustrating the Text

Beware the power of groupthink.

News: Groupthink is the phenomenon where individuals set aside their own beliefs and adopt the opinion of the rest of the group. The driving force for groupthink is the desire to keep the peace rather than disrupt the unity of the crowd.[2] This phenomenon can have disastrous results, as noted by *Time* magazine when it published an article blaming groupthink for the Penn State University cover-up of a child abuser. The men who covered for the sex offender were intelligent, highly educated men known for their moral strength.[3] And yet together they decided to try to cover the offenses, which led to greater pain. The point is that we need to be careful regarding the values and beliefs of the people we allow into our inner circle. All of us are susceptible to being swayed by others to compromise what we believe and how we live. Ask your listeners to consider whom they are listening to. Are the beliefs, attitudes, and values of these people consistent with the perspective of the Bible? Are these people drawing them closer to the Lord or further away from him?

Identify your potential idols, and take practical steps to avoid idolatry.

Christian Life: When people hear the word "idol," they often think of a figure made of stone that is worshiped and adored by the uneducated. But an idol is anything we love more than the Lord. An idol is anything we look to, instead of the Lord, for our ultimate security. American culture is infatuated with celebrities, signified no better than by the popular television show *American Idol*. Modern-day examples of idols include money, power, success, possessions, relationships, and acceptance. Take a moment to share with your listeners the idols you deal with (or have dealt with) in your life and how you fight against them.

There is no love without justice.

Scenario: There was a couple who desperately loved their young child. In their minds their toddler was a miracle, as the doctors had pronounced that the couple would never be able to have children of their own. But the doctors were proved wrong, and the happy couple was raising their bundle of joy. Out of an "attitude of love" the parents gave the toddler everything he wanted. Learning quickly that he preferred sugar over vegetables, he refused to eat anything except candy, cookies, and ice cream. Rather than forcing the child on a sleeping schedule, the parents let him stay up as long as he wanted. When confronted by friends, the parents bristled and confidently proclaimed they did not want to say "no" to the child, fearing that would not be a loving response. What do you think would be the impact of this style of parenting? Is discipline an act of love? Are demands on the child consistent with love? Is God's discipline an act of love?

Covenant Renewal

Big Idea *The people of God confess their allegiance to the Lord.*

Understanding the Text

The Text in Context

Covenant commitment is the focus of Joshua's last words in chapter 23, and hence it is not surprising that a covenant renewal follows in chapter 24. The context implies that Joshua is in his last days, since 23:1–2 describes him as "old," and 24:29 begins the account of his death and burial with the phrase "after these things." Chapter 24 consists of two major parts: covenant renewal and its ceremonial affirmation

(24:1–28) and the burials of Joshua, Joseph, and Eleazar (24:29–33). Subdividing the covenant renewal ceremony facilitates better teaching of the text: (1) Joshua's first speech and the people's response (24:1–18) and (2) Joshua's second speech and his dialogue with the people, who formally confirm the covenant (24:19–28). In the present commentary unit, the historical prologue dominates the first speech. It consists of four paragraphs: the patriarchs (24:2–4), the exodus (24:5–7), the wilderness (24:8–10), and the conquest (24:11–13).

Historical and Cultural Background

Joshua 24 describes a covenant renewal ceremony at Shechem. It reflects the treaty form that is well attested in Hittite suzerain/vassal treaties from about 1400 to 1200 BC. The covenant renewal entered into by the Israelites shows Joshua's familiarity with the general format of ancient treaties (also Deuteronomy). Since the covenant

As Joshua renews the covenant between Yahweh and the people of Israel, he follows a format similar to that found in Hittite suzerain-vassal treaties of the same period. Pictured is the treaty between Suppiluliuma and Hukkana from the thirteenth century BC. It contains a preamble, stipulations, divine witnesses, and curses and blessings.

document itself is not given in chapter 24, the similarities of the underlying covenant and the Hittite treaties are reconstructed by scholars. Also the biblical covenant is an *adaptation* of the treaties, designed to highlight the theological import of the covenant. In the biblical account, the great suzerain is the Lord, and the vassals are the Israelites. The typical features of the Hittite treaty, although not always in this order, are emulated in Joshua 24. (1) An introduction identifies the Hittite king and the vassal (24:2b). (2) A historical prologue recounts the Hittite king's favorable treatment of the vassal in the past, designed to motivate the vassal to accept the terms of the treaty (24:2c–13). (3) The terms incumbent on the vassal explain what is demanded by the Hittite king (24:14–24, the core in 24:14–15). (4) The deposit of the treaty and the witnesses to the treaty are described (24:25–27). A public reading of the treaty was common, but it is not reported in Joshua 24. However, this feature is the focus of the renewal ceremony in 8:30–35, fulfilling Deuteronomy 27:2–3.

Interpretive Insights

24:1 *Shechem.* The assembly had gathered at Shiloh for distribution of the land (18:1), but Joshua now gathers them at Shechem (24:25), the place where Jacob called his family to rid themselves of any foreign gods (Gen. 35:2–4). Shechem was a historically appropriate venue for Joshua to call for choosing the Lord over foreign deities (24:23). The city is located in a valley in the region of Samaria with Mount Ebal to its north and Mount Gerizim to its south.

before God. The phrase may refer to the tent of meeting generally (18:1, 10; 19:51);

"holy place" in 24:26 suggests that it has moved to Shechem. Other interpretations are that it refers to the ark of the covenant (8:33) or generally to God's oversight (1 Sam. 23:18).

24:2 *Long ago your ancestors . . . beyond the Euphrates River.* God chose Israel's earliest ancestors ("long ago") in a land far away ("beyond the Euphrates") and superintended their migrations. The "river" (*nahar*; cf. NASB), referring to the Euphrates, is the eastern border of the land promised to Abraham (Gen. 15:18; Josh. 1:4).

24:3 *I took . . . Abraham . . . led him.* This verse reflects the divine promise of Abraham possessing a land and fathering a great nation (e.g., Gen. 12:1–2). "I," referring to the Lord, occurs throughout the historical prologue, showing that he alone superintends the destiny of Israel (Abraham's travels, Gen. 12:1–25:11).

Seir to Esau, but Jacob . . . to Egypt. Seir is the region east of the Arabah that is sometimes equated with the land of Edom, the possession of Esau's descendants (Gen. 32:3). Jacob and Esau part ways, leaving Jacob to settle peacefully in Canaan (Gen. 36:6; 37:1) until his sojourn in Egypt (Gen. 46:1–27).

24:5 *I brought you out.* The prologue assumes that the audience knows the circumstances of Israel's experience in Egypt (Exod. 1:1–13:16). The majority of Joshua's audience probably was not in Egypt, since the adult population (twenty years and older) died in the wilderness (Num. 14:29). "You," then, refers to the community as a whole, identifying the former generation and the present generation as one and the same (Deut. 5:2–3). The present generation, whether it be Moses's or Joshua's audience, faces the same decision to remain faithful to God.[1]

Joshua's declaration, "But as for me and my household, we will serve the LORD" (24:15) reflects both his commitment to the Lord and the patriarchal culture, where a decision by the head of the family was a decision for all the members of the household. This stele from fourteenth-century BC Egypt shows a family unit worshiping the deity Mnevis, the sacred bull for the ancient city of Heliopolis.

24:6 *your people . . . you . . . them.* The text has "your fathers" (*'abotekem*), meaning their ancestors. "You" (pl.) and "them" (lit., "your fathers") show the solidarity of the past and present. For crossing the sea, see Exodus 13:17–22.

24:7 *with your own eyes.* Although not all of Joshua's audience were actually present at Sinai, the people as a collective nation have witnessed God's historic salvation (24:17; Deut. 4:6–8).

for a long time. The people sojourned for about thirty-eight and a half years.

24:8 *the land of the Amorites.* The Amorites dwelled on both sides of the Jordan (Num. 13:29; Josh. 11:3). The name can refer to a particular group (3:10) or to all the inhabitants of the land (Gen. 15:16).

24:9–10 *Balak . . . Balaam . . . curse . . . blessed.* The Moabite king Balak hires Balaam to pronounce curses against Israel, but instead Balaam can only bless the Israelites at the Lord's instructions (e.g., Num. 22:12). (Cf. the comments on 13:22.) "Curse" and "bless" are common covenant vocabulary (e.g., Deut. 27–28).

24:11 *Jericho . . . also the Amorites.* Joshua shifts from the wars east of the Jordan to the victories in the west. "Jericho" is the only city named in the speech, because it was the first and chief victory (e.g., 8:2; 9:3; 10:1). The naming of the "seven nations" inhabiting Canaan appears only here in the book (cf. Deut. 7:1–2; Acts 13:19).

24:12 *I sent the hornet . . . Amorite kings.* The singular "hornet" is substituted for the plural, indicating a swarm of hornets. Since there is no biblical evidence of hornets used as a weapon in battles, it probably is metaphorical, meaning "terror" (cf. the parallel in Exod. 23:27–28).[2] On the Amorite kings, see Joshua 13:8–12.

24:14 *ancestors worshiped.* That the people have retained the figurines obtained from their ancestors may be for their material value, since idols were often made of precious metals and jewels (Judg. 18:18; cf. Gen. 35:2–4). "Worshiped" (*'abad*, "serve") is the common word for cultic worship (Exod. 20:5). It occurs four times in this verse and eighteen times in the chapter, making it the prominent idea. (Cf. the comments on 23:16.)

24:15 *Beyond the Euphrates . . . Amorites.* These two references in context refer to the deities that were worshiped geographically outside and within Canaan.

But as for me and my household. "But as for me" is a strong contrast with the preceding sentence. "Household" indicates the solidarity of a family unit, led by the decision of the family's patriarch. The eldest male member of a "household" (*bayit*, "house"), as the head of the household, was the social representative of the whole, although a woman too could be considered the representative (Rahab, 2:12). Dependents in the "household" included biological offspring and others who became identified with the household through purchase (slaves) or covenant (e.g., Gen. 14:14; 17:27).

24:16 *Far be it from us to forsake.* "Far be it" (*halilah*) is another strong adversative (22:29). "Forsake" (*'azab*), meaning "abandon/leave," is the antonym to covenant allegiance (Deut. 31:16).

24:18 *because he is our God.* The Israelites respond by summarizing the history that Joshua has described (24:17–18). "Because he is our God" occurs at the start of the Hebrew text (24:18), emphasizing the identity of the Lord.

Theological Insights

Since this passage is a covenant renewal, knowledge of the concept of covenant is necessary to understand the passage's theology. Covenant is not an agreement based on a reward for services rendered. Rather, covenant between God and his people is based on their relationship. One kind of covenant involves a relationship anchored in bilateral obligations between parties. Another kind of covenant, a royal gift without specific obligations, describes the covenant made with Abraham (Gen. 12:1–3) and David (2 Sam. 7). Specifically, the covenant form that Joshua presents

Abraham's Ancestral Gods

Abraham's ancestral home was Ur in Mesopotamia, whose cultural environment was polytheism. Mesopotamian worship included both national and family deities, but especially important to people were their family gods, who were considered personal and accessible. The family deity typically was a minor god who showed interest in the family and to whom the family showed special religious observance. Terah, father of Abraham and Nahor, took the clan from Ur and settled in Haran, which is located in Paddan-Aram, just east of the Euphrates in northern Mesopotamia. To what degree Abraham practiced idolatry, if at all, is not certain, although "[they] worshiped" (24:2) likely includes him. Abraham, however, at the call of God migrated to Canaan, leaving behind Terah and any loyalty to the clan's deity (Gen. 11:24–12:4). That polytheism persisted in Terah's family is shown by Nahor's descendant Laban, Jacob's father-in-law, who possessed household deities (Gen. 31:19; 35:2–4). Initially, Abraham may have understood the call of Yahweh as the call of a personal family deity, but he soon understood that Yahweh was unlike the Mesopotamian deities—he was the only true God as Creator and Covenant Lord (Gen. 14:18–23).[a]

[a] Walton, *Ancient Near Eastern Thought*, 142–44, 150–51; Mathews, *Genesis 11:27–50:26*, 148–51.

closely resembles the structure of ancient international treaties. Joshua's speech follows the pattern of the treaty outline but varies according to the specific setting of the moment. The Israelites are the beneficiaries of God's grace; their part in the covenant is offering thanksgiving through worship. The clearest evidence of divine grace is that the Lord does not cancel the covenant, despite Israel's repeated failures to obey. He restores his people by various means, including disciplining them (e.g., at Ai; cf. Judg. 2:1–5).

"All the tribes of Israel at Shechem" (24:1) signals the distinctive character of Israel as one people whose unity relies on their devotion to one God.[3] The site of Shechem functions as a geographical recollection of the Israelites' historic past from the time of their fathers, especially Jacob, when the elective promises of God differentiated Israel from all nations. Joshua's first speech centers on the identity of the people of Israel as the uniquely chosen people of God. What distinguishes them from all others is not the possession of the land, for they are cohabitants with the nations in Canaan. What distinguishes them is their sole allegiance to the Lord of the covenant. If they compromise their distinctive worship, which is loyalty to one Lord, and serve other lords, they become no different from the nations they have dispossessed. They retain their identity as the people of God only by undivided worship.

Why do the Israelites still possess idols despite the victories God has afforded them (24:14–15)? Although they stumble in their faith at Ai (chap. 7) and by making the treaty with the Gibeonites (chap. 9), Joshua's generation is for the most part faithful (contrast Judg. 1:11–2:10). Now comes the critical moment to see if it will remain devoted to God. Conquering the land and living in the land offer different kinds of challenges. Remnants of foreign deities in Israel's midst must be eradicated, lest these deities become a spiritual snare (23:13). Joshua presents the case for adhering to the Lord by reciting all that the Lord has done in their national history. They must recognize that *they* do not win the battles; only the Lord can overcome their enemies (24:12b). The covenant renewal calls them to demonstrate their perseverance in faith, not just swear to it. Action follows faith. The people must make a choice to obey; God's blessing is not automatic, despite the people's faithfulness in their recent past. They have a responsible role in the blessing that God has promised to bestow.

Teaching the Text

This passage teaches that God accepts only exclusive and thus proper worship from his people (24:14–15). Acceptable worship must reflect the heart of the inner person, showing authentic devotion to the Lord ("love," 22:5; cf. 23:11; 24:23). Moreover, Joshua 24 shows that a right action must arise out of a faith commitment. Forsaking idols means that Israel rejects the sinful past and embraces Yahwistic faith in the present. Both the covenant renewal at Shechem and Jesus's meeting with the Samaritan woman near Shechem ("Sychar," John 4:5) address what is acceptable worship. Jesus's teaching describes worship as authentic only when offered "in the Spirit and in truth" (John 4:23).[4] Faith followed by a right response of obedience is the proper order, for faith generates godly conduct (e.g., Rom. 1:5; James 1:19–27).

Another important feature of the chapter is Joshua's focus on foreign deities (24:14–16, 20, 23). The worldview presented in the book of Joshua conflicts with the polytheistic culture of the nations. The relevance of idols for today's readers is challenging conceptually insofar as contemporary Western understanding of reality differs dramatically from the way that ancient peoples viewed reality. Christians, like the Israelites, have a distinctive understanding of reality regarding the natural and the spiritual spheres, requiring Christians to take a countercultural position toward the "isms" of modern times—including naturalism, secularism, and the world's religions (Acts 17:16; 1 Thess. 1:8–10). In the same way that Joshua calls Israel to make a decisive choice, Christians must choose to submit to the lordship of Christ and then to live obediently.

Also, the passage shows that for Israel, living in the land among the nations inevitably means it will face temptation to adopt polytheism. The conflict between Israel and the nations is at its core an ideological one (24:14–18). The conflict is not primarily generated by ethnic rivalry or substantial differences in their social and material cultures, such as village life, housing, and sanctuaries. The Israelites' identity is defined by their covenant relationship with God and with one another. The passage reminds Christian readers that Christian identity too, as an individual or as a community, is defined by one's relationship to Christ (Acts 11:26; 1 Pet. 4:16).

Illustrating the Text

Celebrate the examples of God's amazing grace.

Testimony: As Joshua reminds the people of God's grace in the past, it is important for us to follow his example as leaders and remind the people of the Lord's amazing grace. Recruit a few people to share stories of how their lives and the church as a whole have been blessed by the Lord and his grace.

True worship involves faithful relationship.

Scenario: One way to demonstrate the importance of authentic worship is to compare our covenant with the Lord with a marriage covenant. Share the following scenarios with the congregation.

Connie had been strongly encouraging her husband, Tom, to make time for the two of them to go out on a much-needed date. They went out to dinner together, but Tom hardly said a word to her. In fact, he spent most of the evening on his cell phone. Following dinner they took a walk around the lake, but Tom was distant, focused on challenges he was facing in his job. When they returned home, Connie was frustrated. But Tom simply said, "I don't know what you want. I spent the entire evening with you!" In the same way, simply being in a church building does not mean that we are worshiping God. If our hearts and minds are a thousand miles from God, then we have not really worshiped him.

Steve believed his marriage with April was strong, until he discovered that she had been having an affair. April did not seem to understand the seriousness of her unfaithfulness. She explained to Steve, "I don't know why you are so concerned. When I'm home, I'm only loving you!" But just as that answer won't (and shouldn't) satisfy, the Lord desires that we be faithful to loving him not only when we are gathered for worship but at other times as well. Worship comprises all aspects of our lives, as acts of obedience become acts of worship.

The Lord demands true, authentic worship from his people.

Lyrics: "The Heart of Worship," by Matt Redman. In the late 1990s, the pastor at Soul Survivor Church in Watford, England, sensed an attitude of worship apathy in his church. So he decided to get rid of the sound system and the band for a season and call the church to worship with just their voices. The pastor said to his people, "When you come through the doors on a Sunday, what are you bringing as your offering to God?" This new approach reminded the congregation of the purpose of worship, and songwriter Matt Redman wrote "The Heart of Worship" to mark this period.[5] For you, is worship all about the Lord?

Covenant Confirmed

Big Idea *The covenant people worship solely the Lord of the covenant.*

Understanding the Text

The Text in Context

This passage continues the covenant renewal ceremony begun in 24:1–18. The unit is the second round of dialogue between Joshua and the representatives of the people (cf. 24:1). After reciting God's grace in Israel's history in the first speech (24:3–13), Joshua states the implications in his second speech. Even though the Lord fulfills his promises, the people are not always loyal. The second speech therefore accuses the audience of failing to obey. The people emphatically declare that they are loyal, but Joshua's second speech begins in a stern rebuttal—"You are not able to serve the Lord" (24:19a).

The dialogue has three rounds (24:19–24). The tempo moves quickly between Joshua's words and the short responses of the people. (1) Joshua declares that God will not relent in his judgment when they fail (24:19–20). They answer, "We will serve!" (24:21). (2) Joshua charges that their response serves as a witness (24:22a), and they agree that their oath is a witness (24:22b). (3) Joshua stipulates that they must remove any vestige of false worship (24:23). As in the former responses, the people swear to obey (24:24).

Joshua exhorts the Israelites to "throw away the foreign gods that are among you and yield your hearts to the Lord, the God of Israel" (24:23). Ishtar was the Mesopotamian goddess of love and war and is depicted on this plaque (eighth century BC).

Next, the text describes the formal features of the covenant: its recording and the placement of a stone (24:25–26). Joshua identifies the stone as a witness to the covenant (24:27). No response is called for, so Joshua dispatches the tribes to their land inheritance (24:28). In this vein of thought, the last unit of the book, in 24:29–33, describes the final resting place in the land of three leading figures—Joshua, Joseph, and Eleazar.

Historical and Cultural Background

Who were the "foreign gods" in Joshua's day (24:20, 23), and what were they like? The nations perceived the world around them as alive with deities. Heaven and earth were essentially integrated, and the deities were within a closed system of existence. They were coextensions of the physical world—hence the cosmos was deified. Fertility between the deities was a primary means of generating the cosmos. In Mesopotamia the primary deities were Ishtar, the goddess of fertility and war, and Marduk, the patron deity of Babylon and the king of the gods. The chief deity of the Egyptians was Amon-Re, a merger of the creator god Amon and the sun god Re. For the Canaanites the primary active deity was Baal, who was the storm and fertility god.[1] Israel's God, however, is different. (1) He exists above and apart from the natural world, not bound by it, and it is not a coextension of himself. (2) He has no sex and no fertility partner; he created the universe by the authority of his spoken word. (3) He relates to his people by covenant promises.

Interpretive Insights

24:19 *to serve*. (See the comments on 24:14.) The language reflects the second of the Ten Commandments, prohibiting the worship of idols (Exod. 20:5; Deut. 5:9).

a holy God. The construction places emphasis on God's character as the reason for Israel's inability to serve the Lord. "For" or "because" (*ki*) begins the clause, explaining the rationale for Joshua's assertion (cf. ESV,

Key Themes of Joshua 24:19–28

- Joshua challenges the people to consider the consequences of the covenant.
- The people confidently agree to the stipulations and consequences.
- Joshua records the covenant in the Book of the Law.
- Joshua establishes a stone as a witness, and the people accept it as a witness.

HCSB). Since the people are not *inherently* holy, they inevitably will displease the Lord.

a jealous God. Here, another emphatic construction occurs. "Jealous" (*qanno'*) is the second echo in this verse of the second commandment (Exod. 20:5, "jealous," *qanna'*), indicating that the Lord condemns those who reject him (cf. Deut. 4:24).

He will not forgive. "Forgive" (*nasa'*) is derived from the word "to bear, carry," which is used of "bearing one's guilt or sin" (e.g., Lev. 5:1 ESV), or oppositely, "to carry away one's guilt or sin" (= forgiveness). That God does not forgive reflects the third commandment, against taking the holy name in vain (Exod. 20:7; Deut. 5:11).

24:20 *If you forsake the* LORD. The conditional clause "if" (*ki*) is the preference of most English translations, but the term may be understood as temporal, "When you forsake." This latter translation correlates well with Joshua's claim in verse 19 that the people will certainly not remain faithful.

he will turn. As a consequence of its failure, the Lord brings against the nation the curses of the covenant. "Turn" or "return" (*shub*) resonates with Deuteronomy 30:1–10; the words "turn" and "the Book of the Law" occur in both passages. (See "Theological Insights," below.)

bring disaster . . . make an end. The essential idea is that the Lord will "harm" (*hera'*) the people by bringing the curses of the covenant against them. The verb "make an end" means "to destroy," as in "to finish off" (*killah*), which also describes the curse of pestilence (Deut. 28:21).

after he has been good. The Lord shows his kind treatment of Israel by establishing it in the "good land" (23:13–16; cf. 21:45). The Lord's goodness is related to covenant blessing (e.g., Deut. 28:63; 30:5; Jer. 32:40). That the people disobey "after" (*'ahar*) his good purposes occur for them underscores the travesty of Israel's expected betrayal.

24:21 *No!* The emphatic negative "no" (*lo' ki*) occurs at the start of the sentence (cf. 5:14).

24:22 *witnesses against yourselves.* A witness to a covenant agreement may be an inanimate object (cf. the comments on 24:27, below) or God himself (e.g., Jer. 42:5). In this verse, the witness is the people's own confession. The idea is that the people have taken an oath of veracity before God (Deut. 5:20; Prov. 21:28). That "witnesses" (*'edim*) is plural indicates that they individually function as witnesses against one another.[2]

24:23 *throw away . . . yield your hearts.* The term "throw away" (*sur*) also occurs in verse 14. The passage perhaps echoes the command of Jacob to his household, "Get rid [*sur*] of the foreign gods" (Gen. 35:2). "Yield" (*natah*) means "to incline, bend, turn." "Hearts" expresses the inner will of the people (cf. the comments on 22:5). The centerpiece of Deuteronomic theology is the Shema, which calls for a perfectly obedient "heart" (Deut. 6:4–6).

24:24 *serve the LORD our God and obey him.* As in the Shema (Deut. 6:4), the possessive pronoun of "our God" (*'elohenu*) contrasts with the "foreign gods" (24:20,

23). Reference to the "LORD" (Yahweh) as Israel's God recalls the historical significance of his saving acts (24:17, 18). The third and final expression of submission (24:21, 22) explicitly adds the idea of obedience.

24:25 *On that day Joshua made a covenant . . . at Shechem.* Naming the day and site emphasizes the immediacy and significance of the covenant renewal. "Make [lit., "cut"] a covenant" (*karat b'rit*) is an idiom that reflects the practice of cutting into parts a sacrificial animal to seal the commitment of the parties (e.g., Gen. 15:10; Jer. 34:18). Joshua too authored a covenant with the Gibeonites on behalf of the congregation (9:15).

he reaffirmed . . . decrees and laws. "Reaffirmed" (*sim*) indicates "to establish," sometimes used of promulgating new law (e.g., Gen. 47:26). To what degree Joshua may have added new statutes to the Book of the Law is uncertain (24:26). The combination of "decrees and ordinances/laws" (*hoq umishpat*) occurs also in Exodus 15:25 ("a ruling and instruction").

24:26 *these things.* This phrase refers to the "decrees and laws" (24:25) that represent the covenant as a whole (synecdoche).

Book of the Law of God. The precise nature of this book is uncertain, since the phrase occurs only once more in the Old Testament (Neh. 8:18). It is probably a synonym for the "Book of the Law of Moses" (23:6). The reference to God indicates that what Joshua has added is equal to that of divine revelation (cf. "Chief Theological Themes" in the introduction).

stone . . . oak . . . holy place. Three features pertaining to the making of a covenant occur here. (1) The stone is treated as a person (personification) who can hear (24:27)

and witness in a court of law (cf. Gen. 31:45). The stone's size and material evoke the idea of permanency, thus a witness surviving the lives of the human parties. Stones functioned as memorials to Israel's crossing the Jordan (chap. 4). They also were overlaid with plaster and inscribed, bearing the content of a covenant agreement (8:32; cf. the Ten Commandments, Deut. 4:13). (2) The oak tree, especially noted for its immense size and shade, was an effective symbol for fecundity provided by the gods. This particular word for "oak" (*'allah*) occurs only here in the Old Testament and may be a corruption of the more frequent reference "terebinth" (*'elah*; cf. LXX's *tereminthos*, ESV). Trees were connected with holy places and were central to idol worship (e.g., Isa. 44:14; Hosea 4:13). The Hebrews recognized fertility as a blessing from the Lord's creative power (e.g., Deut. 28:4). (3) "Holy place" is the tent of meeting, deemed holy because of God's presence. It is his residence among the homes of the Israelites—the hub of Israel's life as the people of God. The practice of placing a copy of a covenant in the sanctuaries of the respective parties to a treaty was typical in ancient treaties (e.g., Deut. 31:24–26; 1 Sam. 10:25).

24:27 *See!* The term *hinneh* (lit., "behold, look here") draws special attention to the stone as a witness, indicating that the people acknowledge its meaning.

a witness against us. By the word "us," Joshua includes himself as a part of the community under obligation to the covenant.

if you are untrue. The clause can be conditional or negative purpose, "lest you" or "so that you will not" (cf. ESV, HCSB). The meaning of "untrue" (*kahash*) is "denial," but the word also is used as "conceal" for Achan's crime (7:11; NIV: "lied").

Theological Insights

The theological tension created in Deuteronomy continues in Joshua. The blessings of the covenant demonstrate grace because of God's love for the fathers. Yet the people must abide by the stipulations, or they will receive the curses, which include expulsion from the land. Both ideas are recurring in Joshua. In this particular commentary unit, the text emphasizes divine retribution against a rebellious people ("turn," 24:20). Deuteronomy 30 describes the outcome of the blessings and curses of the covenant (Deut. 27–29), foretelling that the people of Israel ultimately do repent and are restored to their land. The question is by what motivation they repent. Is it the expulsion (the curse), or is it the circumcision of the heart (Deut. 30:6) that God performs on them? The people are not "able to serve the LORD" (24:19), because they cannot "circumcise [their own] hearts" (Deut. 10:16). Until God works on their hearts, they can experience only partial, temporary obedience. In the case of Joshua's covenant renewal, the historical prologue testifies to God's favor toward their ancestors, indicating that the blessings are in place and will continue, but there is also human responsibility. The issue facing the Israelites is whether they will thrive in the land or be destroyed. However, both Deuteronomy and Joshua show that expulsion is temporary, and future generations will once again dwell in the land under the favor of God's blessing. The blessing that the people enjoy under Joshua is not complete since there are pockets of continued Canaanite resistance. Yet the people can look forward to a complete, permanent possession of the land that the Lord promises someday will be Israel's (e.g., Deut. 7:22; Josh. 11:22; 13:13; 17:13; 23:12–13).

"After [God] has been good to you" (24:20) introduces the judgment that awaits Israel if it abandons its love of the Lord. That Joshua's mood is harsh can be explained by this verse. In Israel's history (24:3–13) the Lord showered favor on a recalcitrant people whose chief characteristic was stubborn rebellion (Deut. 9:6). Despite his patience, they continued in their rebellion, always trying the Lord's mercy. The passage shows that even in the midst of divine discipline, divine good is available. The Lord's continued kindness points to the depth of their ingratitude and also justifies the severity of the ensuing punishment. In the ancient world, an international treaty required the subjugated party to obey the stipulations of the treaty or face the great king's military invasion. However, in the relationship between God and his people judgment is not the last word. Blessing follows punishment, showing that the Lord does not permanently abolish his covenant with Israel.

Teaching the Text

Joshua declares that God is "holy" and "jealous" (24:19, 26; cf. 5:15). This passage invites teaching God's character. Today "jealousy" has a negative meaning, denoting the irrational envy of a human being toward another. A better term explaining the Lord's "jealousy" for contemporary audiences "zealous." The Scriptures show that God is zealous by nature for that which belongs to him (e.g., Exod. 34:14). The Lord is zealous to reestablish what is right, seeking the proper response to honor him (e.g., Nah. 1:2; Zech. 8:2). Since Jesus Christ is Lord of all (Col. 1:15–20), he is deserving of reverence (Heb. 3:3). He does not require worship because of his pride; on the contrary, Jesus receives honor because of his humility before the Father (Phil. 2:7–11). Human jealousy in the Christian community essentially is selfishness and leads to strife (James 3:14, 16).

The Israelites in this passage respond to the covenant offer by expressing an unflappable desire to be bound to God (24:16–18, 21, 24). They have found by their own experience in capturing the land that he is worthy of covenant commitment, for he is a faithful God. They also recognize that their decision at this point means either continued life in the land or expulsion (24:20;

Deut. 11:26–28). For Christian readers this is a reminder that fervency too characterizes discipleship (Matt. 10:22; Rom. 12:11; Col. 1:2–23). What motivates God's people in the book of Joshua is the outpouring of his provision, and Christians will devote themselves to service when they understand more fully the indescribable mercies of God toward us (Rom. 5:5–8; 12:1).

Also, the idea of "witness" to Israel's faith is important for understanding God's work among his people and the appropriate response of his people. The "witness" of Israel's confession and of the memorial stone signifies the people's unreserved submission to the covenant (24:21–22, 24, 27). Previously, memorial stones built at the Jordan were a reminder to future generations of their salvation by the hand of God and served as an encouragement to continue to trust the Lord when facing enemies (4:6–7, 20–24). The Transjordan tribes similarly erected an altar as a "witness" to their fidelity to God and of the unity of the people (22:26–34). Similar features of a witness to the Lord's salvation and to the authenticity of those who believe appear in the New Testament. The divine witness to the gospel is the Holy Spirit, whom God gives to believers—the internal testimony (John 16:7–11; 1 John 5:6). Working in tandem with the Spirit's witness is human testimony—the external witness—given by the first disciples and by subsequent generations (John 15:26–27). Another witness is the Holy Scriptures, the written repository of the divine Word (John 21:24). Christians pass along what they receive so that others may be faithful caretakers of the truth (1 Cor. 15:3; 2 Tim. 2:2).

Illustrating the Text

Be zealous for the Lord.

Film: *Braveheart*. In this 1995 movie, we see zealousness in action through William Wallace, a thirteenth-century Scottish warrior who leads his people in a war against England for Scottish independence. Wallace has an amazing ability to motivate his people to fight. In one scene, Wallace proclaims, "You've come to fight as free men . . . and free men you are. What will you do with that freedom? Will you fight?" His zealous passion for independence mobilizes the people to action. People today tend to be zealous about many trivial things. But how many people are truly zealous for the Lord and for obedience to God?

Christian martyrs provide an example of service and sacrifice.

Quote: Justin Martyr. Church history provides poignant examples of Christian martyrs willing to make the ultimate sacrifice in service to the Lord. Consider the words of Justin Martyr (ca. AD 150):

> For if we looked for a human kingdom, we would deny our Christ, so that we might not be killed. We would try to escape detection, so that we might obtain what we hope for. But since our thoughts are not fixed on the present, we are not concerned when men cut us off; since death is a debt which must at all events be paid.[3]

Zeal for the Lord and a willingness to sacrifice come when we know God and understand that our mission is for him and his kingdom. Are you willing to sacrifice for the kingdom?

Funerals in Faith

Big Idea *God is always faithful to his promises.*

Understanding the Text

The Text in Context

The final paragraph of Joshua narrates the conclusion to the whole book. "After the death of Moses the servant of the LORD" begins the book (1:1), and the similar language, "Joshua . . . the servant of the LORD, died," initiates the conclusion to the book (24:29). By the idea of witness in 24:25–28, the conclusion ties to the immediate context of the covenant renewal ceremony in 24:1–28. Although the word "witness" does not occur in verses 29–33, the motif is apparent. The burying of the three leaders in the land of their inheritance evidences a faith in the promises of the Lord. They receive their inheritance (in Joseph's case symbolically) because of their perseverance in trusting the Lord.

The word "died" (*mut*) brackets the passage, referring to Joshua and Eleazar (24:29, 33). In between is the burial of Joseph's bones (24:32). (1) The death and burial of Joshua in his inheritance appears in verses 29–30, followed by a brief description of the spiritual character of Joshua's generation in verse 31. (2) After the report regarding Joseph in verse 32, the narrative ends with the death and burial of the high

priest Eleazar in verse 33. Interestingly, all three figures are interred "in the hill country of Ephraim" (24:30, 33). Joseph was born in the land of promise but died outside the land in Egypt (Gen. 30:23–24; 50:26), whereas Joshua and Eleazar were born in Egypt and die in Canaan (Exod. 6:23; Num. 11:28). Scripture does not tell Joshua's birthplace, but it was likely in Egypt (Exod. 33:11b); he first appears in Exodus 17:9.

Historical and Cultural Background

Burials at ancient Syro-Palestinian sites cannot be differentiated into Canaanite and Israelite remains. There are, however, correspondences between the burial sites in Palestine and what the Bible portrays. From the patriarchs to the time of the judges, family members commonly were buried together in underground caves. Abraham was buried in the cave of Machpelah that he had purchased for his family's burial site (Gen. 23:20; 25:9). Jacob and Joseph were buried on family land (Gen. 49:29–32; 50:13; Josh. 24:32). Theologically, the Hebrew forefathers whose graves were in their homeland reflected the promise of God's gift of the land. Bench tombs also appeared in the time of the judges and monarchy. Rooms in the cave had benches at waist height on three sides of the cave. Once the bodies decomposed, leaving only bones, they were removed and placed in a repository (1 Kings 13:31; 2 Kings 22:20).[1]

Interpretive Insights

24:29 *After these things.* The period between the making of the covenant and the death of Joshua is probably short, since he is "old" (13:1; 23:1–2; cf. Deut. 31:2). The expression brings to a conclusion his faithful leadership in exceptional times in the history of Israel.

servant of the Lord. (See the comments on 1:1.) This is an appropriate title for Joshua since "serve" (*'abad*) characterizes the covenant renewal in verses 1–28. Joshua never compromises his worship of the Lord.

a hundred and ten. Joseph died at the same age (Gen. 50:22). Longevity is a mark of divine blessing (Ps. 90:10), which adds to the esteem of Joshua's role in history (Judg. 2:8).

24:30 *Timnath Serah . . . Mount Gaash.* (Cf. Timnath Serah at 19:50.) The addition "the hill country of Ephraim" probably distinguishes Timnath Serah from another city named Timnath. The site of Mount Gaash remains unidentified; it possessed significant streams of water (2 Sam. 23:30; 1 Chron. 11:32).

24:31 *Israel served the Lord throughout the lifetime.* The statement "Israel served the Lord" occurs only here in the Old Testament, giving a high commendation to Joshua and his generation. The same could not be said during Moses's leadership (Exod. 32; Num. 25). Israel has not yielded to idolatry during Joshua's leadership. Although the phrase "throughout the lifetime" (lit., "all the days of your

bench where corpse was placed (notice chiseled out areas for the head)

bone repository chamber

bench where corpse was placed

bench where corpse was placed

Joshua, Eleazar, and the bones of Joseph are each buried in the "land of [their] inheritance" (24:30) in the promised land. Although their interment is not described, one type of burial site found in Israel is the bench-cut tomb. This photo shows a bench-cut tomb with a bone repository chamber that was excavated at Ketef Hinnom in Jerusalem and dated to the seventh to sixth century BC.

[Joshua's] life") is a common expression, perhaps it is an echo of the promise in 1:5 (cf. Moses, 4:14).

elders who outlived him. Joshua's witness has left a legacy of faith, but unfortunately it lasts no longer than his contemporaries (Judg. 2:10–11). The elders in Joshua's time play a critical role in spiritual leadership, war, worship, and decision making (7:6; 8:10, 33; 23:2; 24:1).

who had experienced everything the LORD *had done for Israel.* "Experienced" translates "know" (*yada'*), which indicates that it was their personal story, not a matter of simply hearing about God's mighty deeds. The wicked generation to follow only heard of it. Similar wording occurs in Judges 2:7, but there it is the word "seen" (*ra'ah*), indicating that they are eyewitnesses to the events (cf. Josh. 23:3). Another contrast with the Judges account is the words "everything" ("all") in Joshua and "great" in Judges. The difference is the tendency toward inclusivity in the Joshua account, whereas the emphasis in Judges is Israel's repute. This verse gives the last of many acknowledgments that the Lord was responsible for securing the land on behalf of Israel (e.g., 4:23; 10:30, 42; 23:3).

24:32 *Joseph's bones.* Compare Genesis 50:25–26. That Israel returns the bones of Joseph completes the circle of Israel's sojourn in and homecoming from Egypt.

Shechem . . . Jacob bought . . . silver. (Cf. Gen. 33:18–19.) "Shechem" refers both to the person Shechem, son of Hamor, and to the population of Shechem at the time of Jacob. The Shechemites are also Hivites, one of the seven nations the Lord promises to conquer (3:10). The Gibeonites who voluntarily submit to the Israelites are also Hivites (9:7). Jacob purchased a tract from the Shechemites at his return from Paddan Aram and made it his residence (Gen. 28:10–22; 31:3; 35:1–15). It foreshadows God's promise to restore Israel to Canaan. Dealings with the Shechemites became a hindrance to Jacob (Gen. 34), but now the former Canaanite city is in the hands of his descendants. "Silver" translates the word *q^esitah*, which indicates a monetary value or weight (Gen. 33:19; Job 42:11). That Jacob purchases the field for a significant price reflects his prosperity and his right of ownership. Joseph's bones rightly rest in the land that his descendant Ephraim possesses.

24:33 *Eleazar son of Aaron died.* The last verse of the book reports the death of the high priest, who has played a significant role in the distribution of the land (e.g., 14:1). He marks the transition, as do Joshua and the bones of Joseph, from the Egyptian sojourn and wilderness period to the close of the conquest. The mention of Aaron not only asserts Eleazar's priestly credential but also reminds the reader that Aaron died in the wilderness outside the land, as did his generation, for unbelief (Num. 20:28).

buried at Gibeah . . . Phinehas. The information regarding Phinehas's inheritance of Gibeah is new information. "Gibeah" names cities belonging to Judah (15:57) and to Benjamin (18:28), the latter being the birthplace of Saul (1 Sam. 10). Here, it is "Gibeah of Phinehas" (*gib'at pin^ehas*). It may mean "Gibeah belonging to Phinehas," or it may be taken as a place name, "Gibeath Phinehas" (cf. Gibeath Haaraloth, 5:3). In either case, it is apparent that Phinehas somehow came to own this plot. The city

Joseph is buried at Shechem on land that his father, Jacob, had purchased for one hundred pieces of silver. Before coins, payments of silver were made by cutting off appropriate weight pieces from coils such as the ones shown here.

is not named among those designated for the Levites (Josh. 21), and no land went to the high priestly lineage of Aaron (Num. 18:20). Phinehas is especially important in the history of Israel as a crusader but also a peacemaker (Num. 25:7–13; Josh. 22:13, 30–32).

Theological Insights

Although the passage appears to be an unimportant historical postscript and theologically thin, it provides an appropriate conclusion to the theological message of the author. The implications of the passage bundle together key ideas or the effects of those ideas that have dominated the book. These include divine promise, the Divine Warrior, Israel's possession and inheritance of the land, Israel's faith and faithfulness, exclusive worship of the Lord, the unity of God's people across the ages, and the relationship of God with his people.

The relationship of God with his people especially leaps out since the idea of death and burial is primary in the passage. Is the covenant relationship restricted to the present life of the people? What does the passage say regarding death and the afterlife?[2] Is there an expectation for more to come in realizing the blessing of inheritance? The book of Joshua taken alone offers no direct evidence for an afterlife, although it is a natural corollary. That the generation that succeeds Joshua does not follow the example of Joshua's obedience indicates that the people will not be able to hold on to the land permanently (Judg. 2:6–10). Butler comments: "Such a generation forced Israel to look ahead to a new day, when a new Joshua appeared on the scene as the servant of God totally fulfilling the task of God and bringing the promise of a new kingdom of God unlimited by physical boundaries or human death."[3] By Joshua's own admission the people do not have a heart for obedience (24:19); therefore, he sternly warns them to be vigilant. Since Joshua does not gain Israel's permanent possession, all Israel must look forward to "another Joshua," who will assure the full *permanent* inheritance of the blessings (Ps. 95:7–8; Heb. 3:15–4:8).

There is little in the Old Testament that addresses the subject of an afterlife in an explicit way. That there is an afterlife, however, is implied from a few texts, such as the expression of joining one's ancestors (e.g., Gen. 25:8; Judg. 2:10) and the posthumous appearance of Samuel (1 Sam. 28:15; some scholars point to Job 19:25–27; Ps. 73:23–26; Isa. 26:19; Dan. 12:2). The theology of an afterlife can be derived from the essential character of the covenant promises made to Abraham and his descendants. The covenant promises apply to future generations, and since not all generations (e.g.,

Abraham, Moses) enjoyed the full blessings of inheritance in their lives, it is theologically expected that there is a spiritual afterlife of blessing. Also, that the Lord is the God of the living indicates that his rule over his people includes not only this present life but the life to come (cf., e.g., Exod. 3:6; Matt. 22:32). Unlike the lifeless idols, he is the living God (3:10; cf. Jer. 16:18).

Teaching the Text

The lives of these three men—Joshua, Joseph, and Eleazar—provide examples of the lessons learned from the message of the book. These are not intended to be models for imitation, but they function as exhibits for what the book entails (cf. Heb. 11:22). These men's deaths remind readers of the men's lives. They received the promised inheritance and exhibited the faithfulness of the Lord toward Israel. They also represented the faith and obedience that the book repeatedly demands of Israel. God used Joshua as his vehicle of leading his people from the wilderness to settlement in the land. Joshua went against impossible odds, believing that God accomplishes his promises. Joseph, though far removed from the land, recognized that the promises remained, and he acknowledged that his life was evidence of God's preservation of his people (Gen. 50:19–20). The Lord used Joseph in Egypt to preserve the people of God until the time was ready for their departure. Eleazar is more vital than commonly acknowledged. As the successor to his father, the high priest Aaron, Eleazar was used by the Lord as the mediator of his will for the distribution of the land by casting lots (e.g., Num. 27:21; Josh. 14:2). His name

occurs before Joshua's when the narration describes the distribution of the land (14:1; 17:4; 19:51; 21:1; cf. 18:10), which accords with the divine directive (Num. 34:17). Eleazar's life spanned the Egyptian sojourn and the conquest. He was the chief overseer of the tent of meeting and the witness to the appointment of Joshua as Moses's successor (Num. 3:32; 27:19). He understood the power of God to defeat Israel's enemies, for he was involved in the wars of Moses (Num. 31:12).

The passage also conveys the transgenerational unity of the covenant, although these heroes lived in different eras and had different roles. What the generations fundamentally hold in common is their relationship to God and to one another as community by virtue of the covenant. The concept of community as transgenerational explains how promises made to one generation are also promised to future generations, evidenced by ritual observance of circumcision and Passover (5:2–12; cf. Gen. 17:7–10; Exod. 12:24–27). That the promises transcend any one generation is shown by the mention of "Phinehas" in the text and his possession of Gibeah. He is a figure whose life links the conquest generation and the one to follow. Although not yet successor to Eleazar as high priest, he takes the priestly role of protecting the sanctity of the altar and of exercising a mediatory role between the tribes (Josh. 22). He represents future generations that must maintain their fathers' faith (Judg. 20:28). The promises are not finally fulfilled with the conquest of the land, for the "rest" promised by the Lord includes future descendants of faith (Josh. 1:13–15). The writer to the Hebrews shows that the conquest's "rest" stands for the eternal rest that the Lord has for all who believe, now and those to come (Heb. 4:8).

Teachers can address the questions surrounding life and death for the believer and unbeliever. In the Old Testament, longevity is a blessing that is sometimes tied to obedience (e.g., Exod. 20:12; Deut. 4:4) and to wisdom (Prov. 3:16). Yet long life is not an absolute promise, because covenant believers sometimes die as a *consequence* of their faith (e.g., Ps. 44:22; Rom. 8:36), and innocent people also sometimes suffer injustice (Hab. 1:4). Death is the common human experience, whether one is a faithful believer or not, and afterward both stand before God's judgment (Rom. 14:11–12; Heb. 9:27–28). Life everlasting is a gift that the Lord bestows on those who trust Jesus Christ as Savior (John 5:24; Rom. 3:21–26).

Illustrating the Text

Be overcome by the shadow of death, not death itself.

Biography: *Death and the Life After*, by Billy Graham. In his book Graham shares a story about Dr. Donald Grey Barnhouse, one of America's greatest preachers. Barnhouse was on his way with his three children to preach at his wife's funeral. As Graham tells the story, a large truck passed them on the highway, casting a shadow over his car. Barnhouse turned to his oldest daughter, who was grieving the loss of her mother, and asked, "Tell me, sweetheart, would you rather be run over by that truck or its shadow?" The little girl responded, "By the shadow, I guess. It can't hurt you." Her father responded, "Your mother has not been overrun by death, but by the shadow of death. That is nothing to fear." Barnhouse went on to use Psalm 23 as the basis of his message at his wife's funeral, using this powerful image as the backdrop.[4] As Christians who have put their faith in the work of God through Jesus Christ, we will never be overcome by death, but only by the shadow of death.

What is the legacy you want to leave for the generations to come?

Quote: *Raising Godly Children in an Ungodly World*, by Ken Ham and Steve Ham. As we come to the end of the book of Joshua, we are reminded that our lives speak not just to our generation but to the generations to come. In the prologue to their book, one of the brothers writes about the godly impact of their parents.

> [My father] was an uncompromising witness and defender of the gospel. God used him to lay a rock solid foundation for our family and prepare us not only for this present life—but also for an eternity with our Creator. I cannot fathom the value of this inheritance which he left me. There is no doubt in my mind that the legacy of my father and mother, together with the Lord's calling on my life, is the reason I came to be in the ministry.[5]

Ask your listeners to decide on three gifts, apart from material possessions, that they want to leave to the generations to come. How do they want to be remembered? How do they want to impact the generations to come? Now, what can they do to create that legacy?

Notes

Introduction to Joshua

1. The Hebrew Bible is called TaNaK, referring to the tri-partite arrangement of Torah, Nevi'im, and Ketuvim, meaning "the Law, the Prophets, and the Writings" (cf. Luke 24:44).

2. Younger, *Ancient Conquest Accounts*, 241–47.

3. McConville and Williams, *Joshua*, 106.

4. Hawk, *Joshua in 3-D*, 178–80; Hawk, *Every Promise Fulfilled*, 56–93.

5. E.g., Boling and Wright, *Joshua*, 55–59; Butler, *Joshua*, xx–xxiii; Hawk, "Joshua, Book of."

6. E.g., Hess, *Joshua*, 26–41; Pitkänen, *Joshua*, 51–64.

7. For further reading, see Hess, "War in the Hebrew Bible"; Howard, *Joshua*, 180–87; Copan, *Is God a Moral Monster?*, 158–206; Flannagan, "Genocide of the Canaanites?"

8. For further reading, see Waltke, *Old Testament Theology*, 512–87; McConville and Williams, *Joshua*, 95–108; Saucy, *Progressive Dispensationalism*, 50–57; and Bateman, *Three Central Issues in Contemporary Dispensationalism*.

Joshua 1:1–18

1. Hess, "Joshua," 2:9–13; Arnold and Beyer, *Readings from the Ancient Near East*, 96–97.

2. For details, see Howard, *Joshua*, 119–20; Harstad, *Joshua*, 92.

3. Richard Dawkins, *The God Delusion* (London: Black Swan, 2007), 340–41.

4. Billy Graham, *Just As I Am: The Autobiography of Billy Graham* (New York: HarperCollins, 1997), 139.

5. Joshua Rhett Miller, "Sudanese Woman Sentenced to Death for Apostasy Gives Birth in Prison," FoxNews.com, May 27, 2014, http://www.foxnews.com/world/2014/05/27/su danese-woman-sentenced-to-death-for-apostasy-reportedly -gives-birth-in-prison/.

Joshua 2:1–24

1. Hess, "Joshua," 2:19–20.

2. John Cecil, *The Works of the Rev. John Newton* (Philadelphia: Uriah Hunt, 1831), 1:89.

3. "John Newton: Reformed Slave Trader," *Christian History* website, August 8, 2008, http://www.christianitytoday .com/ch/131christians/pastorsandpreachers/newton.html.

4. Brother Andrew, John Sherrill, and Elizabeth Sherrill, *God's Smuggler* (Grand Rapids: Chosen Books, 2001), 166.

Joshua 3:1–17

1. There is debate regarding the literary and chronological relationship of these two chapters; see, e.g., Pitkänen (*Joshua*, 129–32) and Hess (*Joshua*, 97–98), who argue for coherence, and Nelson (*Joshua*, 55–60, 65–68) and Butler (*Joshua*, 41–44), who represent the view of multiple sources, citing various discrepancies.

2. Charles Montaldo, "Velma Barfield—The Death Row Granny," About.com, August 15, 2014, http://crime.about .com/od/serial/p/velma_barfield2.htm.

3. Billy Graham, *Just As I Am: The Autobiography of Billy Graham* (New York: HarperCollins, 1997), 681–83.

Joshua 4:1–24

1. Steven Gertz, "What Is the Origin of the Anchor as a Christian Symbol, and Why Do We No Longer Use It?," *Christian History* website, August 8, 2008, http://www.christianity today.com/ch/asktheexpert/sep13.html.

2. Jack R. Van Ens, "Keeping the Wide-Angle View," *Leadership Journal*, January 1, 1989, http://www.christianity today.com/le/1989/winter/89l1032.html.

Joshua 5:1–12

1. "Teaching Visually Impaired Skiers," OutdoorsForAll .org, https://outdoorsforall.org/wp-content/uploads/2014/05 /OFA-Material-Visual.pdf.

2. "Promissory Note," Investopedia.com, http://www .investopedia.com/terms/p/promissorynote.asp.

Joshua 5:13–15

1. Some scholars consider 5:13–15 a fragment of a fuller account that gave the task (e.g., Nelson, *Joshua*, 81–82).

See Butler, *Joshua*, 57, who answers this viewpoint. Others believe that the commander, identified as "the Lᴏʀᴅ" (*Yahweh*) in 6:2, continues speaking in 6:2–5, which gives the task (see Hubbard, *Joshua*, 187; Harstad, *Joshua*, 252; Hess, *Joshua*, 128–29; Goslinga, *Joshua, Judges, Ruth*, 67). Howard, *Joshua*, 159, contends that the passage as it stands is original and is independent of chapter 6.

2. Bray, *God Is Love*, 160.

3. "From a Distance Lyrics," MetroLyrics.com, http://www.metrolyrics.com/from-a-distance-lyrics-bette-midler.html.

4. Matthew Simpson, *Funeral Address Delivered at the Burial of President Lincoln* (New York: Carlton and Porter, 1865), 16.

5. Dave Gibbons, *Xealots: Defying the Gravity of Normality* (Grand Rapids: Zondervan, 2011), 145–46. Gibbons writes this piece in light of John the Baptist's statement regarding Jesus in John 3:30.

Joshua 6:1–27

1. Hawk, *Joshua*, 91–98.

2. Hess, *Joshua*, 135.

3. Howard, *Joshua*, 176.

4. McConville and Williams, *Joshua*, 176.

5. Redpath, *Victorious Christian Living*, 106. This *mis*-interpretation of Jericho is sometimes reinforced by the parable of the good Samaritan, in which the city Jericho appears (Luke 10:30).

6. Rich Mullins, "His Master's Voice," *Release Magazine*, September/October 1994; available online at http://www.kidbrothers.net/words/release-magazine/release-magazine-sepoct94.html.

7. Kenny Luck, "Sexual Atheism: Christian Dating Data Reveals a Deeper Spiritual Malaise," CP Opinion, *Christian Post*, April 10, 2014, http://www.christianpost.com/news/sexual-atheism-christian-dating-data-reveals-a-deeper-spiritual-malaise-117717/.

8. Corrie ten Boom, *The Hiding Place* (Peabody, MA: Hendrickson, 1971), 84.

9. Ibid., 94.

Additional Insights

1. For further reading, see Copan, *Is God a Moral Monster?*, 205; Bennett, *Studying Islam*, 93, where Bennett identifies three different Islamic views on jihad: the classical, the critical, and the reformist's.

Joshua 7:1–15

1. Milgrom, *Leviticus 1–16*, 345–47.

2. Maranda M., "Judgment vs. Correction," *Revealing Truth Today* (blog), July 11, 2012, http://revealingtruthtoday.wordpress.com/tag/judgment-vs-correction/.

Joshua 7:16–26

1. Howard, *Joshua*, 196–97.

2. Ibid., 198n97.

3. Butler, *Joshua*, 86.

4. Hess, *Joshua*, 154.

5. Creach, *Joshua*, 75.

6. Hill and Walton, *Survey of the Old Testament*, 190.

7. Jeffry C. Davis and Philip Graham Ryken, eds., *Liberal Arts for the Christian Life* (Wheaton: Crossway, 2012), 16.

8. Dennis L. Thompson, ed., *Moral Values and Higher Education* (Provo, UT: Brigham Young University Press, 1991), 116.

9. Annie Laurie Gaylor, "Oliver Wendell Holmes, Jr.," Freedom From Religion Foundation, https://ffrf.org/news/day/dayitems/item/14246-oliver-wendell-holmes-jr.

10. "Victimless Crime," https://www.princeton.edu/~achaney/tmve/wiki100k/docs/Victimless_crime.html.

Joshua 8:1–29

1. *ANET*, 255.

2. *ANET*, 278–80.

3. See Cole, *Numbers*, 78–82, for discussion.

4. Butler, *Joshua*, 88.

5. Harris, "Joshua," 58.

6. Ron Moses, *The 15 Secrets of Millionaires* (n.p.: Ron Moses, 2012), 152.

7. "Funny Directions to Follow," Inspire21.com, http://www.inspire21.com/stories/humorstories/funnydirections.

8. *The King of Queens*, "Holy Mackerel," season 5, episode 103.

Joshua 8:30–35

1. Nelson, *Joshua*, 116–17, describes the variant placing of the MT, LXX, and Qumran Joshua.

2. Seger, "Shechem"; for a full discussion of Shechem's relevance for dating the exodus and conquest, see Walton, "Exodus, Date of."

3. Hawk, *Joshua*, 133.

4. Ibid., 134.

5. For a detailed correspondence between 8:30–35 and the Pentateuch instructions, see Howard, *Joshua*, 214; Butler, *Joshua*, 90.

6. United States Constitution, article II, section 1, cited by "Fifty-Seventh Presidential Inauguration, January 21, 2013," Joint Congressional Committee on Inaugural Ceremonies, http://www.inaugural.senate.gov/days-events/days-event/presidents-swearing-in-ceremony.

7. "Biography: Jim Jones," PBS.org, http://www.pbs.org/wgbh/americanexperience/features/biography/jonestown-bio-jones/.

8. Jennifer Rosenberg, "The Jonestown Massacre," About.com, http://history1900s.about.com/od/1970s/p/jonestown.htm.

Joshua 9:1–27

1. Hubbard, *Joshua*, 283, uses the catchy phrase "trick and treaty."

2. For a survey of these nations, see Satterthwaite and Baker, "Nations of Canaan."

3. Butler, *Joshua*, 104.

4. For proposed sites, see Hubbard, *Joshua*, 289 and n. 33.

5. Hawk, *Joshua*, 138–49.

6. Ibid., 148.

7. Hamlin, *Joshua*, 80–81.

8. Marcus Luttrell and Patrick Robinson, *Lone Survivor: The Eyewitness Account of Operation Redwing and the Lost Heroes of SEAL Team 10* (New York: Little, Brown, 2007); *Lone Survivor*, produced by Peter Berg, released on December 25, 2013.

9. Sami Yousafzai and Ron Moreau, "The Afghan Village That Saved Navy SEAL Marcus Luttrell," *Daily Beast*, November 8, 2013, http://www.thedailybeast.com /articles/2013/11/08/the-afghan-village-that-saved-navy-seal -marcus-luttrell.html.

10. Laura Hillenbrand, *Unbroken: A World War II Story of Survival, Resilience, and Redemption* (New York: Random House, 2010), 379.

Joshua 10:1–15

1. For details, see Hess, *Joshua*, 29–30.

2. Creach, *Joshua*, 93.

3. Ann Conner, *Enter the Open Door* (Maitland, FL: Xulon, 2008), 242.

Additional Insights

1. *HALOT* 1:226.

2. *HALOT* 2:840–42.

3. For a summary and evaluation of these views, see Howard, *Joshua*, 241–49; and Hom, "Day Like No Other," 217–23.

4. For a full explanation, see Walton, "Joshua 10:12–15."

Joshua 10:16–43

1. For more on these issues, see Copan, *Is God a Moral Monster?*; Flannagan, "Genocide of the Canaanites?"; Hess, "War in the Hebrew Bible"; Wright, *Old Testament Ethics*; and Cowles, Merrill, Gard, and Longman, *Show Them No Mercy*.

2. Hamlin, *Joshua*, 95.

3. Tim Challies, "Hymn Stories: A Mighty Fortress Is Our God," Challies.com, July 7, 2013, http://www.challies .com/articles/hymn-stories-a-mighty-fortress-is-our-god.

4. "A Mighty Fortress Is Our God," HymnSite.com, http://www.hymnsite.com/lyrics/umh110.sht.

5. Abraham Lincoln, "Proclamation Appointing a National Fast Day," *Collected Works of Abraham Lincoln*, ed. Roy P. Basler et al. (New Brunswick, NJ: Rutgers University Press, 1953), 6:156.

Joshua 11:1–15

1. Nelson, *Joshua*, 151, for example, divides the chapter based on temporal markers: 11:1–9, 10–20, and 21–23; Hawk, *Joshua*, 169, has 11:1–5, 6–9, 10–15.

2. Ben-Tor, "Hazor."

3. Mathewson, *Joshua and Judges*, 65.

4. Palmer Chinchen, *True Religion: Taking Pieces of Heaven to Places of Hell on Earth* (Colorado Springs: David C. Cook, 2010), 55.

5. Wilbur Rees, "Three Dollars [*sic*] Worth of God," Faith-Forward.org, http://www.faith-forward.org/three -dollars--worth-of-god.htm.

6. Georgie, "23 Funny Letters to God from Kids," Pop hangover.com, December 4, 2012, http://www.pophangover .com/20610/23-funny-letters-to-god-from-kids/.

Joshua 11:16–12:24

1. For commentary on the locations of the many sites named in 11:16–12:24, see Pitkänen, *Joshua*, 232–46.

2. Younger, *Ancient Conquest Accounts*, esp. 227–28, 230–32, 241, 251.

3. For "Galilee," see Hess, *Joshua*, 226–29, who has a useful chart naming the cities.

4. McConville and Williams, *Joshua*, 59.

5. Davis W. Houck, *FDR and Fear Itself: The First Inaugural Address* (College Station: Texas A&M University Press, 2002), 3.

Joshua 13:1–33

1. The text of verse 4 is uncertain, with ancient and modern versions differing; see Butler, *Joshua*, 146, for details.

2. Simon Tomlinson, "Prince William Expected to Inherit £10 million from Diana's Estate as He Turns 30 Today," MailOnline, *Daily Mail*, June 21, 2012, http://www.daily mail.co.uk/news/article-2162474/Prince-William-expected -inherit-10million-Dianas-estate-turns-30-today.html.

Joshua 14:1–15

1. Boling and Wright, *Joshua*, 351.

2. Nelson, *Joshua*, 178n5.

3. McConville and Williams, *Joshua*, 66.

4. Trillia Newbell, "Dear Pastor: From a Black Female Congregant," CP Blog, *The Christian Post*, April 2, 2012, http://blogs.christianpost.com/guest-views/dear-pastor-from -a-black-female-congregant-9100/.

5. Billy Graham, *Nearing Home: Life, Faith, and Finishing Well* (Nashville: Nelson, 2011), 34.

6. Eryn Sun, "Joni Eareckson Tada on Wilberforce Award, 'Better Off Dead Than Disabled' Mentality," *Christian Post*, March 16, 2012, http://www.christianpost.com/news/joni -eareckson-tada-on-wilberforce-award-better-off-dead-than -disabled-mentality-71536/.

Joshua 15:1–63

1. Hess, "Joshua," 2:58–61; Kitchen, *Reliability of the Old Testament*, 179–82.

2. Hess, *Joshua*, 244–45.

3. William H. Bartsch, *December 8, 1941: MacArthur's Pearl Harbor* (College Station: Texas A&M University Press, 2003).

4. Marc Fisher, "Clinton's Pastor with a Past," *Washington Post*, September 28, 1998, http://www.washingtonpost .com/wp-srv/style/daily/clinpastor0928.htm.

5. Jessica Bennett, "Poll: How Much Is Beauty Worth at Work?," *Newsweek*, July 18, 2010, http://www.newsweek .com/poll-how-much-beauty-worth-work-74305.

Joshua 16:1–17:18

1. Howard, *Joshua*, 356.
2. House, *Old Testament Theology*, 208.
3. Kathy Weiser, "Old West Legends: The Donner Party Tragedy," *Legends of America*, last updated April 2012, http://www.legendsofamerica.com/ca-donnerparty4.html.
4. P. Solomon Banda, "Deputy: Dad Likely Saved Girl in Deadly Rock Slide," Associated Press, October 1, 2013, http://bigstory.ap.org/article/5-hikers-killed-colo-rock-slide-easy-trail.

Joshua 18:1–19:51

1. Hess, "Joshua," 2:68.
2. McConville and Williams, *Joshua*, 74–75.
3. Bob Smietana, "Statistical Illusion: New Study Confirms That We Go to Church Much Less Than We Say," *Christianity Today*, April 1, 2006, http://www.christianitytoday.com/ct/2006/april/32.85.html.
4. Paul Schwartzman, "Peggielene Bartels: Secretary by Day, King of Otuam, Ghana, by Night," *Washington Post*, September 16, 2009, http://www.washingtonpost.com/wp-dyn/content/article/2009/09/15/AR2009091503393.html.

Joshua 20:1–9

1. "Fled" (*katapheugō*) in Heb. 6:18 also occurs in the LXX in Num. 35:25–26; Deut. 4:42; 19:5; and Josh. 20:9, which describe the killer's flight to a city of refuge. On the rendering "fled for refuge" in Heb. 6:18, see, e.g., HCSB, ESV, and NRSV. Koester, *Hebrews*, 328, observes that in antiquity people sought refuge in temples; in Israel the altar (1 Kings 1:50) and cities of refuge provide protection. Hebrews 6:19 indicates the place of refuge is in the sanctuary. Johnson, *Hebrews*, 171, attributes *katapheugō* to the wanderings of the patriarchs or the travels of Israel in the exodus wilderness (cf. Heb. 11:8–16).
2. "Elijah Parish Lovejoy Was Killed by a Pro-Slavery Mob," *America's Story from America's Library*, Library of Congress website, http://www.americaslibrary.gov/jb/reform/jb_reform_lovejoy_1.html.

Joshua 21:1–42

1. Watkins, "Shiloh"; Gilmour, "Shiloh."
2. Harstad, *Joshua*, 661–62.
3. Henry Adams, *The Education of Henry Adams* (Stilwell, KS: Digireads.com, 2007), 162: "A teacher affects eternity; he can never tell where his influence stops."
4. Kit Yarrow, "Worst. Gift. Ever. The 6 Kinds of Presents You Should Never Give," *Time*, November 30, 2012, http://business.time.com/2012/11/30/worst-gift-ever-the-6-kinds-of-presents-you-should-never-give/.

Joshua 21:43–45

1. For an extensive discussion of "rest" (*nuah*), see Oswalt, "*nuakh*."

Joshua 22:1–9

1. *Everybody Loves Raymond*, "Christmas Present," season 5, episode 11. See also Joanna Wilson, "*Everybody Loves Raymond* Christmas (2000)," *Christmas TV History* (blog), May 15, 2013, http://www.christmastvhistory.com/2013/05/everybody-loves-raymond-christmas-2000.html.
2. Derek Thompson, "This Is Why You Don't Go to the Gym," *Atlantic*, January 13, 2012, http://www.theatlantic.com/business/archive/2012/01/this-is-why-you-dont-go-to-the-gym/251332/.
3. Jason Fox, *The Game Changer* (Hoboken, NJ: Wiley, 2014), 26.

Joshua 22:10–34

1. Van Groningen, "*qeṣep*, wrath."
2. McConville and Williams, *Joshua*, 84–85.
3. Milgrom, *Leviticus 1–16*, 250, 724.
4. Jane Englsiepen, "Trees Communicate," *Ecology*, October 8, 2012, http://www.ecology.com/2012/10/08/trees-communicate/.
5. Tim Challies, "Counterfeit Detection (Part 1)," Challies.com, June 27, 2006, http://www.challies.com/articles/counterfeit-detection-part-1. This article draws from his interview with one of Canada's foremost experts on counterfeit currency.
6. Melody Warnick, "Lending a Helping Hand," *Woman's Day*, http://www.womansday.com/life/personal-stories/lending-a-helping-hand-112631.

Joshua 23:1–11

1. Creach, *Joshua*, 114.
2. Donald B. DeYoung, *77 Science Activities for Illustrating Bible Lessons* (Grand Rapids: Baker Books, 2013), 66–68.
3. Ibid., 68.
4. Anna Johnson, "3 Ultra-Athletes Run across Sahara," *USA Today*, February 20, 2007, http://usatoday30.usatoday.com/news/world/2007-02-20-sahara-crossing_x.htm.
5. Association for Psychological Science, "Research Shows Temptation More Powerful Than Individuals Realize," Phys.org, August 3, 2009, http://phys.org/news168523630.html.

Joshua 23:12–16

1. See Bray, *God Is Love*, 140–41, 398.
2. Kendra Cherry, "What Is Groupthink?," About.com, http://psychology.about.com/od/gindex/g/groupthink.htm.
3. Lawrence J. Cohen and Anthony T. DeBenedet, "Penn State Cover-Up: Groupthink in Action," *Time*, July 17, 2012, http://ideas.time.com/2012/07/17/penn-state-cover-up-group-think-in-action/.

Joshua 24:1–18

1. McConville, *Deuteronomy*, 124.
2. Hess, *Joshua*, 304.
3. Hawk, *Joshua*, 262–63.
4. Harstad, *Joshua*, 780.
5. David Schrader, "Song Story: Matt Redman's 'The Heart of Worship,'" Crosswalk.com, March 25, 2004, http://www.crosswalk.com/church/worship/song-story-matt-redmans-the-heart-of-worship-1253122.html.

Joshua 24:19–28

1. Walton, *Ancient Near Eastern Thought*, 87–112.
2. Hubbard, *Joshua*, 559.
3. Justin Martyr, *First Apology* 11. Translation from "Martyrdom Quotes," Christian History for Everyman, http://www.christian-history.org/martyrdom-quotes.html.

Joshua 24:29–33

1. Hachlili, "Burials"; McCane, "Burial; Techniques."
2. Johnston, "Death and the Afterlife."

3. Butler, *Joshua*, 284.
4. Billy Graham, *Death and the Life After* (Nashville: Nelson, 1987), 73–74.
5. Ken Ham and Steve Ham, *Raising Godly Children in an Ungodly World: Leaving a Lasting Legacy* (Green Forest, AR: Master Books, 2006), 20–21.

Bibliography

Recommended Resources

Copan, Paul. *Is God a Moral Monster? Making Sense of the Old Testament God*. Grand Rapids: Baker Books, 2011.

Harstad, Adolph L. *Joshua*. Concordia Commentary. St. Louis: Concordia Publishing House, 2004.

Hess, Richard S. *Joshua*. Tyndale Old Testament Commentaries. Downers Grove, IL: InterVarsity, 1996.

Howard, David. *Joshua*. New American Commentary. Nashville: Broadman & Holman, 1998.

Hubbard, Robert L. *Joshua*. NIV Application Commentary. Grand Rapids: Zondervan, 2009.

McConville, J. Gordon, and Stephen N. Williams. *Joshua*. The Two Horizons Old Testament Commentary. Grand Rapids: Eerdmans. 2010.

Select Bibliography

Arnold, Bill T., and Bryan E. Beyer, eds. *Readings from the Ancient Near East: Primary Sources for Old Testament Study*. Encountering Biblical Studies. Grand Rapids: Baker Academic, 2002.

Ash, P. S. "Borders." In *Dictionary of the Old Testament: Pentateuch*, edited by T. Desmond Alexander and David W. Baker, 101–4. Downers Grove, IL: InterVarsity, 2003.

Averbeck, Richard E. "Tabernacle." In *Dictionary of the Old Testament: Pentateuch*, edited by T. Desmond Alexander and David W. Baker, 807–27. Downers Grove, IL: InterVarsity, 2003.

Baker, David. "*r*‛‛" In *New International Dictionary of Old Testament Theology and Exegesis*, edited by Willem A. VanGemeren, 3:1154–58. 5 vols. Grand Rapids: Zondervan, 1997.

Bateman, Herbert W., ed. *Three Central Issues in Contemporary Dispensationalism: A Comparison of Traditional and Progressive Views*. Grand Rapids: Kregel, 1999.

Beitzel, Barry J. *Moody Atlas of the Bible*. Chicago: Moody, 2009.

Bennett, Clinton. *Studying Islam: The Critical Issues*. New York: Continuum International, 2010.

Ben-Tor, Amnon. "Hazor." In *The Oxford Encyclopedia of Archaeology in the Near East*, edited by Eric M. Meyers, 3:1–5. 5 vols. New York: Oxford University Press, 1997.

Boling, Robert G., and G. Ernest Wright. *Joshua*. Anchor Bible. Garden City, NY: Doubleday, 1982.

Bray, Gerald. *God Is Love: A Biblical and Systematic Theology*. Wheaton: Crossway, 2012.

Bruce, F. F. *The Epistle to the Hebrews*. Rev. Grand Rapids: Eerdmans, 1990.

Brueggemann, Dale A. *Numbers*. Cornerstone Biblical Commentary. Carol Stream, IL: Tyndale, 2008.

Butler, Trent. *Joshua*. Word Biblical Commentary. Waco: Word, 1983.

———. *Understanding the Basic Themes of Joshua*. Dallas: Word, 1991.

Carpenter, E. "*qahal*." In *New International Dictionary of Old Testament Theology and Exegesis*, edited by Willem A. VanGemeren, 3:888–92. 5 vols. Grand Rapids: Zondervan, 1997.

Cole, Dennis R. *Numbers*. New American Commentary. Nashville: Broadman & Holman, 2000.

Collins, C. John. *The God of Miracles: An Exegetical Examination of God's Action in the World*. Wheaton: Crossway, 2000.

Cowles, C. S., Eugene Merrill, Daniel Gard, and Tremper Longman III. *Show Them No Mercy: Four Views* on God and Canaanite Genocide. Grand Rapids: Zondervan, 2003.

Creach, Jerome F. D. Joshua. Interpretation. Louisville: John Knox, 2003.

Davis, D. R. Joshua: No Falling Words. Fearn, Ross-Shire, Scotland: Christian Focus, 2000.

Els, P. J. J. S. "'aheb." In New International Dictionary of Old Testament Theology and Exegesis, edited by Willem A. VanGemeren, 1:277–99. 5 vols. Grand Rapids: Zondervan, 1997.

Flannagan, Matthew. "Did God Command the Genocide of the Canaanites?" In Come Let Us Reason, edited by Paul Copan and William Lane Craig, 225–50. Nashville: Broadman & Holman, 2012.

Fürst, D. "Paideuō." In New International Dictionary of New Testament Theology, edited by Colin Brown, 3:775–80. 3 vols. Grand Rapids: Zondervan, 1986.

Garrett, Duane. "Levi, Levites." In Dictionary of the Old Testament: Pentateuch, edited by T. Desmond Alexander and David W. Baker, 519–22. Downers Grove, IL: InterVarsity, 2003.

Geivett, Douglas R., and Gary R. Habermas, eds. In Defense of Miracles: A Comprehensive Case for God's Action in History. Downers Grove, IL: InterVarsity, 1997.

Gilmour, G. "Shiloh." In Dictionary of the Old Testament: Historical Books, edited by B. T. Arnold and H. G. M. Williamson, 893–95. Downers Grove, IL: InterVarsity, 2005.

Goslinga, C. J. Joshua, Judges, Ruth. Grand Rapids: Zondervan, 1986.

Grudem, Wayne. Systematic Theology: An Introduction to Biblical Doctrine. Grand Rapids: Zondervan, 1994.

Günther, W., and H.-G. Link. "Love." In New International Dictionary of New Testament Theology, edited by Colin Brown, 2:539–47. 3 vols. Grand Rapids: Zondervan, 1986.

Hachlili, Rachel. "Burials." In Anchor Bible Dictionary, edited by David Noel Freedman, 1:785–94. 6 vols. New York: Doubleday, 1992.

Hamlin, E. John. Joshua: Inheriting the Land. International Theological Commentary. Grand Rapids: Eerdmans, 1983.

Harris, J. Gordon. "Joshua." In Joshua, Judges, Ruth, by J. Gordon Harris, Cheryl A. Brown, Michael S. Moore, 3–119. Peabody, MA: Hendrickson, 2000.

Hawk, Daniel L. "Altars." In Dictionary of the Old Testament: Pentateuch, edited by T. Desmond Alexander and David W. Baker, 33–37. Downers Grove, IL: InterVarsity, 2003.

———. Every Promise Fulfilled: Contesting Plots in Joshua. Louisville: Westminster John Knox, 1991.

———. Joshua. Berit Olam. Collegeville, MN: Liturgical Press, 1999.

———. "Joshua, Book of." In Dictionary of the Old Testament: Historical Books, edited by B. T. Arnold

and H. G. M. Williamson, 563–75. Downers Grove, IL: InterVarsity, 2005.

———. Joshua in 3-D. Eugene, OR: Cascade, 2010.

Hess, Richard S. "Joshua." In Zondervan Illustrated Bible Background: Old Testament, edited by John H. Walton, 2:3–93. 5 vols. Grand Rapids: Zondervan, 2009.

———. "War in the Hebrew Bible: An Overview." In War in the Bible and Terrorism in the Twenty-First Century, edited by Richard S. Hess and Elmer A. Martens, 19–32. Winona Lake, IN: Eisenbrauns, 2008.

Hill, Andrew, and John Walton. A Survey of the Old Testament. 2nd ed. Grand Rapids: Zondervan, 2009.

Hom, Mary K. "A Day like No Other: A Discussion of Joshua 10:12–14." Expository Times 115/7 (2004): 217–23.

Horton, Michael. The Christian Faith. Grand Rapids: Zondervan, 2011.

House, P. Old Testament Theology. Downers Grove, IL: InterVarsity, 1998.

Hughes, R. Kent. Living on the Cutting Edge. Westchester, IL: Crossway, 1987.

Ibrahim, M. "Jordan Valley." In The Oxford Encyclopedia of Archaeology in the Near East, edited by Eric M. Meyers, 3:248–51. 5 vols. New York: Oxford University Press, 1997.

Johnson, L. T. Hebrews, A Commentary. New Testament Library. Louisville: Westminster John Knox, 2006.

Johnston, P. S. "Death and the Afterlife." In Dictionary of the Old Testament: Historical Books, edited by B. T. Arnold and H. G. M. Williamson, 215–19. Downers Grove, IL: InterVarsity, 2005.

Keener, Craig S. Miracles: The Credibility of the New Testament Accounts. 2 vols. Grand Rapids: Baker, 2011.

Kitchen, Kenneth A. On the Reliability of the Old Testament. Grand Rapids: Eerdmans, 2003.

Koester, Craig R. Hebrews: A New Translation with Introduction and Commentary. Anchor Bible. New York: Doubleday, 2001.

LaSor, William S., David A. Hubbard, and Frederic W. Bush. Old Testament Survey: The Message, Form, and Background of the Old Testament. 2nd ed. Grand Rapids: Eerdmans, 1996.

Lewis, C. S. Miracles: A Preliminary Study. New York: Macmillan, 1947.

Longman, Tremper, III, and Daniel G. Reid. God Is a Warrior. Grand Rapids: Zondervan, 1995.

MacDonald, W. "Christology and the Angel of the Lord." In Current Issues in Biblical and Patristic Interpretation, edited by G. Hawthorne, 324–35. Grand Rapids: Eerdmans, 1975.

Mathews, Kenneth A. Genesis 11:27–50:26. New American Commentary. Nashville: Broadman & Holman, 2005.

Mathewson, Steven D. Joshua and Judges. Oxford: The Bible Reader's Fellowship, 2003.

McCane, Byron. "Burial; Techniques." In *The Oxford Encyclopedia of Archaeology in the Near East*, edited by Eric M. Meyers, 1:386–87. 5 vols. New York: Oxford University Press, 1997.

McConville, J. Gordon. *Deuteronomy*. Apollos Old Testament Commentary. Downers Grove, IL: InterVarsity, 2002.

———. "Jericho." In *Dictionary of the Old Testament: Historical Books*, edited by B. T. Arnold and H. G. M. Williamson, 541–44. Downers Grove, IL: InterVarsity, 2005.

Merrill, Eugene. *A Kingdom of Priests*. 2nd ed. Grand Rapids: Baker, 2008.

———. "ysr." In *New International Dictionary of Old Testament Theology and Exegesis*, edited by Willem A. VanGemeren, 2:479–82. 5 vols. Grand Rapids: Zondervan, 1997.

Milgrom, Jacob. *Leviticus 1–16*. Anchor Bible. New York: Doubleday, 1991.

———. *Numbers*. JPS Torah. Philadelphia: Jewish Publication Society, 1990.

Naudé, Jackie A. "qdš." In *New International Dictionary of Old Testament Theology and Exegesis*, edited by Willem A. VanGemeren, 3:877–87. 5 vols. Grand Rapids: Zondervan, 1997.

Nelson, Richard D. "Joshua." In *Dictionary of the Old Testament: Historical Books*, edited by B. T. Arnold and H. G. M. Williamson, 559–62. Downers Grove, IL: InterVarsity, 2005.

———. *Joshua: A Commentary*. Old Testament Library. Louisville: Westminster John Knox, 1997.

Oswalt, John. "nuakh." In *New International Dictionary of Old Testament Theology and Exegesis*, edited by Willem A. VanGemeren, 3:56–59. 5 vols. Grand Rapids: Zondervan, 1997.

Pitkänen, Pekka M. A. *Joshua*. Apollos Old Testament Commentary. Downers Grove, IL: InterVarsity, 2010.

Redpath, Alan. *Victorious Christian Living: Studies in the Book of Joshua*. London: Pikering & Inglis, 1955.

Ross, Allen P. *Recalling the Hope of Glory*. Grand Rapids: Kregel, 2006.

Satterthwaite, Philip, and David W. Baker. "Nations of Canaan." In *Dictionary of the Old Testament: Pentateuch*, edited by T. Desmond Alexander and David W. Baker, 596–605. Downers Grove, IL: InterVarsity, 2003.

Saucy, Robert L. *The Case for Progressive Dispensationalism*. Grand Rapids: Zondervan, 1993.

Schneider, W. "*Krima*." In *New International Dictionary of New Testament Theology*, edited by Colin Brown, 2:362–67. 3 vols. Grand Rapids: Zondervan, 1986.

Seger, Joe D. "Shechem." In *The Oxford Encyclopedia of Archaeology in the Near East*, edited by Eric M. Meyers, 5:19–23. 5 vols. New York: Oxford University Press, 1997.

Shepherd, J. E. "*Shekel*." In *New International Dictionary of Old Testament Theology and Exegesis*, edited by Willem A. VanGemeren, 4:237. 5 vols. Grand Rapids: Zondervan, 1997.

van Groningen, G. "*qeṣep*, wrath." In *The Theological Wordbook of the Old Testament*, edited by R. Laird Harris, Gleason L. Archer Jr., and Bruce K. Waltke, 2:808–9. 2 vols. Chicago: Moody, 1980.

Vogt, Peter T. *Deuteronomic Theology and the Significance of Torah*. Winona Lake, IN: Eisenbrauns, 2006.

Waltke, B. K. *Old Testament Theology*. Grand Rapids: Zondervan, 2007.

Walton, John H. *Ancient Israelite Literature in Its Cultural Context*. Grand Rapids: Zondervan, 1989.

———. *Ancient Near Eastern Thought and the Old Testament: Introducing the Conceptual World of the Hebrew Bible*. Grand Rapids: Baker Academic, 2006.

———. "Exodus, Date of." In *Dictionary of the Old Testament: Pentateuch*, edited by T. Desmond Alexander and David W. Baker, 258–72. Downers Grove, IL: InterVarsity, 2003.

———. "Joshua 10:12–15 and Mesopotamian Omen Texts." In *Faith, Tradition, and History*, edited by A. R. Millard, J. K. Hoffmeier, and D. W. Baker, 181–90. Winona Lake, IN: Eisenbrauns, 1994.

Watkins, L. "Shiloh." In *The Oxford Encyclopedia of Archaeology in the Near East*, edited by Eric M. Meyers, 5:28–29. 5 vols. New York: Oxford University Press, 1997.

Weeks, Harry. "Timnath-heres." In *Anchor Bible Dictionary*, edited by David Noel Freedman, 6:557–58. 6 vols. New York: Doubleday, 1992.

Woudstra, Marten. *The Book of Joshua*. New International Commentary on the Old Testament. Grand Rapids: Eerdmans, 1981.

Wright, Christopher J. H. *Old Testament Ethics for the People of God*. Downers Grove, IL: InterVarsity, 2004.

Younger, K. Lawson, Jr. *Ancient Conquest Accounts: A Study of Ancient Near Eastern and Biblical History Writing*. Journal for the Study of the Old Testament: Supplement Series 98. Sheffield: Sheffield Academic, 1990.

Image Credits

Unless otherwise indicated, photos are copyright © Baker Publishing Group and Dr. James C. Martin. Unless otherwise indicated, illustrations and maps are copyright © Baker Publishing Group.

The Baker Photo Archive acknowledges the permission of the following institutions and individuals.

Photos on pages 13, 32, 45, 64, 71, 94, 96, 134, 137, 159, 162, 177, 183 © Baker Publishing Group and Dr. James C. Martin. Courtesy of the British Museum, London, England.

Photo on page 180 © Baker Publishing Group and Dr. James C. Martin. Courtesy of the British Museum, London, England, on loan from Berlin.

Photo on page 36 © Baker Publishing Group and Dr. James C. Martin courtesy of the Egyptian Ministry of Antiquities and the Aswan Museum, Elephantine Island.

Photo on pages 9 © Baker Publishing Group and Dr. James C. Martin. Courtesy of the Egyptian Ministry of Antiquities and the Museum of Egyptian Antiquities, Cairo, Egypt.

Photos on pages 151, 168 © Baker Publishing Group and Dr. James C. Martin. Collection of the Israel Museum, Jerusalem, and courtesy of the Israel Antiquities Authority, exhibited at the Israel Museum, Jerusalem.

Photo on page 42 © Baker Publishing Group and Dr. James C. Martin. Collection of the Israel Museum, Jerusalem, and courtesy of the Israel Antiquities Authority, exhibited at the Rockefeller Museum, Jerusalem.

Photos on pages 83, 93, 184, 188, 192 © Baker Publishing Group and Dr. James C. Martin. Courtesy of the Musée du Louvre; Autorisation de photographer et de filmer. Louvre, Paris, France.

Photos on pages 81, 201 © Baker Publishing Group and Dr. James C. Martin. Courtesy of the Oriental Institute Museum, University of Chicago.

Photos on pages 63, 186 © Baker Publishing Group and Dr. James C. Martin. Courtesy of the Turkish Ministry of Antiquities and the Istanbul Archaeological Museum, Turkey.

Photo on page 126 © Baker Publishing Group and Dr. James C. Martin. Courtesy of the Turkish Ministry of Antiquities and the Museum of Anatolian Civilizations, Ankara, Turkey.

Photo on page 1 © Baker Publishing Group and Dr. James C. Martin. Courtesy of the Vatican Museum.

Photo on page 120 © Baker Publishing Group and Dr. James C. Martin. Courtesy of the Wohl Archaeological Museum and Burnt House, Jerusalem.

Additional image credits

Photo on page 66 courtesy of The British Library, Creative Commons CC0 1.0 Universal Public Domain Dedication, http://www.bl.uk/catalogues/illuminatedmanuscripts/ILLUMIN.ASP?Size=mid&IllID=53744.

Photo on page 49 © Gregory Gerber / Shutterstock.com.

Photo on page 153 © Kim Walton.

Photso on pages 69, 104 © Kim Walton. Courtesy of the British Museum, London, England.

Photo on page 28 © Library of Congress, Prints & Photographs Division, [LC-DIG-matpc-00450].

Photo on page 7 © Library of Congress, Prints & Photographs Division, Lamb Studios Archive, [lambdc 07666].

Photo on page 34 © Marie-Lan Nguyen / Wikimedia Commons. Courtesy of the National Roman Museum - Baths of Diocletian.

Photo on page 77 courtesy of Ralph K. Hawkins.

Photo on page 30 © Steve F-E-Cameron / Wikimedia Commons, CC-BY-3.0.

Photo on page 59 © The Yorck Project / Wikimedia Commons.

Photo on page 123 © Zev Radovan / Bridgeman Images.

Contributors

General Editors
Mark. L. Strauss
John H. Walton

Associate Editors, Illustrating the Text
Kevin and Sherry Harney

Contributing Author, Illustrating the Text
Donald C. Porter

Series Development
Jack Kuhatschek
Brian Vos

Project Editor
James Korsmo

Interior Design
Brian Brunsting
William Overbeeke

Visual Content
Kim Walton

Cover Direction
Paula Gibson
Michael Cook

Index

Canaan
  boundaries of, 14
  new life in, 36
Canaanites, 25, 37, 81
  deities of, 188
  dispossession of, 136
  failure to dislocate, 135–36, 158
  intermarriage with, 133, 180, 181, 182–84
  intermingling with, 166, 176
  sinfulness of, 55
  subjected to forced labor, 133, 134
capital punishment, 15, 58, 64
Carmel, 111
casting lots, 58, 65, 121, 124, 152
caves, 97
celestial omen texts, 93–95
ceremonies of victory, 97
chariots, 135
cherubim, 27
Christians, as countercultural, 190
Christian unity, 136
church, 79
  attendance, 142–43
  leaders and laity of, 154
circumcision, restoration of, 36–37, 39–40
circumcision of the heart, 38, 40, 178, 196
cities of refuge, 5, 144–49
"cities you did not build," 129
"commander of the LORD's army," 36, 42–46, 48
command/obedience pattern, 48
commands, 163
community solidarity, 15, 64, 66, 145, 163
confession of sin, 62
conquest, 1, 10, 13, 16, 54–55, 100
  summary of, 108–13
consecration, 5, 25, 36, 40, 45
covenant, 4, 6, 39, 159, 163, 186–87, 189–90, 192
  blessings of, 194, 195
  curses of, 194, 195
  loyalty to, 165–66, 171
  renewal of, 180, 182, 186–90, 192–97, 198
  transgenerational unity of, 202
covenant law, 31
coveting, 59, 63, 65
crossing the sea. See exodus
cry for deliverance, 89–90
cultic worship, 188
curse, 82–83, 188
curses. See covenant, curses of

Dan, 127, 139, 140
Danites, 142
David
  and capture of Jerusalem, 129
  kingdom of, 111, 116
Day of Atonement, 27
Dead Sea, 26, 127

death, 201, 203
Debir, 128
deception, 68
  of Achan, 58,
  of the Gibeonites, 68, 80, 82–84
  of Rahab, 22
deliverance, 69
destruction, 50. See also *haram*
Deuteronomistic History, 2
Deuteronomistic theology, 2
devoted things, 21. See also *herem*
discipline, 60, 61
disobedience, 77
  and death, 72
divination, 94
divine and human agency, 4, 6–7, 68, 71
Divine Warrior, 6, 16, 43, 71, 84, 88, 103, 105, 112, 178, 181, 201
"Do not be afraid," 14, 87, 98
dry ground, 32

eastern tribes. *See* Transjordan tribes
Ebenezer, 150
elders, 14, 81, 175, 200
Eleazar, 8, 120, 121, 142, 151, 202
  death of, 198, 200
enemies, 97, 158, 160
Ephraim, 120, 132, 133, 134, 136
Esau, 187
eternal inheritance, 142
eternal rest, 11, 203
Euphrates River, 14, 187
Eve, temptation of, 63, 82
evil, 183–84
exile, 116
exodus, 36, 37, 39, 177, 188
exogamy, 183

faith, 35, 105, 112, 119
faithfulness to God, 13, 142, 174, 176
false worship, 192
family deities, 189
fear, 35, 111, 113
  of chariots, 135
  of the Lord, 31, 98
  in the nations, 20, 36
Feast of Tabernacles, 171
Feast of Unleavened Bread, 38, 39, 171
Feast of Weeks, 171
fellowship offerings, 76
fertility gods, 177, 193
foreigners, 76, 78, 146, 148
foreign gods, 190, 193, 194
forgiveness, 72, 85
forsaking the Lord, 189

Gad, 114, 116
Gadites, 15

Japhletites, 133
Jarmuth, 96
javelin, 70
Jebusites, 25, 81, 104, 129, 130
Jephunneh, 129
Jericho, 21, 42, 49–52, 108, 110, 132, 140, 188
Jerusalem, 96, 111, 140
  failure to take possession of, 127, 129
  sanctuary in, 141
Jesus, miracles of, 22, 27–28
jihad, 54
Jordan River, crossing over, 13, 24–28, 32
Joseph
  bones of, 198, 200, 202
  tribes of, 120, 132–36
Joshua
  authority of, 163
  contrition of, 58, 59, 62
  death of, 181, 186, 198
  faithfulness of, 37, 51
  faith of, 99, 202
  farewell address, 174–78, 180–84
  fulfillment of promises to, 142
  leadership of, 48, 135, 141–42, 172
  as the new Moses, 8, 9, 12, 84
  obedience at Gilgal, 88–89
  ordination of, 13
  reads the law, 77–78
  as servant of God, 31
Joshua (book)
  authorship of, 8–9
  dating of, 8
Jubilee, 51
Judah, inheritance of, 126–30
judges, 14, 175
Judges (book), 200
judgment, 60
justice, 149

Kadesh Barnea, 98, 99
Kedesh, 111
Kenaz, 121–22
Kenizzites, 121–22, 124, 129
Khirbet Rabud, 128
Khirbet Seilun, 139, 150
kindness, 21
kings, execution of, 71, 89
Kiriath Arba, 123
Kishon, 104
Kohathites, 152

Lachish, 96, 98
land, 5–7, 123–24
  distribution of, 13, 114–18, 156
  holiness of, 39, 44
  inventory of, 108
  as metaphor for the Christian life, 11
  promise of, 1, 10–11, 117

Lasharon, 111
Late Bronze Age, 8, 18, 55
Law of Hammurapi, 19
law of Moses, 3–4, 74–76, 78, 163. *See also* torah
leaders, 175
leadership, 8, 16, 84, 85, 135
Lebanon, 14, 115
Leshem, 140
Levites, 116, 139, 152
  cities of, 140, 144, 150–54
  inheritance of, 114, 118, 121
Levitical priests, 5, 8, 76
life, 72
lists of boundaries, cities, and territories, 122
livestock, 164
living in the land, 190–91
longevity, as a blessing, 199, 203
Lord of all the earth, 26, 48
Lord of hosts, 43, 169
Lord's Supper, 34, 40
love
  for enemies, 10, 100
  for God, 165
lying, 22, 58, 59, 65

Maakah, 116
Makir, 116
Makirites, 133–34
Makkedah, 97
Manasseh, 15, 114, 116, 120, 132, 133–34, 136
manna, 39
manslaughter, 145, 147
Marduk, 193
meditation, on the law, 14
Mediterranean Sea, 14, 127, 128
Megiddo, 111
memorials, 31, 33, 90, 194–95, 197
mercy seat, 27
merism (literary device), 14, 50
Merom, 104
"Mighty One," 170
Mikmethath, 133
milk, 38
miracles, 22, 26–27, 33, 46, 89–90, 177
  as local not global, 92
Misrephoth Maim, 105
Mizpeh, 104, 105
Moses
  death of, 12
  as servant of the Lord, 110, 122
most holy place, 27
Mount Ebal, 74–76, 78, 187
Mount Gerazim, 74–75, 78, 187
Mount Hermon, 115, 116
Mount Horeb, 2
Mount Sinai, 2, 188
murder, 145

names of God, 170–71
Naphoth Dor, 104
Naphtali, 140
nationalism, 10, 47
natural and supernatural, 27, 33
naturalism, 190
necks of kings, 97, 98
Negev, 98, 128
Noah, offering of, 78
northern kings, defeat of, 98, 99, 102–6, 109

oak, 195
oaths, 157, 176
obedience, 3, 4, 14, 16, 22, 79, 135–36, 165, 166, 182, 190, 201
  vs. disobedience, 56
  and life, 15, 72
  reward for, 117
  and spiritual rest, 161
officers, 14, 175
Og, 110, 115, 116
omen language, 95
opposition to the gospel, 113
Othniel, 122, 128, 130
outstretched arm, 70

Passover, 36, 38–40
pasturelands, 151, 152, 165
patriarchs, promises to, 157
Pentateuch, 2
Pentecost, 171
Peor, 169–70
Perizzites, 25, 81, 134–35
persevering faith, 124
Pharaoh, hardening of heart, 109–10
Philistines, 115, 176
Phinehas, 8, 153, 168, 169, 170, 200–201, 202
polytheism, 19, 21, 113, 183, 189, 190–91
possession of the land, 110, 158, 160, 201
prayer, 73, 90
presence of the Lord, 2, 42, 44
promise and fulfillment, 1, 3, 22, 48, 72, 106, 111–12, 129, 153, 158–60
prosperity in the land, 3, 6, 164, 165, 184
prostitution, 20, 22

Qur'an, 54–55

racial superiority, 10
Rahab, 18–23, 50, 51–52, 66, 80, 83, 84, 100, 101, 124, 130, 177
ram's horn, 51
rebellion, 15, 169
refuge, 145
regeneration, 178
remembrance, 31, 175
repentance, 64–65, 101
Rephaites, 110, 134–35

reproach, 38
resident aliens, 82, 146
rest, 3, 15, 110, 112, 113, 158, 160, 175, 202–3
Reuben, 114, 116
Reubenites, 15
reverence, 43
reward, 117, 166
ritual contamination, 64
rocks, pile of, 64, 65
royal cities, 87
royal land grant, 13
ruin, 71

sacred, 5
sacred assemblies, 90
sacrificial system, 147–48
Samaritan woman, 190
Samson, 140
sandals, 44
Scripture, authority of, 78–79
second commandment, 193
secularism, 190
seed, 11
Seir, 187
Septuagint, 2
serpent, deception of, 81–82
servant of the Lord, 12, 14, 111, 199
serving God, 164, 188, 193
seven (number), 49
Shechem, 74–75, 186, 187, 189, 190, 194
Shechemites, 200
Shema, 194
Shiloh, 139, 141, 150–51, 165
Shittim, 19–20, 24
Sidon, 105
Sidonians, 115
sign
  miracles as, 22
  stones as, 31
Sihon, 110, 115
silence, at destruction of Jericho, 49, 50
Simeon, 127, 139, 140
sin
  of Peor, 169–70
  as pervasive, 60
  perverseness of, 65
  power of, 59
  of previous generation, 40
six-plus-one pattern, 48–49
snares, 181
Solomon, kingdom of, 116
soul, 164
southern kings, defeat of, 86, 96–99, 108–9
special days, 90
"spirit of wisdom," 8
spying of the land, 18
steadfastness in the Lord, 166

stealing, 58, 59, 65
stone memorials, 31–32, 33, 194–95
stoning, 64
"strong and courageous," 12–13, 14, 16, 30, 124
suffering, 184
sun, standing still, 88, 92–95
surprise attack, 88
sword, 43
syncretism, 172

Taanach, 111
Tappuah, 111
temptation, 59–61, 63
Ten Commandments, 31, 58, 59, 63, 65, 76, 163, 193
tent of meeting, 6, 138, 139, 141, 142, 165, 187, 195
theophany, 44
third commandment, 193
thousand (word), 57, 69
three days, 14–15, 21
Timnath Serah, 140–41
Tirzah, 111
tithing, 152
torah, 2, 3, 14, 78
"to the right or to the left," 14
town lists, 122, 126, 127, 128, 139, 151
Transjordan, 110, 133, 152
Transjordan tribes, 15, 114–18, 172–73, 176
    altar of, 168–72
    blessing of, 162–66
traps, 181
tribal allotments, 110, 114–18, 120–21, 138–42
trouble, 50, 63
"turn away," 180–81
twelve spies, 18, 20, 142

twelve stones, 30–31
two memorials, 30–34

uncleanness, 147
unfaithfulness, 169, 174
unintentional sins, 148
unity, 7
    of family of God, 33, 172–73
    of Israel, 171–72
Urim and Thummim, 121

Valley of Achor, 50, 63, 64
Valley of Aijalon, 90, 92
Valley of Hen Hinnom, 127
vassal, 187

walls of Jericho, 52
warfare, 54–55, 68–69
western foothills, 98
wide-angle view, 35
wilderness generation, 112, 188
will of God, and casting lots, 124, 152
witnesses, to a covenant, 171, 187, 194–95, 197, 198
women, ownership of land, 129
woodcutters and water carriers, 82–83
word of God, 1, 3–4
worship, 141, 142–43, 164, 166, 190
worship of other gods, 180
wrath of God, 46, 60, 170

Yahweh, 32, 99
Yahwism, 3

Zarethan, 26
Zebulun, 140
Zelophehad, daughters of, 120, 129, 132, 134, 135, 136